40

OUR BIG BLUE BACKYARD

OUR BIG BLUE BACKYARD

NEW ZEALAND'S OCEANS AND MARINE RESERVES

JANET HUNT

For all the creatures of the oceans, great and small

A RANDOM HOUSE BOOK published by Random House New Zealand
18 Poland Road, Glenfield, Auckland, New Zealand
in association with NHNZ

For more information about our titles go to www.randomhouse.co.nz

A catalogue record for this book is available from the National Library of New Zealand

Random House New Zealand is part of the Random House Group
New York   London   Sydney   Auckland   Delhi   Johannesburg

First published 2014

© 2014 text Janet Hunt; images as credited on page 297

The moral rights of the author have been asserted

ISBN 978 1 77553 654 3

This book is copyright. Except for the purposes of fair reviewing no part of this publication may be reproduced or transmitted in any form or by any means, electronic or mechanical, including photocopying, recording or any information storage and retrieval system, without permission in writing from the publisher.

Design: Janet Hunt and Megan van Staden
Cover photograph: photonewzealand / Darryl Torckler
(snapper, Goat Island)
Image previous page: Little pied shag over the waters
of the Hauraki Gulf, Waiheke Island

Printed in China by Everbest Printing Co Ltd

CONTENTS

	INTRODUCTION	7
1	**OUR VERY BIG BLUE BACKYARD**	15
2	**MARINE RESERVES** ✿ LEADING THE WAY	39
3	**HARBOURS & KNIGHTS** ✿ THE FAR NORTH	59
4	**HAURAKI GULF MARINE PARK** ✿ TĪKAPA MOANA	101
5	**ROCKS & ISLANDS** ✿ THE BAY OF PLENTY	145
6	**BLACK SANDS & VERY SMALL DOLPHINS** ✿ TARANAKI	165
7	**WHALE RIDER WORLD** ✿ EAST CAPE & SOUTHERN HAWKE'S BAY	185
8	**CITYSIDE** ✿ KAPITI & TAPUTERANGA	193
9	**SOUNDS & BOULDERS** ✿ TOP O' THE SOUTH	205
10	**TE WAIPOUNAMU** ✿ UPCOMING WEST COAST	219
11	**CANYONS & PENINSULAS** ✿ SOUTH ISLAND EASTSIDE	231
12	**FIORDS & MUTTONBIRDS** ✿ SOUTH OF THE SOUTH	247
13	**WAY, WAY OFFSHORE** ✿ THE KERMADEC & SUBANTARCTIC ISLANDS	265
	CONCLUSION	289
	GLOSSARY, BIBLIOGRAPHY, ILLUSTRATION & TEXT CREDITS	291
	INDEX	299
	ABOUT THE AUTHOR	304

THE SEA, OUR SAVIOUR

Today, the sea at *mid-morning*
    is invested with a colossal indifference;
    but not without stylish nonchalance

Ensparked by sunlight, the waves
    are like agitated coils of tin foil
    rolling in . . .

I've worked it out, the boring, daily
    thing it does is influenced not only
    by current, wind and tide but also
    by the regularity with which
    the pull of the sun and moon in concert
    remoulds by day, by night its
    coming & going, ebb and flow.

At high tide, we fish, chuck out
    a line or two, a curtain of nets,
    close meshed. We wait.

Later, with eyelids opening to a tremor
    of interest, we pull in the nets. Well,
    it's like it's been always, you know?
    It's our living: the sea, our saviour.

On shore again, we seek out the pooled
    rocks at low tide, delicately
    plucking the prickle-needled king
    (sea-egg), opening it, and scooping
    out the vulnerable and tremulous
    orange segments, clinging inside
    its globular shelter. And well . . .

Slurp is all you hear, as we hold it
    a-dangle above our gaping mouths,
    dropping it quickly into a
    ngungly-snuckly, throat-contraction flat out
    right the way on past the
    Adam's-apple check-out, slithery-gump
    O, sexy!
m-m-m-m-m and m-m-m-m-m—
my millennial thanks to you,
    Tangaroa!

— Hone Tuwhare, from *Piggy-Back Moon*

INTRODUCTION

A couple of years ago, four women met on a north-facing beach on a bright spring morning. A pied shag slowly rotated outstretched wings on a rock just offshore. One of the four carried the ashes of a dear friend. They crossed the sandy foreshore to a small headland and waded thigh-deep into the clear waters. With some difficulty, they uncorked the container and released its contents. The grains spiralled with the tide as it surged against the rocks; they winked and sparkled, catching the light as they descended and mixed with the drifting sands below. The four laughed. One placed a rose and a sprig of pōhutukawa on the surface and the flowers lifted and rocked in the swell. Another fell over and they laughed some more.

It seemed right. It was good.

The sea. How absolutely it is interwoven with the fabric of our lives, especially here in New Zealand. It underwrites consciousness, a silver-blue-grey-green expanse, shimmering, restless, alive. It changes constantly, its surface fashioned by wind, current and undersea landform into gentle swell or turbulence of jagged peaks. It breathes, it moves, it murmurs, sighs or thunders according to mood. It is to be feared but is also a place of light and reflection, of great presence and beauty. It is the kingdom of a god of many names: Tangaroa, Poseidon, Neptune. It has been with us forever, one of the essential trio of air and land and sea that make up this place we call home.

The majority of Kiwis live within 50 kilometres of the ocean: on it, in it and sometimes under it, we flock to it whenever we can. It is inseparable from days off, Sunday picnics and holidays. Insert your own snapshots here but there is a good chance they will include toddlers at the water's edge; school outings; New Year carnivals; sunburn and fossicking on the rocky shore; pipi boiling over a driftwood fire at sunset; the crackle of dry salt on the skin; the ouch-ouch-ouch of running over hot sand to the water; grit in clothes and other places; belly-flops on mudflats; body surfing and being dumped in the surf.

Yet all these encounters are on the periphery. We skim the sea's surface, skirt its margins and scavenge beguiling fragments from another world. Few of us truly encounter its depths or comprehend how utterly different the rules are, how alien it is, beneath the waves.

And, even as we celebrate the positive and the wonderful, our pleasure is tempered by awareness of shadows beyond the campfire. Despite its gleaming surface, the ocean is not at all blue and benign. The sea is vast and untamed and it behaves in ways that we do not fully understand; as individuals we are helpless before it and yet it is with disbelief that we increasingly acknowledge our impact as a species: like the apparently unending skies, the sea is not immune to our collective predations and our carelessness.

IF YOU ROTATE A GLOBE so that New Zealand faces you dead centre, you can't help but notice that it is one of the most maritime nations on

Earth. From the north, the main islands are long and thin, and extend from 34° to 47° latitude south; they sprawl across the junction of two of the planet's great water masses, the subtropical seas that flow now tempestuously, now lazily from the north and the subantarctic waters, hooning like biker-boys from the south: from west to east, the islands' landmasses form the boundary of the Pacific Ocean and the Tasman Sea, taking the slap and pull of weather from either side.

New Zealand has an Exclusive Economic Zone (EEZ) of some 4.4 million square kilometres enclosing an abundance of marine environments from the shallower waters of the continental shelf to the abyssal depths beyond. It is home to countless communities of plants and animals, from the tiniest millionth-of-a-millimetre microbe through to that rare, most massive of living creatures, the blue whale, and is stocked with endemic life — animals and plants that are found nowhere else in the world.

THIS BOOK IS A COMPANION to the Natural History New Zealand (NHNZ) documentary series of the same name. We take a similar approach to our subject, conveying the beauty and complexity of the whole through showing and describing the individual and particular. The series focuses on six sites, three in the north — Northland Harbours, Goat Island and Poor Knights Islands — and three in the south — Kaikōura, Open Bay Islands and Stewart Island. To an extent, the book covers the same territory but because the format is different and the brief is wider, it uses marine reserves as a window through which to observe that vast and astonishingly different, astoundingly beautiful, utterly terrifying other world.

Marine reserves are, of course, the merest fraction of what is on offer. At the time of writing, there are 38 — not enough, but growing. However, because they are selected to be typical and representative and, despite the fact that some are relatively new and have not yet really hit their straps, they are increasingly the best examples of coastal ecosystems, often pristine, largely undisturbed and, above all, not fished. They are the finest measure we have of how things were and how they could be again, the bright spots in an otherwise gloomy picture.

So, the framework of the book is New Zealand's marine reserves — what they are, how they came to be, where they are from north to south. It is not, however, a guide book. Those who want to visit the reserves will find that there are maps, directions and information about what to see online.

Instead, the books casts its net a little wider, taking a sample here, a snapshot there. It includes stories about the people who spend time in and on the sea, especially those who study it and record its creatures, as well as glimpses of the lives and habits of selected marine creatures, and occasionally marine plants. Some are found all around our coasts, while others, like the great whites, are mainly in one area.

Hone Tuwhare, whose poem opens this book, was a lover of the sea and especially of its bounty. He lived on its shores at Kākā Point, south of Dunedin, watched the waves riding towards his little crib all the way from Chile, and daily celebrated its being. Like him, in the end, we may offer our 'millennial thanks to you, Tangaroa!'

AS ALWAYS IN THE MAKING of a book, there's a large cast behind the name on the front cover. My love and appreciation firstly to family and friends and above all my partner and co-conspirator, Peter Haines.

Then, my appreciation for unstinting generosity of a wide circle of associates, experts and accomplices: you offered accommodation, shared time, experiences and anecdotes, provided information and images, answered queries and contributed in myriad ways, no matter how small.

In no particular order, my thanks to: Josie and Bill Whall, Rob Tuwhare, Pita Rikys, Ed Skelton, Mark Arthur, Chris Turver, Ian Skipworth, Tara Sutherland, Mike Lee, Virginia King, Warren Farrelly, Tui Foster, Brent Stephenson, Darryl Torckler, Leigh Torres, Howard Lynk (www.victorianmicroscopeslides.com), Jeanne Gallagher (Algarita), Dave Rayner (Aerius Helicopters), Adrienne and Scott (Glass Bottom Boat), Pip Gill (Whale Watch Kaikōura), Kate Malcolm and the team (Dive! Tutukaka) and Inglewood's ever-cheerful and helpful librarians.

I am indebted to the kindness of marine experts Bill Ballantine, Wade Doak, Roger Grace and Malcolm Francis, and, in their wake, Samara Nicholas, Brady Doak, Peter Crabb and Vince Kerr. Thanks to divers and cameramen Dave Abbott, Winston Cowie, Steve Hathaway, Max Quinn,

Stefan Mutch and Kina Scollay, who willingly shared photos and stories.

The science and expertise of many organisations lies behind marine reserves, among them DOC, NIWA, GNS Science, MPI, Massey University, University of Auckland, University of Waikato, University of Otago and the Museum of New Zealand Te Papa Tongarewa. I am grateful for the assistance of a number of their staff, especially Vivian Ward, Riley Elliott, Tessa Mills, Callum Lilley, Jamie Quirk, Debbie Freeman, David Carlton, Hannah Hendriks, Don Neale, Bruce Hayward, Tracy Farr, Kate Neill, Susan Pepperell, Emily King, Brett Gartrell, Chris Battershill and Colin Miskelly; your timely responses to questions, your suggestions, solutions and knowledge and expertise is beyond price.

My thanks also, to many 'friends' groups, both for your immediate assistance and in wider appreciation of the hours you spend out there regardless of season or weather — on coasts, in wetlands, on and in the water, monitoring conditions, counting critters and removing pests. You also engage in the time-consuming, often tedious, painstaking but equally important tasks of making proposals, writing submissions and objections, talking to the public . . . the list is endless. The outcome, however, is that the rest of us, and especially children, get to see more in the oceans than just kina barrens. My thanks especially to Danielle Hart (Whāingaroa Environment Centre), Anne McDermott (Fiordland Guardians), Jo-Anne Vaughan (Friends of Mangarākau Swamp), Kent Xie, Michael Coote and Haru Sameshima (Forest & Bird, Motu Manawa), Murray Hosking (Friends of Taputeranga), David Gray and Ross Garrett (Sir Peter Blake Marine Education & Recreation Centre), Anne Scott and Elise Smith (Ngā Motu Marine Society), and Clare Pinder and Lynne and Danny Boulton (Sustain Our Sounds). My apologies if I have overlooked anyone.

Finally, my gratitude to the teams at Natural History New Zealand and Random House New Zealand, whose vision stands behind this book, especially Barbara Larson, Judith Curran, Nicola Legat, Wayne Poll, Sue Hallas, Megan van Staden and Anna Bowbyes — thanks, everyone.

NEW ZEALAND MARINE RESERVES 2014

New Zealand's marine reserves are mostly signposted by yellow triangles.

NORTH ISLAND

Poor Knights Islands: 1981, 2400 ha.
Whāngārei Harbour: 2006, 254 ha.
Cape Rodney–Ōkakari Point (Goat Island): 1975, 518 ha.
Tāwharanui: 2011, 400 ha.
Long Bay–Ōkura: 1995, 980 ha.
Motu Manawa (Pollen Island): 1995, 500 ha.
Te Matuku: 2003, 690 ha.
Te Whanganui-a-Hei (Cathedral Cove): 1993, 840 ha.
Tūhua (Mayor Island): 1992, 1060 ha.
Te Paepae-o-Aotea (Volkner Rocks): 2006, 1267 ha.
Te Tapuwae-o-Rongokako: 1999, 2452 ha.
Parininihi: 2006, 1800 ha.
Tapuae: 2008, 1404 ha.
Te Angiangi: 1997, 446 ha.
Kapiti: 1992, 2167 ha.
Taputeranga: 2008, 854 ha.

SOUTH ISLAND

Long Island–Kokomohua: 1993, 619 ha.
Horoirangi: 2006, 904 ha.
Tonga Island: 1993, 1835 ha.
Westhaven (Te Tai Tapu): 1994, 536 ha.
Pōhatu (Flea Bay): 1999, 215 ha.
Akaroa: 2014, 475 ha.
Ulva Island/Te Wharawhara: 2004 1075 ha.

FIORDLAND

Piopiotahi (Milford Sound): 1993, 690 ha.
Te Hāpua (Sutherland Arm): 2005, 449 ha.
Hāwea (Clio Rocks): 2005, 411 ha.
Kahukura (Gold Arm): 2005, 464 ha.
Kutu Parera (Gaer Arm): 2005, 433 ha.
Te Awaatu Channel (The Gut): 1993, 93 ha.
Taipari Roa (Elizabeth Island): 2005, 613 ha.
Moana Uta (Wet Jacket Arm): 2005, 2007 ha.
Taumoana (Five Fingers Peninsula): 2005, 1466 ha.
Te Tapuwae-o-Hua (Long Sound): 2005, 3672 ha.

UPCOMING

Kahurangi: 8466 ha.
Punakaiki: 3558 ha.
Hikurangi: 10,416 ha.
Waiau Glacier Coast: 4641 ha.
Tauparikākā: 16 ha.
Hautai: 847 ha.

OFFSHORE

Kermadec Islands: 1990, 748,000 ha.
Auckland Islands/Motu Maha: 2003, 498,000 ha.
Bounty Islands/Moutere Hauriri: 2014, 105,000 ha.
Antipodes Island/Moutere Mahue: 2014, 217,000 ha.
Campbell Island/Moutere Ihupuku: 2014, 113,000 ha.

Existing marine reserves, 2014

* Upcoming marine reserves

△ Kermadec Islands

- Poor Knights Islands
- Whāngārei Harbour
- Cape Rodney–Ōkakari Point (Goat Island)
- Tāwharanui
- Long Bay–Ōkura
- Motu Manawa (Pollen Island)
- Te Whanganui-a-Hei (Cathedral Cove)
- Te Matuku
- Tūhua (Mayor Island)
- Te Paepae-o-Aotea (Volkner Rocks)
- Parininihi
- Tapuae
- Te Tapuwae-o-Rongokako
- Te Angiangi
- Westhaven (Te Tai Tapu)
- Kahurangi*
- Kapiti
- Taputeranga
- Punakaiki*
- Long Island–Kokomohua
- Horoirangi
- Tonga Island
- Waiau Glacier Coast*
- Hikurangi*
- Tauparikākā*
- Pōhatu (Flea Bay)
- Hautai*
- Akaroa

FIORDLAND
- Piopiotahi (Milford Sound)
- Te Hāpua (Sutherland Arm)
- Hāwea (Clio Rocks)
- Kahukura (Gold Arm)
- Kutu Parera (Gaer Arm)
- Te Awaatu Channel (The Gut)
- Taipari Roa (Elizabeth Island)
- Moana Uta (Wet Jacket Arm)
- Taumoana (Five Fingers Peninsula)
- Te Tapuwae-o-Hua (Long Sound)

- Ulva Island/Te Wharawhara
- Bounty Islands/Moutere Hauriri
- Antipodes Island/Moutere Mahue
- Auckland Islands/Motu Maha
- Campbell Island/Moutere Ihupuku

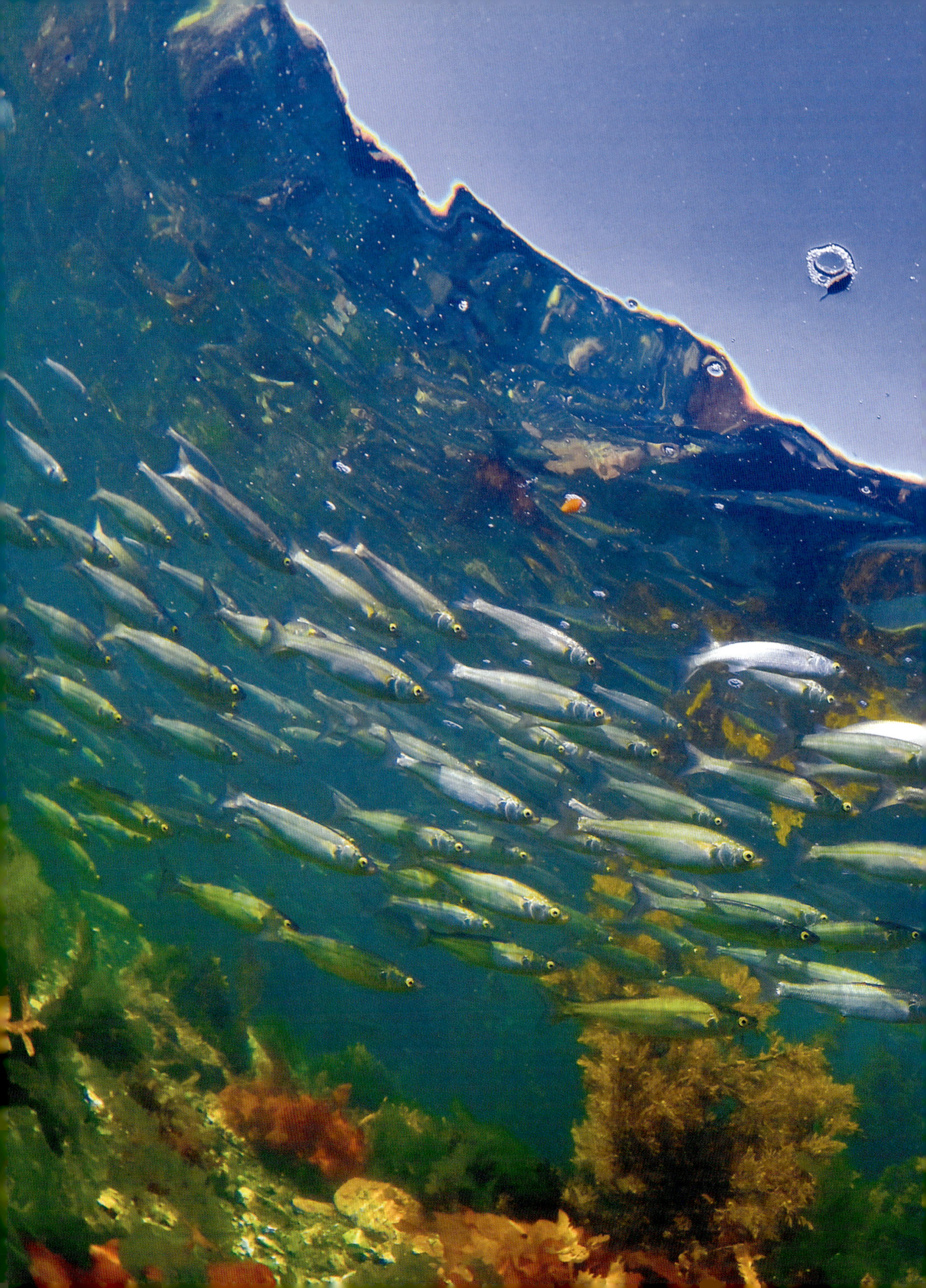

1
OUR VERY BIG

BLUE BACKYARD

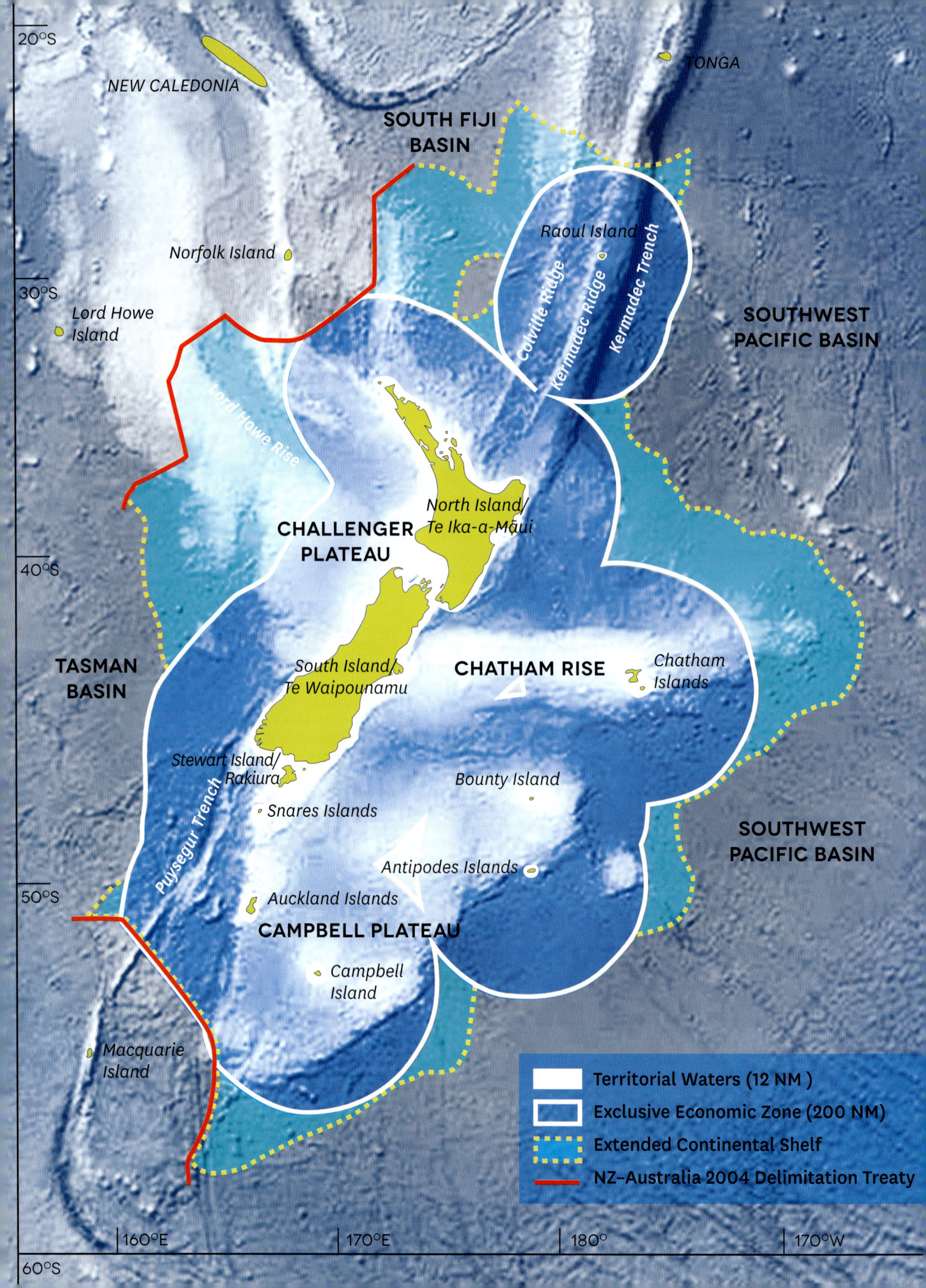
20°S
NEW CALEDONIA
TONGA
SOUTH FIJI BASIN
Raoul Island
Norfolk Island
30°S
Lord Howe Island
Colville Ridge
Kermadec Ridge
Kermadec Trench
SOUTHWEST PACIFIC BASIN
Lord Howe Rise
North Island/ Te Ika-a-Māui
CHALLENGER PLATEAU
40°S
TASMAN BASIN
South Island/ Te Waipounamu
CHATHAM RISE
Chatham Islands
Stewart Island/ Rakiura
Puysegur Trench
Bounty Island
Snares Islands
SOUTHWEST PACIFIC BASIN
Antipodes Islands
50°S
Auckland Islands
CAMPBELL PLATEAU
Campbell Island
Macquarie Island
Territorial Waters (12 NM)
Exclusive Economic Zone (200 NM)
Extended Continental Shelf
NZ–Australia 2004 Delimitation Treaty
160°E
170°E
180°
170°W
60°S

Ladies and gentlemen, please fasten your seat belts — from the comfort of your own computer chair take a spin and see Zealandia and the Pacific as Kupe and James Cook could never have imagined. Just fire up Google Earth and away we go . . . Like a bird with extraordinary powers, you can soar in the stratosphere or swoop closer to Earth if you fancy.

You will instantly identify the roughly triangular shape of the continent of Zealandia and the welt-like boundary dividing the Australian and Pacific plates. Follow it from the Kermadec Trench in the north, fly south along the east coast of New Zealand, cross the South Island to the Alpine Fault and zoom down to the Puysegur Trench.

Drop to only 322 kilometres for some close-up flying, and take a peek at Macquarie Island in the south. It is a smudge of emergent land perched atop a steep ridge with a deep chasm on either side. On your ride, you can see every crease and fold in the planet's surface, every sag and wrinkle, every tear and blip. It's truly amazing.

IT'S NOT JUST BIG, IT'S HUMUNGOUS!

New Zealand is among the smaller countries in the world by land area: the combined total of the North, South and Stewart islands, plus around 330 offshore islands, islets and rock stacks is 267,707 square kilometres, according to GNS Science, similar to Japan or the United Kingdom. By comparison, our seas are around 4,400,000 square kilometres, one of the largest Exclusive Economic Zones (EEZ) in the world. This means that even if the majority of us are entirely landlubbers in habit and outlook, 'New Zealand' is, in fact, vastly more marine than terrestrial.

This is because of a combination of two things: first, the provisions of international law and second, our location and geology.

PREVIOUS:
A calm day on Wellington's south coast: yellow-eyed mullet in Ōwhiro Bay lagoon.

TO GET A HANDLE on the first, we need to go back in time. From 1702 it was held that the high seas belonged to all aside from a strip of water around a maritime nation's coast. This strip was the width of three nautical miles, the distance a person 1.750 metres tall can see from the beach to the horizon and also the approximate reach of a cannon shot — on that basis, a somewhat defensive measure.

In those days, when the only ways to get about were to seize the oars or hoist a sail, it must have seemed that the seas were a source of abundant, infinite bounty. *Wrong!* They may be vast but they are, of course, as finite as the atmosphere — as eventually became apparent.

In 1945 the United States abandoned the three-mile limit and unilaterally extended its jurisdiction out to the continental shelf; others followed and by the late 1960s the oceans were exploited and polluted as never before. Oil was drawn from as deep as four kilometres below the surface, minerals were extracted from a multitude of locations and fishing vessels with previously undreamed-of capacity swept the seas without restraint. The oceans had become an arena of international tension and conflict.

Enter the United Nations. In 1967 Malta's ambassador Arvid Parvo challenged the world to take action. His appeal set in motion a process that spanned 15 years and ultimately became what former UN Secretary General Boutros Boutros-Ghali described in 1994 as one of the greatest achievements of the 20th century: the comprehensive regulation of the seas and its resources. The Third United Nations Conference on the Law of the Sea was convened in New York in 1973; nine years later, in 1982, a constitution for the seas was adopted, the United Nations Convention on the Law of the Sea, or UNCLOS.

A cannon shot: the measure of a nation's territorial limit.

Cum Priuile Reg. Israel excudit

UNCLOS binds more than 160 signatory sovereign states to its provisions, including 'navigational rights, territorial sea limits, economic jurisdiction, legal status of resources on the seabed beyond the limits of national jurisdiction, passage of ships through narrow straits, conservation and management of living marine resources, protection of the marine environment, a marine research regime and . . . a binding procedure for settlement of disputes between states'.

Of particular importance to New Zealand was the determination of sovereign area. The three-mile limit, which had clearly passed its use-by date, was replaced by the 12-nautical-mile Territorial Sea. Within its confines, all states are free to enforce any law, regulate for any use and to exploit any resource while still allowing 'innocent passage' for naval and merchant vessels of other nations. In addition, signatories were given control of a further 12 nautical miles, known as the Contiguous Zone, essentially a protective buffer for the Territorial Sea.

It was the next ruling, however, that had the greatest implications for New Zealand, which, along with Pacific countries and many others, argued for greater control of its fisheries. In a revolutionary move, the EEZ extended a coastal state's interest from 12 to 200 nautical miles from land, conferring the right to explore and exploit, conserve and manage the living and non-living natural resources within the zone, including the seabed and subsoil.

New Zealand's land area is comparatively modest but under this provision, a long, skinny shape and 18,000-kilometres of coastline amounts to a very healthy EEZ once you add 200 nautical miles all round. But then, because New Zealand also has islands and island groups that are well offshore, the EEZ mushrooms — some 1000 kilometres northeast to the subtropical waters of the Kermadec Islands, around 850 kilometres east to the Chatham Islands, Antipodes Islands and Bounty Island, and south 465 kilometres to the Auckland Islands and 700 kilometres to Campbell Island. Draw a circle of 200-nautical-mile radius (370.4 kilometres) around each of these islands or island groups, and there — you might think — you have it: New Zealand's enormous EEZ.

But it doesn't end there. The convention's Article 76 provides for nations to exercise additional control over what is termed the Extended Continental Shelf, effectively aligning the zone's boundary to the physical form of the seafloor. This means a coastal state can claim to a maximum of either 350 nautical miles from shore or 100 nautical miles from the 2500-metre contour line, whichever is greater. This extension confers exclusive rights to non-living resources and sedimentary species, although there are no special rights to fisheries in this zone.

NEW ZEALAND RATIFIED UNCLOS IN 1996. In the same year, the New Zealand Continental Shelf Project team, a coalition of Ministry of Foreign Affairs and Trade, Land Information New Zealand (LINZ), the National Institute of Water and Atmospheric Research (NIWA) and the Institute of Geological and Nuclear Sciences (now GNS Science) undertook a decade-long, $44 million survey of the continental shelf. Depth, seismic, gravity, magnetic and geologic data were ultimately compiled into a supporting report for submission to the United Nations Commission for the Limits of the Continental Shelf.

New Zealand was the fifth country to do so. In 2008 an additional 1.7 million square kilometres of seabed beyond the existing EEZ were confirmed.

THE DARK SIDE OF THE MOON

HMS *Challenger* (centre-right) in Wellington Harbour, 29 June 1874; painted by able seaman John Arthur.

Planet Earth is overwhelmingly wet. Over 70 percent of its surface is water-covered, with 96.5 percent of that being ocean and around 40 percent of *that* being what is known as 'abyssal plain' — a vast, oozy, featureless expanse several kilometres down that is largely populated by invertebrates known somewhat misleadingly as 'sea cucumbers' (they're animal, not vegetable and have a wonderful family name: *Holothuria*). We fish the ocean's surface, trawl its floor and occasionally the carcass of an unknown creature washes onto a beach, but on the whole, the oceans are one vast enigma. Divers are more or less confined to the upper layers — about 40 metres — and even the best underwater craft rarely ventures deeper than 1000. It's said that we know more about the dark side of the moon than we do about the seas.

But it's not for lack of trying. The foundations of modern oceanography were laid in 1872 when the British Museum, the Royal Society and the British government sent Her Majesty Victoria's Ship *Challenger* on a four-year, 70,000-nautical-mile voyage of discovery. Her crew sampled the seafloor, measured temperatures, observed ocean currents, charted the great sea basins and took a very large number of biological samples — of over 4700 species. It took 15 years to write up the findings, resulting in 50 hefty volumes.

Obtaining samples using simple dredges and trawls gives only a limited picture, however, and often mangles or destroys any soft-bodied creatures. Sonar, which was developed from the first half of the 20th century and accelerated in wartime for use in submarines, also detected the air-filled swim bladders of many fish species, expanding knowledge of the world below. Even then, soundings were difficult to interpret and a range of species such as squid, jellyfish and krill didn't really show on the screen so the picture was still incomplete.

Fast-forward to the present: science has built upon those early years and now employs an extraordinary suite of remote-sensing, photographic, measuring and sampling equipment to 'see' below the waves, including manned and unmanned remote-controlled submersibles with cameras and capture devices that are less damaging to the seafloor.

New Zealand's NIWA is a leader in the use of this technology for oceanic exploration, and keeps a number of research vessels busy including the ocean-going, 70-metre RV *Tangaroa* and its smaller companion, the 28-metre RV *Kaharoa*. Among other achievements, in July 2011 *Tangaroa*

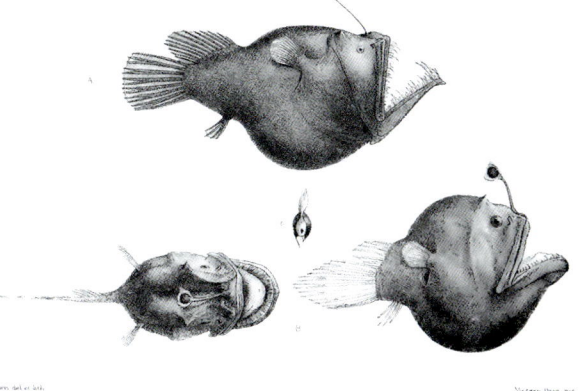

'All are carnivorous, and some of them most rapacious creatures [...] In coming to the surface their body has undergone a change which is merely due to their rapid withdrawal from the pressure under which they lived [...] what is a vigorous fish at a depth of 500 or more fathoms, appears at the surface as a loosely-jointed body, which, if the skin is not of sufficient toughness, can only be kept together with difficulty.' Albert Günther, *Report on the Scientific Results of the Voyage of HMS Challenger During the Years 1873–76* (1887).

Adelie penguins look back as RV *Tangaroa* inspects their world.

undertook a marathon 42-day, 24/7 survey of habitats of significance for marine organisms and biodiversity on New Zealand's continental shelf. Thousands of specimens and samples were taken using sophisticated devices such as the Deep Towed Imaging System — a high-definition video camera, a still camera and lighting apparatus. It was deployed at night and showed both the seafloor and its nocturnal inhabitants. It would have astounded the men of the *Challenger*.

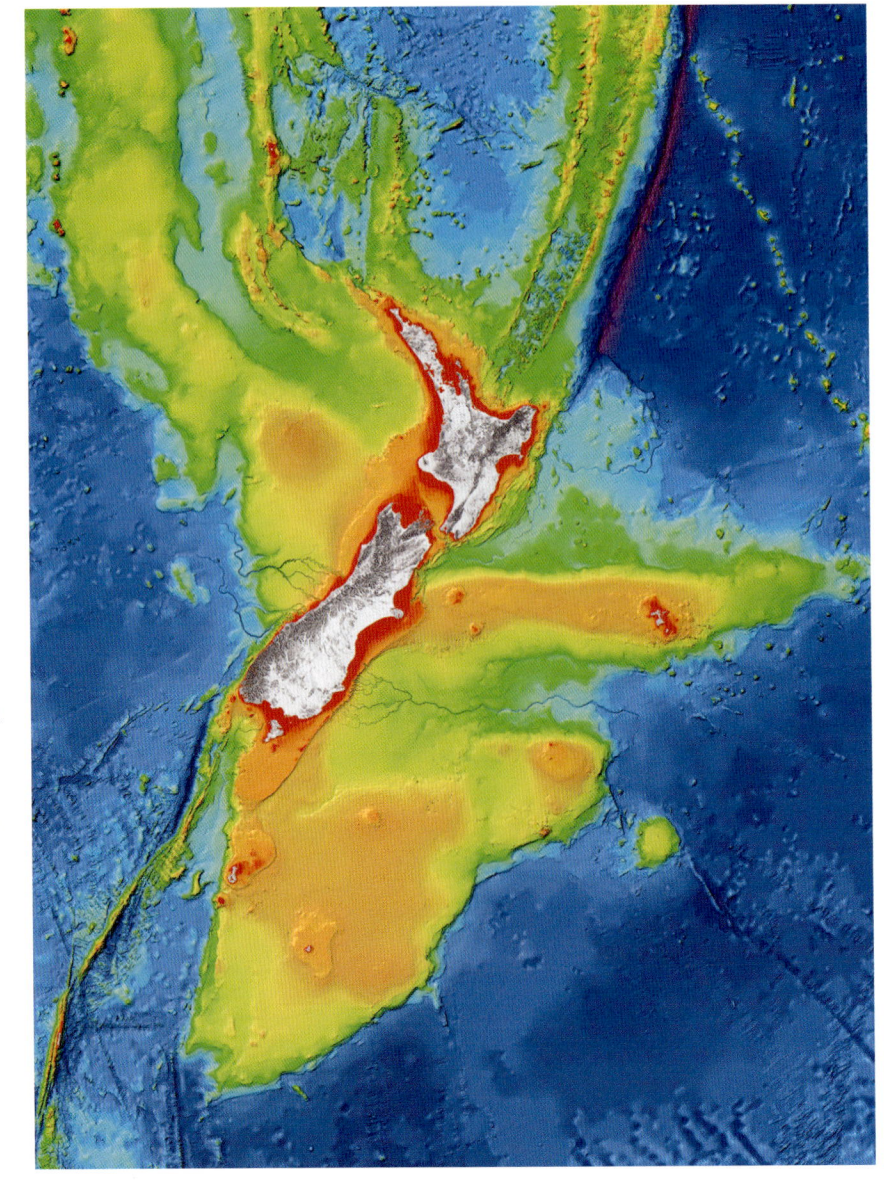

The *Tangaroa* has also, over the course of many expeditions, charted the seafloor and compiled a bathymetric map that enables us to appreciate the full extent of the continent of Zealandia. The continental shelf, plateau and slopes are orange; the shelf edges are pale yellow-green; the surrounding oceanic basins are blue (to 4000 metres and more) and the deep trenches are purple (down to over 8000 metres).

AN EYE ON THE DARK

On 15 August 1934, when pioneering naturalist William Beebe and adventurer, inventor and film-maker Otis Barton were lowered to 922 metres in Barton's bathysphere, they took turns peering through a tiny porthole. As they dropped the first 200 metres, they saw jellyfish, salps and other plankton; another 100 metres, and the growing darkness was lit by the flash and sparkle of illuminated creatures — something with a row of six lights, a fish backlit like a Halloween mask, another with bulging eyes, a cluster of arrow worms and deep sea shrimps with the trick of exploding in a shower of light when alarmed. They turned on a light beam of their own and a large, whale-like shape moved out of eyeshot in the distance. 'The water is filled with lights,' Beebe said.

Thirty years on, oceanographic engineer Jacques Piccard and US naval officer Don Walsh outdid Beebe and Barton when they descended 11,033 metres to the deepest part of the deepest ocean, the bottom of the Mariana Trench. They used a bathyscaphe, a free-diving, self-propelled submersible called the *Trieste*, with reinforced walls 127 millimetres thick. It took them almost five hours to go down and it's said that they saw a flatfish but little else.

For a long time, it wasn't worth anyone's while to return but in March 2012 film-maker and explorer James Cameron repeated the journey in a purpose-designed, one-person vertical submarine named *Deepsea Challenger* (coming to a cinema near you in 2014).

A deep-sea diving suit, ca. 1920.

Knowledge of the deep is continuously expanding. Large gelatinous organisms such as giant salps were not seen using traditional sampling methods.

A LOST CONTINENT: ZEALANDIA

International law defines New Zealand's waters in terms of the Territorial Sea, the Exclusive Economic Zone and the Extended Continental Shelf. They are so extensive because, although the first two of these zones are calculated from the coast outward, the third reflects not our above-water islands but a whole continent, albeit one that is 93 percent under water — Zealandia, one of Earth's two submerged continents, the other being the Kerguelen Plateau in the south Indian Ocean.

Zealandia extends from New Caledonia in the north to beyond Campbell Island in the south, and out to the Chatham Islands in the east. Generally speaking, it is everything above the depth of 2500 metres, the dividing line between continental crust above and oceanic crust below.

IN THE MID–1960S, just as politicians were reconsidering the laws of the sea, scientists' understanding of the composition and workings of the earth underwent radical revision: although it had been suspected since the 1900s, new technologies led to the fundamental game-changer — the confirmation of the theory of plate tectonics. It was realised that the solid outer crust of the earth is a mosaic of 15 or so earth-curved, irregular-edged, giant plates that are in ever-so-slow but ever-so-definite motion, jostling and colliding, stretching, eroding, rising and sinking, riding over and sliding under each other above the hotter, softer, more malleable rock in the mantle below.

New Zealand spans two of these monsters, the Australian Plate to the west and the Pacific in the east: they strain and push in contrariwise directions, one indomitable force in massive confrontation with the other. In the region of the North Island, the Pacific Plate pushes west and slowly sinks beneath the Australian while in the South Island, it is the reverse, with the Australian Plate not only sliding below the Pacific but also — because they are not head-on — shearing and slipping hundreds of kilometres to the northeast at the same time. The outcome of this titanic arm-wrestle, above and below the water, is our volatile, earthquake-prone, mountainous and volcanic landscape.

540 MILLION YEARS AGO New Zealand as we know it did not exist; nor did the continents we today know as Australia, Antarctica, Africa and South America. To the west and south of our present location, there was a single landmass, the supercontinent Gondwana, with the Pacific Plate to its east. For hundreds of millions of years, the Pacific Plate behaved more or less as it does today, pushing, sliding and diving; as it did, it piled ocean sediment into a range of coastal mountains along Gondwana's eastern fringe.

Then, between 100 and 125 million years ago, there was a reversal: as if all that opposing momentum caused the two antagonists to fall away from each other, the pushing and subducting ceased and was replaced by spreading. Hot rock welled up from the mantle and expanded on the inland side of Gondwana's coastal mountains, eventually forming an enormous rift valley between them and the rest of the continent.

Subsequently, starting around 85 million years ago and continuing for some 30 million years, the ocean moved in, forming what we now know as the Tasman Sea. A chunk of Gondwana about half the size of Australia, the new landmass Zealandia, was slowly pushed east and north into the Pacific Ocean. As it cooled, it sank into the soft rock of the mantle and in time was also engulfed by the ocean. By about 35 million years ago, it had been reduced to a chain of islands approximately a third the size of modern New Zealand.

About 25 million years ago, another period of tectonic activity began, with those behemoths, the Australian and Pacific plates, back to their old push-pull ways again. A fresh plate boundary appeared, splitting the fledgling continent along a fracture starting at the 10,000-metre-deep Kermadec Trench in the north and extending as far as the Puysegur Trench in the south. All of the North Island, the northern South Island, a strip of the West Coast and all of Zealandia to the north and west of that line are on the Australian Plate, while the remainder of the South Island east of the Alpine Fault, and Zealandia to the east, is on the Pacific Plate.

Franz Josef Glacier: the erosive power of ice is a major force in shaping the land.

Modern New Zealand came into being over those 25 million years, from a combination of uplift and mountain building caused by the colliding plates and extreme volcanic activity caused by weaknesses in the crust's surface along the plate boundary. Numerous ice ages came and went over the next 2.5 million years: rising and falling sea levels, in tandem with the erosive powers of sun, ice, wind, wave and rain carved the mountains and coasts and dumped their sediments on low-lying land and in the sea.

OF SHELVES & SEAMOUNTS

The shape of our big blue backyard is determined by what lies below — plains, valleys, gorges, mountain ranges and volcanoes, many on a scale that is difficult to comprehend. They lie largely in the deep darkness, sensed by satellites and depth-sounding equipment, but never seen in the way that we see their counterparts on land.

If, however, as in a children's tale, the ocean were to disappear, and we

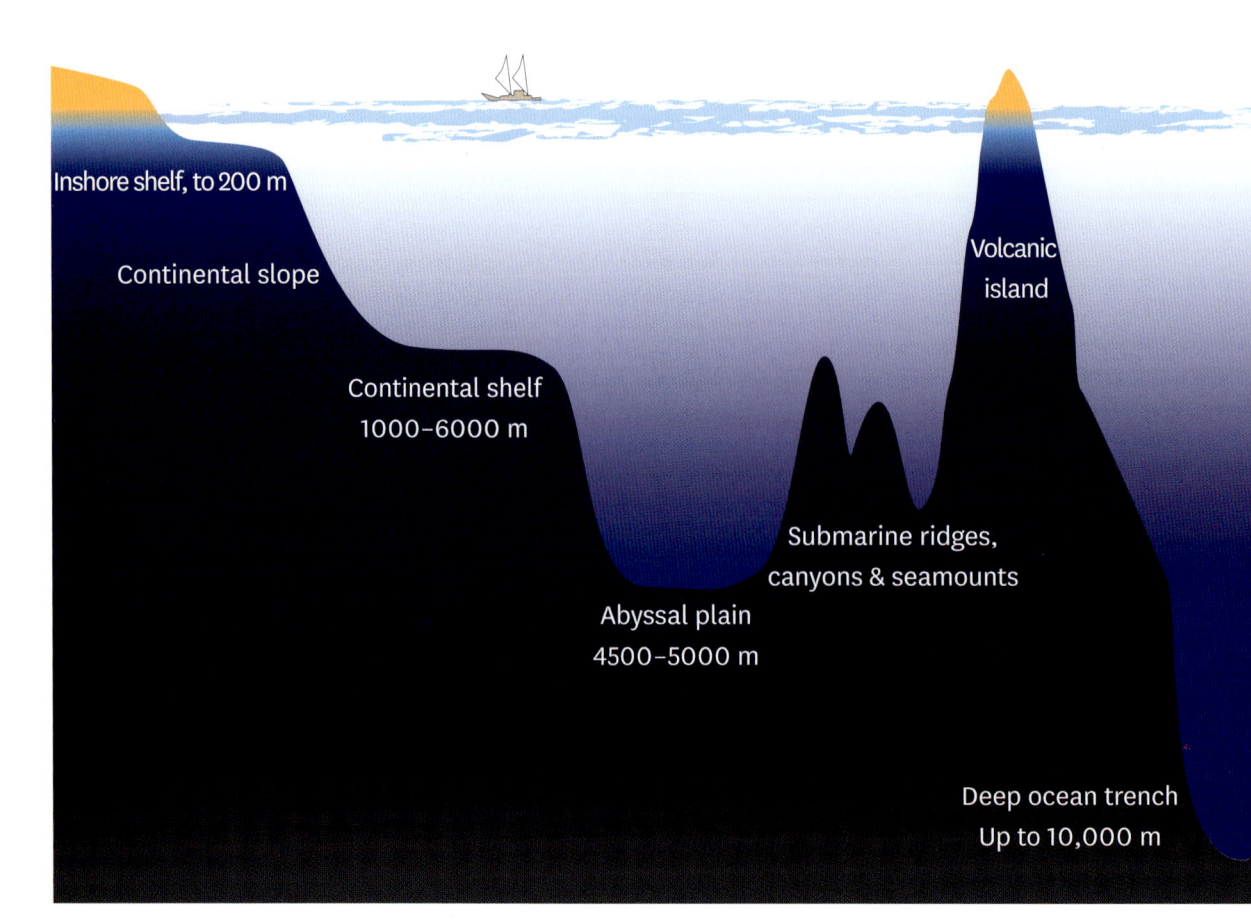

A cross-section of New Zealand's ocean floor. Depending on location, an actual representation would differ enormously in proportion and scale.

Inshore shelf, to 200 m

Continental slope

Continental shelf
1000–6000 m

Submarine ridges, canyons & seamounts

Abyssal plain
4500–5000 m

Volcanic island

Deep ocean trench
Up to 10,000 m

A black smoker: the Brothers volcano in the Kermadec Arc.

could take a look at this astonishing landscape, we would first pass over the inshore shelf, a relatively shallow platform of approximately 130 metres at its deepest. Off Taranaki and Southland, it is over 160 kilometres from the shore to its outer edge, but it is almost non-existent at Kaikōura and only a few kilometres off Fiordland. (Note: this book uses the term 'inshore shelf' to describe this area in preference to the more commonly used 'continental shelf' because the latter has become ambiguous through its use to also describe the far greater landmass of Zealandia.)

The inshore shelf is our playground, where we paddle, swim, surf, dive and fish. It was formed around 20,000 years ago when much of the world was buried in ice and sea levels were 120–130 metres lower than they are today. Shingle, sand and silt were washed off the uplifted land and flattened by wave action into a barren, gradually sloping foreshore.

Beyond the inshore shelf, the ground drops abruptly from 130 metres depth across what is called the continental slope to the continental shelf. It's deep: around three-quarters of New Zealand's EEZ is between one and six kilometres deep but there are spots that are even deeper, such as the Kermadec Trench, which plunges to ten kilometres. For a sense of scale, think of the Grand Canyon, which is a mere 1800 metres at its deepest . . . and multiply by five and a half times.

The standout feature is the rift boundary between the mighty Pacific Plate and its stubborn neighbour, the Australian, but there is much to wonder at elsewhere in this submarine world, including a number of plateaus at depths ranging from 500 to 1500 metres. They include the

Photic zone
0–200 m

Twilight or mesopelagic zone
200–1000 m

Midnight or bathypelagic zone
1000–4000 m

Abyssal zone
4000–6000 m

Hadal zone
off this scale below 6000 m

500,000-square-kilometre Campbell Plateau, the 1400-kilometre-long finger of the Chatham Rise, the 350,000-square-kilometre Hikurangi Plateau, the 30,000-square-kilometre Northland Plateau and the 280,000-square-kilometre Challenger Plateau.

There are hills, mountain ranges and seamounts or underwater volcanoes singly, in clusters or in chains across the continental shelf, both on the plateaus and in deeper water. There are also numerous ridges, troughs, channels and basins, often cleft by steep-sided canyons and pocked with holes.

The continental shelf is surrounded by deep ocean abyss at depths of four and a half to five kilometres, much of it flat and featureless. To the west lies the Tasman Basin, with the South West Pacific Basin to the south and east. There are two lesser basins, the South Fiji Basin north of the Northland Plateau and the Norfolk Basin west of the North Island's mid-west coast.

WATER, FROM TOP TO BOTTOM

Plant material in the sea is so different from plant material on land that it's hard to think about it in the same breath. They only have one thing in common, they're green and they manufacture their own food.

But the ones in the sea are microscopic — if you say 'microscopic' real quick, that sounds like a size grouping! But within phytoplankton there is the same range of size as there is in terrestrial plants — and terrestrial plants go from a moss to a kauri tree, which is a thousand times. But within phytoplankton there are the ones that are a thousand times bigger than another one and all of them need a microscope so you can see them. In fact, the smaller ones need an electron microscope!

— Dr Bill Ballantine

Scientists often describe the way the water changes as it deepens by talking about the 'water column'. Imagine a giant cylinder extending from the sea's surface to its floor: from top to bottom, it passes through a series of watery zones that are determined by many factors including location, chemistry (especially salinity but also dissolved oxygen, carbon dioxide and minerals),

What you get varies according to place, season and time of day, but sea water is full of microscopic life — diatoms, larvae, eggs, zooplankton (copepods) and bacteria. This sample is from Auckland harbour, June 2014.

clarity (which in turns affects the amount and quality of light which enters it), temperature and movement (by current, tide and wind). And, of course, the plants and animals that make their homes in each zone.

The surface layer is by far the busiest. It is sometimes also called the photic zone because the presence of light is its key characteristic. It extends from the surface to about 200 metres, the distance that light will penetrate before giving way to darkness — the greater part of the ocean. Only the upper 80 or so metres are sufficiently lit to support photosynthesis although there is gloomy light a wee way below that. Temperatures in this zone are likely to be similar to those on the surface.

The photic layer's blue-green colour is a giveaway: it is sometimes called a 'marine meadow' because it's loaded with phytoplankton — thousands of species of minuscule, single-celled floating plants, millions per litre, that harness the light in the sunlit upper waters and are the power house of the whole ocean — the basis of the food web. The very smallest, called 'picoplankton', are similar in size to bacteria, less than one thousandth of a millimetre across.

The majority use chlorophyll, the pigment that makes them green, to process the sun's energy and convert water and carbon dioxide to sugars and the essential-for-most by-product, oxygen. Phytoplankton includes diatoms (microscopic algae with ornate and beautiful silica shells), dinoflagellates (weak swimmers with two small, whip-like tails), phaeophytes (brown algae) and cyanobacteria (blue-green algae).

And so it begins. Phytoplankton are eaten by often equally microscopic animals known collectively as zooplankton. Zooplankton, like phytoplankton, largely drift with the slop and slap of the sea. Some of these creatures will never be any different but others are, as it were, just passing through — larvae of crustaceans, shellfish and fish that will, if they survive, ultimately transit to another phase of existence. Zooplankton includes animals with exotic names such as foraminifera (single-celled organisms up to a centimetre in diameter that are so numerous that their calcite-rich shells are the main constituents of chalk), radiolarians (with shells made of silica) and various ciliates (with tiny hairs around their bodies) and zooflagellates (like dinoflagellates, they have long thread-like structures that give them a limited amount of propulsion).

Larger zooplankton includes jellyfish, siphonophores (colonial animals such as Portuguese man-o'-war) and copepods ('oar-feet'). Copepods may be small but their 10,000 or so species in total form the greatest protein source in the ocean. Krill, also crustaceans and a little larger than copepods (at up to 50 mm), feed on phytoplankton and to a lesser extent, smaller zooplankton. There are over 80 species of krill. These tiny creatures form the major part of the diet of the world's largest animals, the various species of baleen whales. Krill are also eaten by fish, squid, seals and seabirds, including penguins and albatrosses.

Below the photic layer, the twilight or mesopelagic zone extends roughly from 200 to 1000 metres. It is deep blue to black in colour and only dimly lit in daylight hours. It is much colder — with temperatures falling steadily across the zone from around 5°C to 2°C. Pressure at 1000 metres is equal to 100 atmospheres. There are no plants here but this is the dormitory for the majority of the creatures that graze the zone above. At night, in what is said to be the most massive animal migration on the planet, hundreds of millions of tonnes of animals rise through the water column to feed in the now-dark photic layer before descending again at dawn. Among other things, this behaviour means there's less chance of being eaten. Living at cooler depths is also thought to conserve energy because food is metabolised more slowly.

A large range of weird and wonderful creatures inhabits the twilight zone (no vampires — although there are dragonfish and fangfish with teeth so large that adults are unable to close their mouths), including crustaceans, jellyfish-like animals, eels, octopuses, shrimps, squid and many kinds of worm. Many are bioluminescent: as William Beebe noticed, some wink and wink and flash, others glow dimly. In some cases, light is used by predators to confuse and attract prey, in others it is used by prey to confuse and evade predators. Most predators in this zone are slow moving and operate by stealth — they either entice their victims to come to them or just wait, mouths agape, and pounce. Fish that live at this level are often thin and small with dark upper surfaces and large upward-turned eyes and jaws.

IT'S LIGHTS OUT BELOW. The midnight or bathypelagic zone, from 1000 to 4000 metres, is so dark the only visible light is produced by its inhabitants. Pressure is immense and yet as many as 150 species live at these depths. Sperm whales are known to descend this deep hunting for giant squid.

While it doesn't get any blacker in the abyssal zone or plain from 4000 to 6000 metres, the temperature continues to fall until it is not far off freezing. The pressure is extreme. Very few creatures live below 4000 metres aside from invertebrates and tiny crustaceans. That's in some degree because there's very little food: one way or another, virtually everything generated in the upper layers has been intercepted and eaten on its way down.

Below 6000 metres, it's the deep trenches and canyons of the hadal zone. The water temperature is just above freezing but the pressure is beyond extreme — at 8000 metres depth it's 8000 tonnes per square metre. Nevertheless there are living things such as invertebrates, including starfish and tubeworms. And yes, it's very, *very* dark.

From the midnight zone: in February 2013 a dead giant squid was found floating in South Bay, Kaikōura, by Christchurch couple Jack and Sharon Osikai. The creature was eight metres long and weighed approximately 140 kilograms.

HOW SMALL?

It's estimated that there are 100,000 species of diatoms, making them among the most common types of phytoplankton, contributing up to 45 percent of the ocean's primary production. Because they have no means of getting around or even of keeping afloat, they have a range of adaptations such as flat bodies, radiating spines, oil droplets and air-filled floats to keep them in the upper layers of the sea.

Their seemingly endless array of shapes and sizes attracted amateur microscopists in Victorian England in the second half of the 19th century; using an array of specially designed tools, diatoms, butterfly scales and other tiny objects were painstakingly arranged in artistic patterns on slides before being cemented in place.

LEFT: A slide comprised of diatoms, sponge spicules and plates and anchors of Synapta, a genus of slender, transparent holothurians.

TOP RIGHT: A slide preparation cabinet protected the design from dust and air currents during the lengthy process.

OPPOSITE: Ernst Haeckel (1834–1919) was a talented German scientist and artist who, among his many achievements, discovered, described and named thousands of new species. His art includes detailed, multi-colour illustrations of animals and sea creatures such as this selection of copepods.

32 OUR BIG BLUE BACKYARD

1 · OUR VERY BIG BLUE BACKYARD · 33

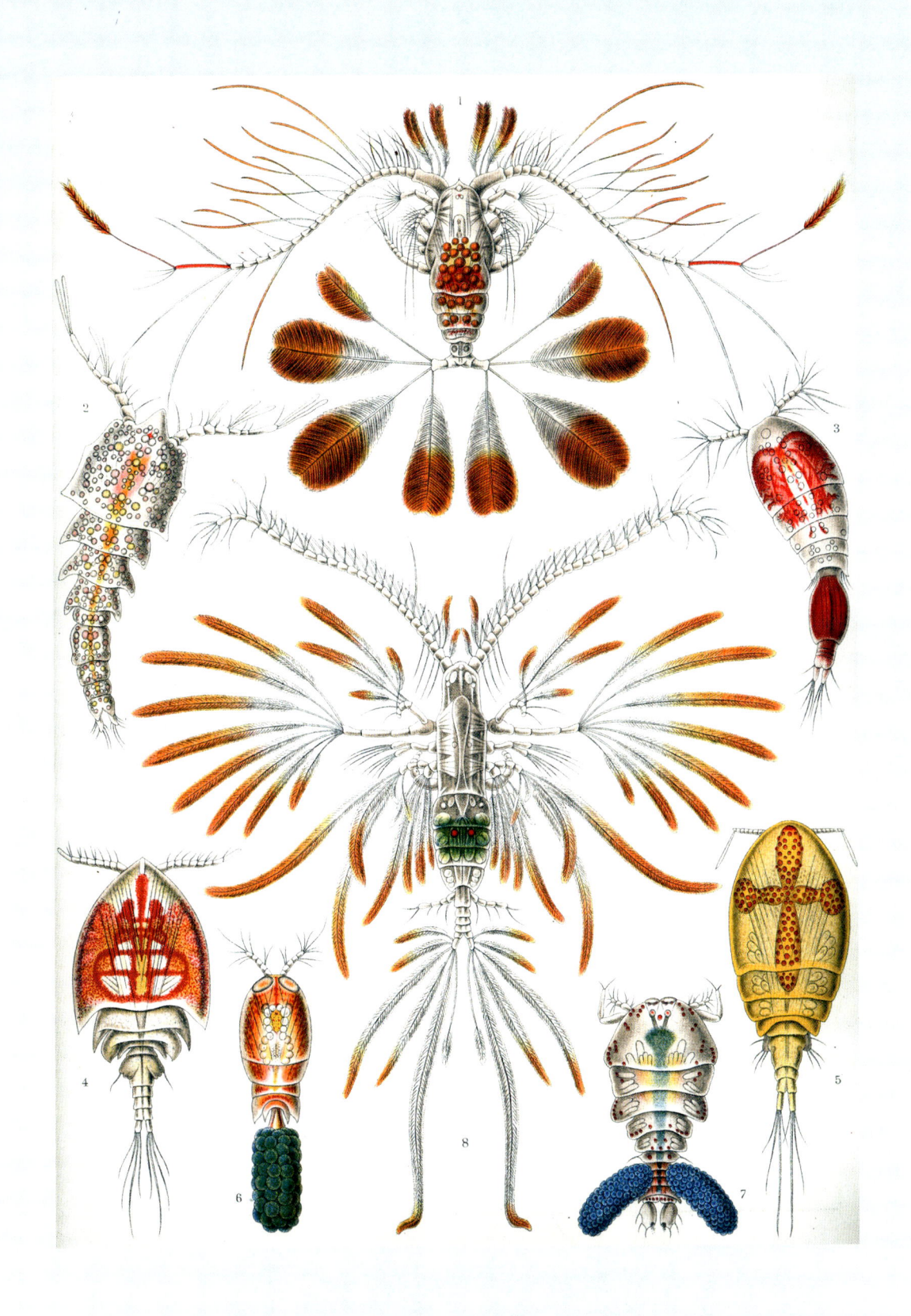

SLOPPING AROUND

Water is water, right, and all much of a muchness? Not so: in the ocean, a lot of what happens is about motion, about currents, tides, waves, eddies, gyres and about the transport, layering and mixing of different bodies of water with different qualities — such as salinity, temperature, nutrients and clarity — all of which has a bearing on the life it supports.

Clearly, the chemistry of seawater is dominated by salt, but even that varies from one location to another depending on circumstances such as the presence of rivers and the amount of evaporation. On average, one kilogram of water contains 35 grams of salts. And while most of it is common salt (sodium chloride), there are also salts of potassium, magnesium, sulphates and carbonates as well as rarer substances such as arsenic, uranium, mercury, titanium and even minuscule amounts of gold (0.00000004 grams/kilogram).

This matters because the amount of salt plus the temperature determines the water's density: less dense, warm water floats above denser, cold water across a boundary called the 'thermocline'. Water does not generally cross between the two densities unless some other agent causes it to move, such as a current flowing up the side of an undersea landform, an upwelling, wind or perhaps a winter storm. It may not seem very significant but unless there is mixing, the layers become more consolidated, one of the reasons we sometimes have phytoplankton blooms in spring when warm water is trapped in surface layers.

In fact, temperature and salt together are the engine that drives overall oceanic circulation. When ice forms on the surface of the sea in the southern polar region it excludes salt, which increases the water's density, causing it to sink. Colder water also sinks. As this colder, denser water flows off the Antarctic continental shelf into the abyssal ocean beyond, it initiates currents that, among other things, are vital to the earth's weather.

NEW ZEALAND LIES IN THE path of two major water systems. The more dominant is the East Australia Current, which flows from the equatorial regions of the Pacific down the east coast of Australia and across the Tasman. When it strikes Cape Rēinga, it splits into the West Auckland and East Auckland currents and continues down both coasts of the North Island bathing northern parts of the country in warm, relatively salty waters. The East Auckland Current forms a number of important depth-stirring eddies in the northeast before eventually flowing past East Cape (where it becomes the East Cape Current) as far as Banks Peninsula, where it is deflected east across a line called the Subtropical Convergence (or Front), over the Chatham Rise to the Chatham Islands and off into the central Pacific.

South of that line, westerly winds drive relatively cold, fresh waters of the Antarctic Circumpolar Current northward. This current is sometimes also called the 'West Wind Drift' and is an important body of water that flows eastwards right around Antarctica.

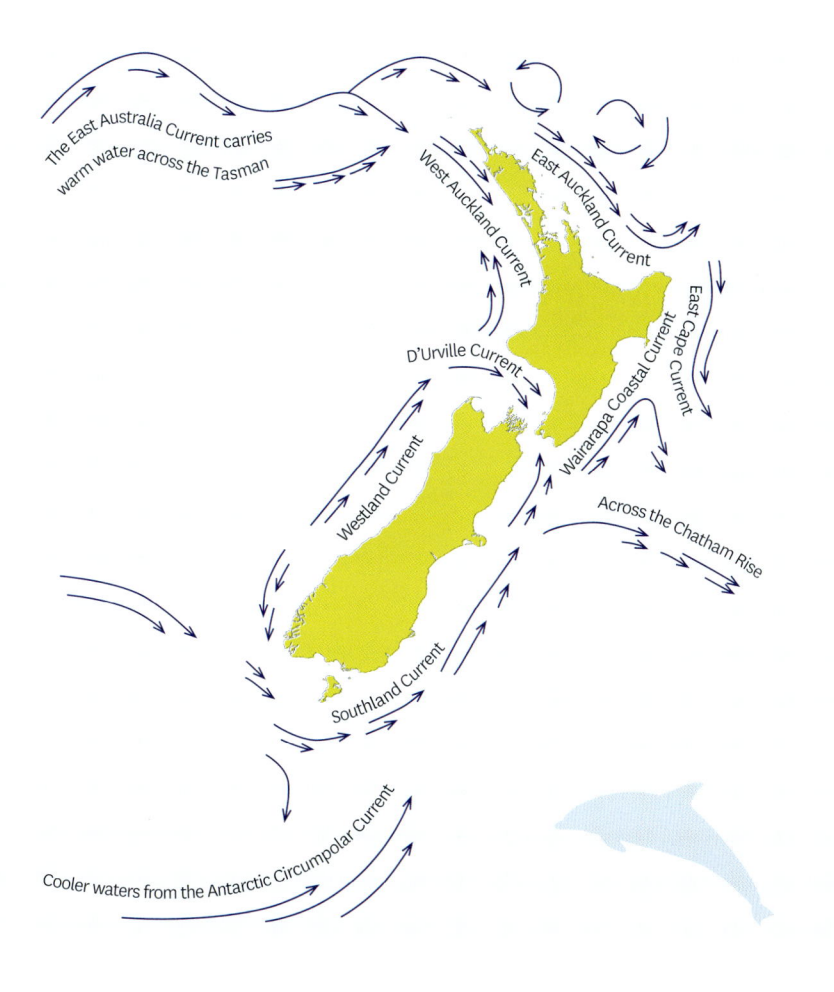

A broad view of New Zealand's ocean currents. In reality, they are complex and are influenced by a multitude of factors, changing by the hour, day and season.

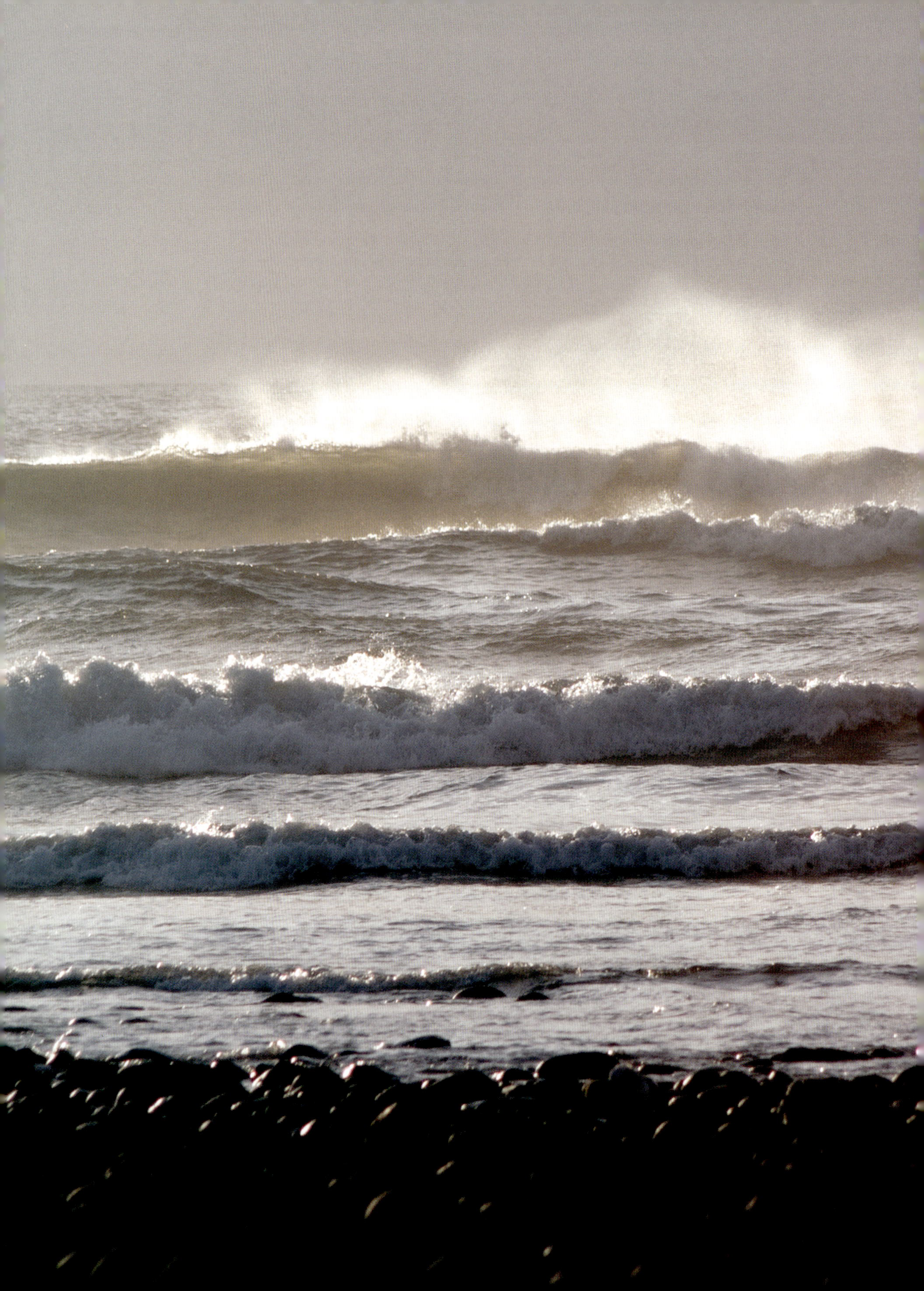

Waves are children of the wind. How hard the wind blows, how long it blows and where it blows from determines how high waves are, how frequent and the distance between them. Waves can be generated locally or in another part of the world entirely, travelling long distances before reaching New Zealand's shores. Waves in the west and in the south of the country tend to be most substantial because they are driven by the westerly winds of the Southern Ocean. Storms also generate very high waves — outside Wellington Harbour, for instance, waves average six metres during storms but at their most extreme, individual waves have been recorded at 13 metres.

When waves break on a beach they slow and lose impetus but on a rocky shore or over a reef they have more impact, oxygenating the water and stirring up the seafloor.

Tides are caused primarily by the gravitational pull of the moon and, to a lesser extent, by the sun. New Zealand's tidal range is between one and three metres, which is small compared with other parts of the world, and the tidal current is not too swift, at approximately two kilometres per hour (one knot).

However, New Zealand is unique in that there are five hours, almost a complete tide cycle's difference, between one coast and the other — when it's high tide on the west, it's low on the east. This causes tidal currents of up to seven knots through parts of the Cook Strait as the waters hurry from one coast to the other. At French Pass in the Marlborough Sounds, the tidal flow resembles a swift river.

Wellings are movements of large bodies of water, either from depths of hundreds of metres to the surface or the reverse. They are caused by a combination of factors including wind and the earth's rotation and are an important means of mixing the layers, especially moving nutrients from one area to another; higher nutrient levels increase the productivity of phytoplankton, initiating a cascade of fruitfulness right across the food web.

East End beach in New Plymouth: Taranaki's wild west coast.

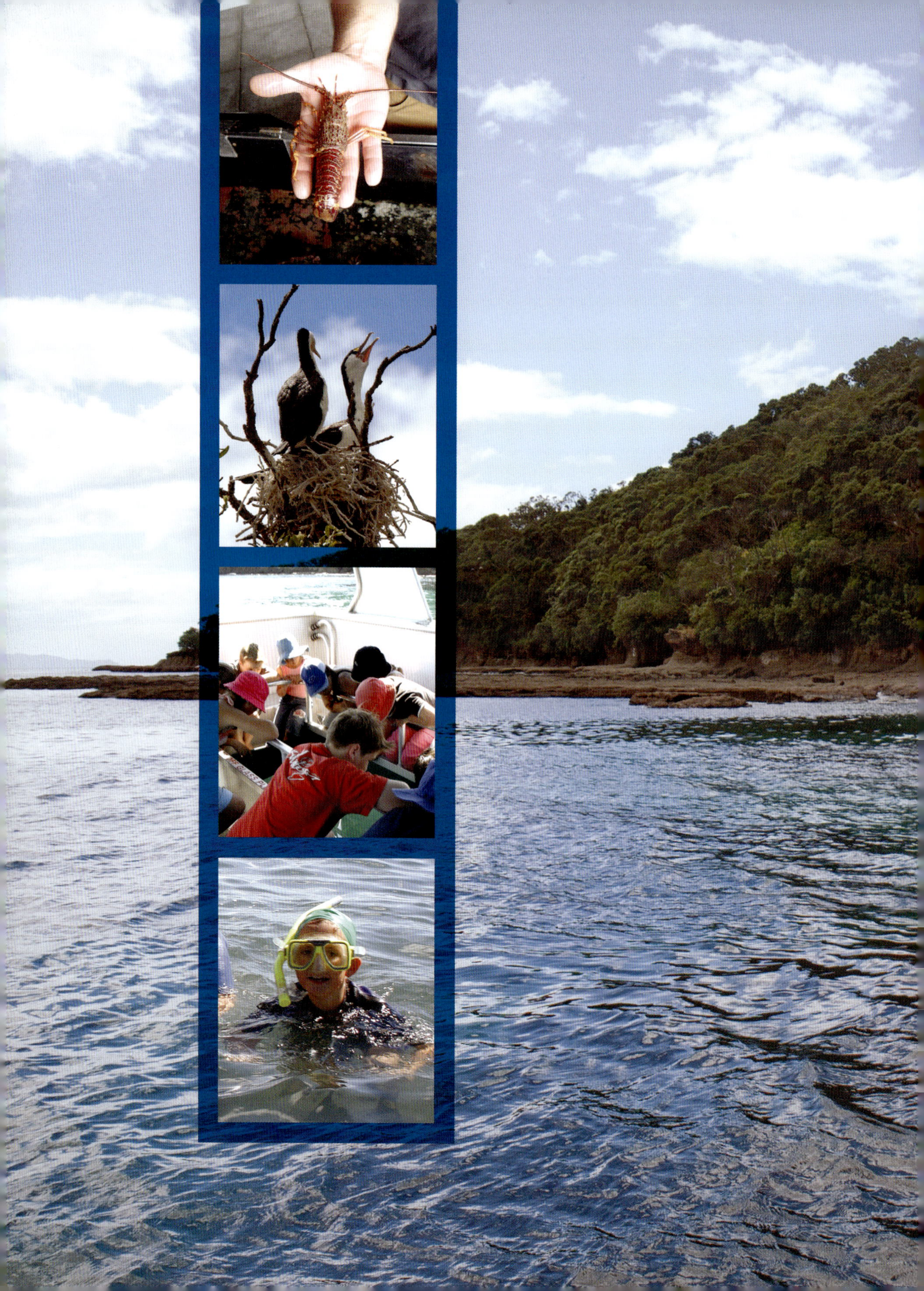

2
MARINE RESERVES

LEADING THE WAY

We really are at the beginning of it all. The trick, of course, is to make sure we never find the end. And that, most certainly, will require a lot more than lucky breaks.

— Bill Bryson, A Short History of Nearly Everything

Why protect the ocean? Why not just let it be? It's very simple: we terrestrial animals are too populous and too good at what we do, and that other *world*, the sea, doesn't have a chance — we fish for leisure or a living and in both cases, devise ever-more-sophisticated aids, from improved lines, hooks and fish-finding sonar to ocean-going fleets and factory ships that process hundreds of tonnes of fish a day. It cannot continue.

NEW ZEALAND HAS ADDRESSED the need for marine conservation by creating a patchwork of areas with varying degrees of protection, including inshore and offshore marine parks, marine reserves, marine mammal sanctuaries and Māori-regulated areas. They are overseen by the Ministry of Primary Industries (MPI) whose brief is to sustain fisheries using the Quota Management System, the Department of Conservation (DOC) which looks after national parks and marine reserves, and iwi, who manage mātaitai, taiāpure and rāhui; see chapter 4 for more about these cultural mechanisms that protect resources.

Offshore, in Benthic Protection Areas, deep-water trawling is prohibited in over 1.2 million square kilometres of seabed, including the seafloor around many of New Zealand's approximately 750 extraordinary and fragile seamounts and active hydrothermal vents.

Under the Wildlife Act 1953 and the Marine Mammals Protection Act 1978, a range of marine creatures are protected in all New Zealand waters, regardless of location. These acts cover all marine mammals, all

PREVIOUS:
Goat Island: a young crayfish from the Goat Island Marine Discovery Centre; shags nesting above the beach; Te Huruhi Primary School students visit in 2011.

seabirds except southern black-backed gulls, all marine reptiles, black corals, gorgonian corals, stony corals, hydrocorals and nine species of fish — deepwater nurse shark, white pointer (great white) shark, whale shark, basking shark, oceanic white-tip shark, manta ray, spinetail devil ray, giant grouper and spotted black grouper.

But of all the protection mechanisms, 'marine reserve' status is the most complete. A reserve is a permanent 'no-take' zone, with straightforward rules: no fishing, no removal of any material whether dead or living, no dredging, dumping, construction or any other activity that would disturb natural processes. As such, it is a yardstick against which all other activity in and on the sea can be measured, whether positive or negative. By its very nature, marine reserve status protects, fosters and in all likelihood restores (it's not guaranteed) biodiversity in an area — a good thing in itself but it is also a backup, if you like, against events outside the reserve.

It's also a Very Good Thing that there is a place that is just let be, where the living things can just, in the words of one of the champions of marine reserves, Dr Bill Ballantine, 'do what they do' — a place that is valued for its own sake.

MAKING A MARINE RESERVE is not as straightforward as fencing off a reserve on land because the sea is inherently more difficult to manage: its waters and the things that live in them are constantly on the move. In general, marine species reproduce by scattering large numbers of eggs to disperse on the currents — they drift like thistledown as they develop and eventually they settle and become adults. This means no part of the ocean stands alone, including a marine reserve. Some of its species come from beyond its boundaries, making it vital to have not just a few reserves but a number that are well placed, with a degree of connection with each other.

On the other hand, making a marine reserve is also very simple — no fences, no weeds, no alien predators, no planting days, no trap-lines . . . it's just a matter of sorting out boundaries and saying 'no take'. All you have to do, as marine scientist Roger Grace says, is 'stop fishing. You don't have to do a damned thing.'

There are many criteria for selection, including special reasons such as exceptional beauty, unique natural features or historical and cultural values, but in the end the essence of a marine reserve is that it is *typical* of its kind and location. Ideally, there will one day be several of each type, including similar or replicated environments and species.

As of the time of writing, 2014, there are 38 marine reserves and seven more on the horizon, some around remote oceanic islands, others within the boundaries of metropolitan Auckland. They include fiords, harbours and open coasts, and cover a range of latitudes and habitats.

Nevertheless, significant areas of inshore seas are not represented: there's a cluster of ten reserves on the east coast of the upper North Island north of East Cape but none on the opposite coast, right down to north Taranaki — there are only three on the North Island west coast, in fact. They are similarly sparse on the South Island, with four in the Golden Bay–Nelson–Marlborough region, two on Banks Peninsula, a nest of ten in the Fiordland area and one on Stewart Island/Rakiura. This paucity will soon be slightly redressed by five to come on the West Coast and one in Kaikōura but there is scope for many more.

The reason there are so few is that their creation is enormously contentious. Time and again, reserves have been proposed and after years of consultation and often heartfelt, sometimes angry debate, have either been radically trimmed in size or canned altogether, to the despair and frustration of their backers. The first marine reserve, at Goat Island northeast of Auckland, is an example.

A crayfish ventures among the sponges in daylight at Goat Island Marine Reserve.

> *In New Zealand, we have discussed marine reserves for 40 years. We established the first reserve at Leigh nearly 30 years ago. We now have 19 reserves scattered round the country. We know that they are practical, and that once established, they are popular and successful. We have carried out enough trials and tests. I want my grandchildren to inherit a full system of marine reserves, just as we inherited a system of reserves on land.*
>
> — Bill Ballantine, 2004

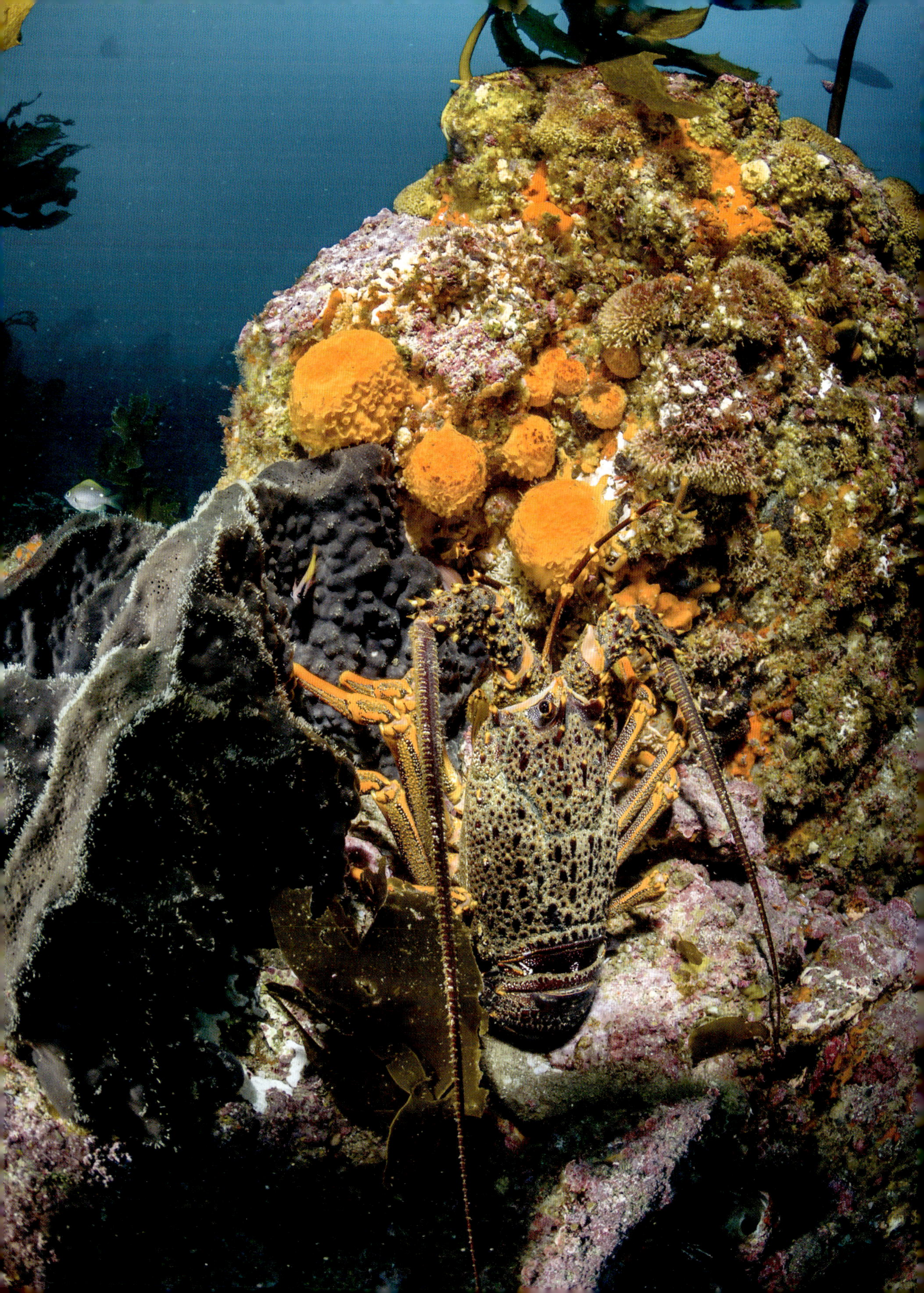

DOWNHILL FROM EVERYWHERE

It's one example only of the many troubles that beset the world's oceans.

In 1997 Captain Charles Moore, environmentalist and skipper of the 50-foot racing catamaran *Alguita* took an unconventional route home across the northern Pacific from Hawaii to southern California. He and his crew passed through the doldrums where few bother to go because of its lack of wind. To their astonishment and horror, they found themselves horizon-to-horizon in a mess of debris. They were at the heart of a gyre, where ocean currents meet and swirl together, carrying a stew of every imaginable plastic — bottles and bottle caps, cigarette filters, combs, cups, toys, syringes, bags, wrappers, fishing lines, nets and bins, rubbish from oil rigs. Worse, it was not only on the surface but, as Moore found when he returned, the trash was suspended to a depth of 30 metres and consisted of not only whole objects but also minute plastic particles — so many that they outnumbered plankton by a ratio of six to one.

Dubbed the 'Great Pacific Garbage Patch', the area is not seen by satellites although it covers approximately twice the size of France; no one had previously been aware of its existence let alone its scale. There are five such areas in the world: the Indian Ocean Gyre, the North and South Pacific gyres, and the North and South Atlantic gyres. They're the hot spots for drifting trash, but lest we think ourselves immune, nowhere is free: plastic debris is found in every sea and on every shore on Earth, from the poles to the tropics. And lest you think it's just a matter of scooping it out — it cannot be cleaned up. It is too huge. All we can do is prevent it from getting worse.

44 • OUR BIG BLUE BACKYARD

Plastics are so enduring and so useful that it's difficult to imagine modern life without them but it's that very durability that makes them so problematic. Every single piece ever manufactured still exists somewhere. Plastics in the ocean break down in sunlight and from wave action, but only to smaller pieces that are even more widespread — in the water, on beaches, on ocean floors and in the food web (the tiniest pieces are called 'mermaid's tears'). Worse still, plastics attract and bond with substances such as DDT and PCBs, concentrating them up to a million times the level of the poisons floating free in the water; so not only are plastics problems in themselves, they are toxic problems.

The plastic trash has been quietly building up, year on year. As the inventory opposite shows, some of it comes from fishing and tourist vessels, oil and gas platforms and from aquaculture facilities. But, as Moore points out, the ocean is 'downhill from everywhere': the bulk, an estimated 80 percent, is consumer plastic, tossed, washed and blown from the land. Scientists estimate that a million seabirds and 100,000 marine mammals and turtles die annually as a direct result of the plastic plague, entangled in it, swallowing or choking on it, poisoned by it.

The impact of plastics is nowhere more tragically illustrated than on the tiny Midway Islands, northwest extensions of the Hawaiian archipelago, over 3000 kilometres from the nearest continent. These days, although criss-crossed by runways and installations from World War II, they are a national wildlife refuge. From above, the islands are blue-green like an opal, washed by azure waters. They appear pristine.

However, the Midways are also at the heart of the North Pacific Gyre and millions of pieces of trash float in the islands' waters and pile their beaches. The Laysan albatrosses that breed on the atolls are surface feeders like all their kind; they mistake the colourful debris for their usual prey of squid and take it home in their gullets for their young, with disastrous consequences. The beaches are littered with decomposing corpses of adult and juvenile birds, their bellies chock-full of human trash — more like 'the cigarette lighter shelf at a convenience store,' says Moore.

New Zealand is not immune from this curse. In 2011, scientists recovered more than 200 plastic fragments from the stomach of a flesh-footed shearwater on Lord Howe Island, just next door to our own backyard. No one knows precisely how much plastic junk enters the oceans annually but estimates range as high as 6.5 million tonnes every year, enough for 13,000 pieces of plastic for every square kilometre of ocean.

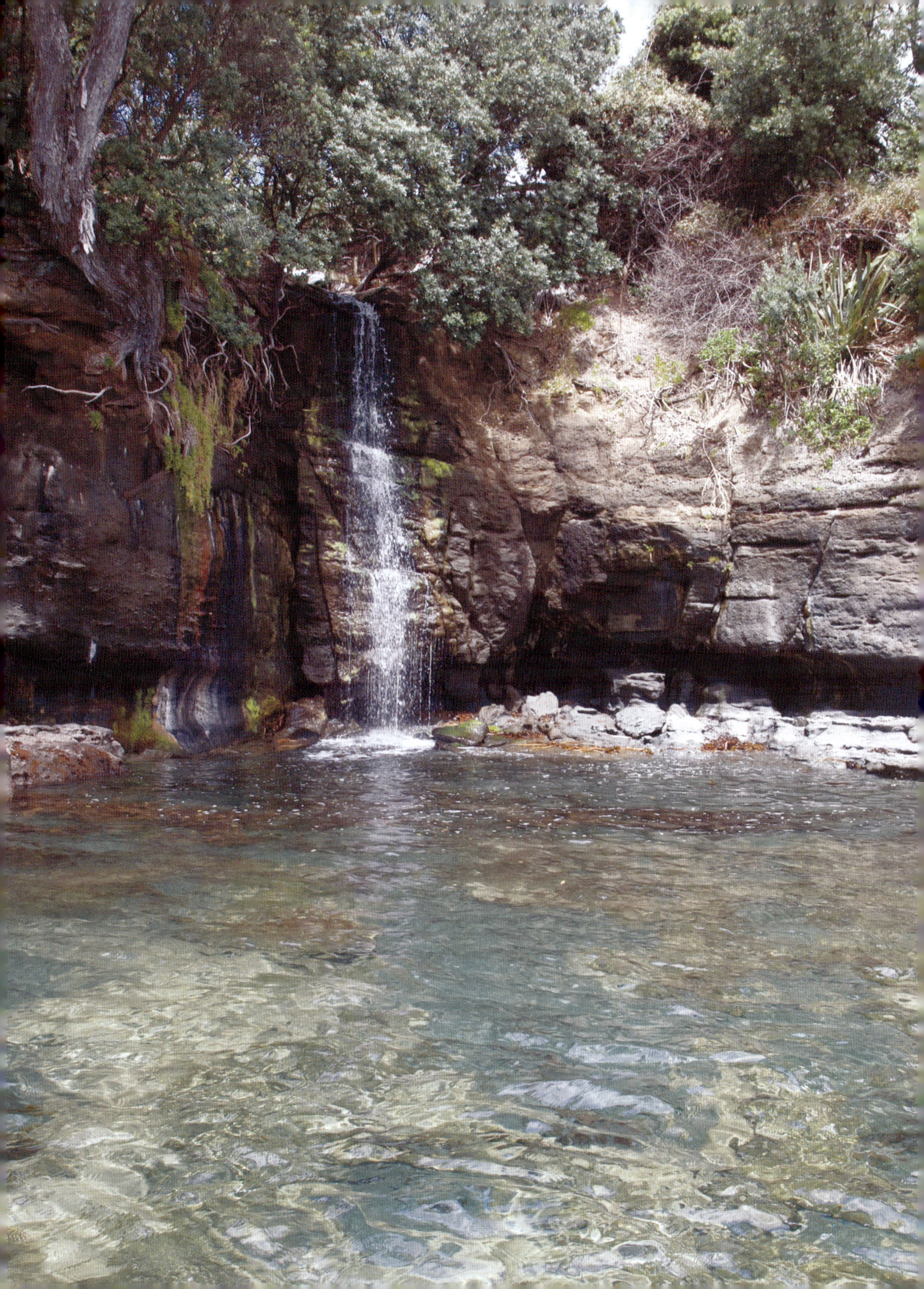

THE FIRST: GOAT ISLAND

New Zealand's first marine reserve is a five-kilometre tract on the east coast at Leigh, north of Auckland. It extends from Ōkakari Point to Cape Rodney and, although its correct title is 'Cape Rodney–Ōkakari Point Marine Reserve', is generally known as either 'Goat Island' or just 'Leigh'.

The area was selected for the University of Auckland's marine laboratory in the late 1950s by Professor John Morton not because it was extraordinary but the reverse — because it was ordinary, a sample of typical northeastern New Zealand coast. Goat Island, named after the animals once released there, is a 25-hectare, low, bush-clad island about halfway along the reserve. Pōhutukawa line the shores, with shags looking down from untidy nests overhanging the beach.

The attraction for the university was the diversity of habitats within a relatively small area: rocky cliffs, ledges and benches are interspersed with sandy beaches along the shore, and there are caves and platforms, underwater reefs, boulders, stacks and sandy seafloors around the island. Some of the rock is hard greywacke, some mud and sandstone. The waters are often calm and clear, ideal for snorkelling and diving, and the island provides shelter for small boats and swimmers. Although the central area had been fished clean of crayfish, pāua and snapper, it was potentially rich in sea life including reef fish, kelp beds, and kina (sea urchins), sponges and other invertebrates.

The laboratory opened in 1964 but already, a year later, it was clear that continued fishing was reducing the marine area's usefulness. Dr Bill Ballantine, then director and sole employee of the laboratory, reports that the matter came up at the first management committee meeting. The chairman, Professor Val Chapman, said: 'We must get a marine reserve!' Everyone looked blank. *Novel idea!*

Despite the long-accepted concept of terrestrial reserves, there was

A small waterfall empties into the clear waters over rock platforms below the University of Auckland Leigh Marine Laboratory.

no provision in law for a maritime equivalent and when the then Marine Department was approached, it was distinctly unenthusiastic, replying, Ballantine says, that 'if anything was to be reserved it should be in areas remote from population centres. They could see no reason to promote any legislation — and in any case, Parliament was very busy.'

Undaunted, Chapman began a letter-writing campaign and the rest of the team, including Ballantine, fell in behind. 'We organised public meetings, lobbied politicians, gave school talks and generally made a nuisance,' he says.

Twelve years of public education, gathering evidence, canvassing, submissions and counter-submissions followed. Diving clubs endorsed the proposal along with the New Zealand Marine Sciences Society and the New Zealand Underwater Association but the journey was anything but smooth.

Those in favour learned, as supporters of every reserve since have learned, that the quantity and quality of public objections is daunting. Most dissenters were passionate and outspoken; some objections were well founded and well argued but many were unreasonable and illogical.

Misinformation, whether deliberately or inadvertently generated, assumed a life of its own and was difficult to defuse. Ultimately, it seemed, many opposers had profound difficulty accepting the loss of an area where they had long been accustomed to untrammelled freedom. One thing was certain: while the innovation and much of the impetus for the reserve stemmed from people associated with the laboratory, unless the hearts and minds of the wider population were won, it was going nowhere.

But win them they did. The supporters' tenacity was rewarded when the Cape Rodney–Ōkakari Point Marine Reserve was formally gazetted in 1975 and two years later, after administrative formalities were sorted, the first signs were erected on the shore. The new reserve extended seaward for 800 metres from the land and for the first time in New Zealand, an area of shore and sea — 547 hectares — was 'no take'. It was, as they say, the dawn of a new era.

Looking south into the Hauraki Gulf. Goat Island is in the foreground; Leigh is across the hills with Ōmaha, Whangateau Harbour and Tāwharanui Peninsula beyond, and Kawau Island, Auckland city, Rangitoto and the gulf in the distance. The keen of eye may even make out mounts Ruapehu and Taranaki on the horizon.

No one could have anticipated what happened. People were accustomed to seeing almost two-thirds of the underwater rock platforms in the reserve covered in pink, encrusting algae and populated mainly by the spiky, round forms of kina, little characters like balled-up hedgehogs, that love above all to eat seaweed. The environment was so desolate, it was termed a 'kina barren', an undersea desert where the natural balance had gone awry.

To everyone's delighted astonishment, this landscape slowly vanished and within ten years had been completely replaced by forests of seaweed — and that was because snapper and crayfish had increased in number and in size, and were eating the kina. Without large numbers of munching, chewing sea urchins, the kelp forests had regenerated and a whole community of reef fish such as red moki, butterfish, silver drummer, parore and blue maomao moved in. A new regime was set, a healthier situation all round — even kina don't do so well in a kina barren.

SCIENCE USES THE TERM 'TROPHIC CASCADE' to describe the domino effect triggered when an animal — such as snapper or crayfish — at or near the top of the food web is removed or replaced and there is a corresponding ripple of consequences.

The 'trophic level' is the position an organism occupies in the sequence of food production. In a simple marine food chain, the first trophic level is that of primary producers, phytoplankton; immediately above are herbivores, tiny zooplankton that eat the phytoplankton; on the third level, are carnivores, the creatures that eat the zooplankton. There might be several of these layers, each successive one having larger creatures but fewer numbers. And so on.

It's easy to imagine what happens if the base of the chain disappears but a change in *any* level sparks a concatenation of reactions and counter-reactions. And, of course, it's always far more multi-dimensional than a chain. As we have seen in the case of the kina, the change doesn't just affect a few species, it alters the structure of the whole ecosystem.

Kina barrens are an excellent example of how our expectations slowly shrink so that in time we accept less and less, and believe the current situation is the way things have always been.

People snorkelling over kina barrens in northeast New Zealand had

No contest: the contrast is obvious between the marine desert of a kina barren and the rich, colourful world (Port Fitzroy, Great Barrier Island) of a kelp forest where kina are still in balance.

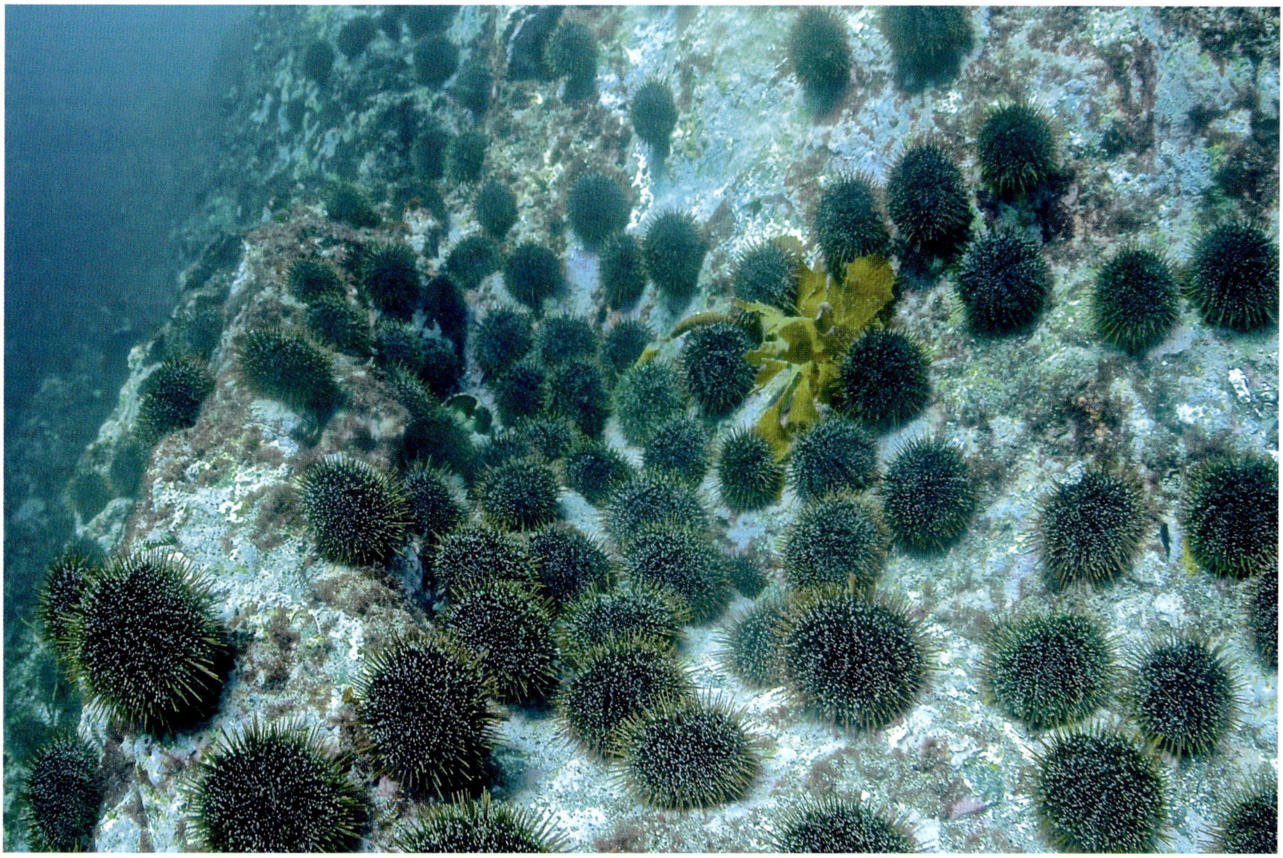

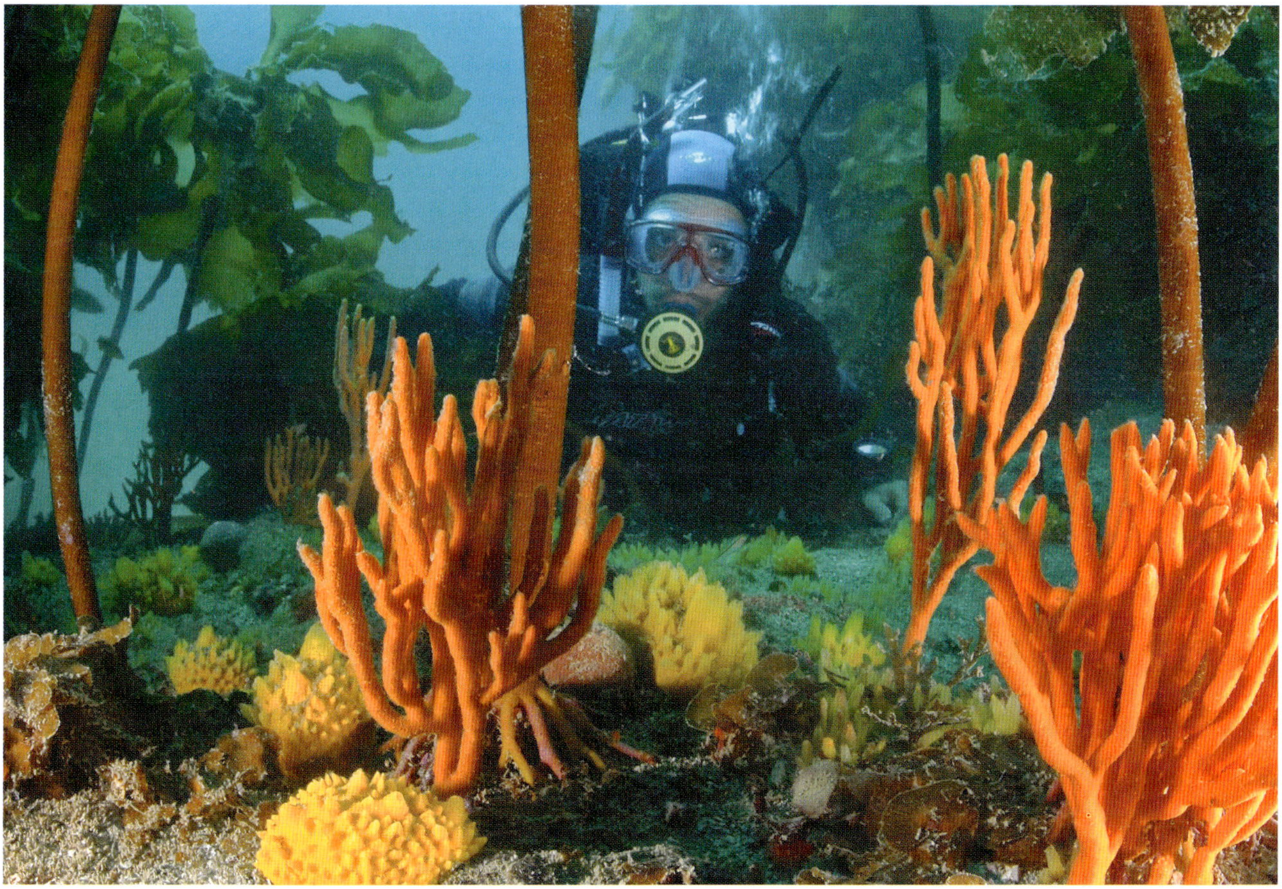

come to accept that they were the order of the day ... until they were shown otherwise.

ONCE THE FISH IN THE RESERVE learned they were safe, they became more approachable; snapper especially, became very tame. People are actively welcomed to marine reserves and suddenly Goat Island was popular not only with scientists but also schools, tourists, snorkellers and divers, who flocked in to see and swim with the fish. There was a significant rise in public support, including from many previous nay-sayers.

Today, a glass-bottom boat ferries visitors around the island, the laboratory on the headland continues its research and in the wider Leigh area there are dive shops, restaurants and accommodation, all centred on the reserve. Over 300,000 people visit annually, many of them in school groups. The reserve is a spectacular success, even with fishers, who find not only that the waters immediately outside the reserve are more bountiful with spill-over fish but also that the reserve is seeding a range of species that disperse up and down the coast. Objections have evaporated like mist on a sunny morning.

Even after almost 40 years, though, it's still relatively early days. Goat Island Marine Reserve will be a 'no-take' zone *forever* and will continue to rebuild and evolve. Ballantine tells of a moment during the campaign when enthusiasm was flagging and achieving the reserve seemed impossible and he went to see Roddy Matheson, a farmer who had overlooked the site all his life. Matheson recalled the coast as he knew it when a child and said simply: 'It used to be quite different round here; I would like my grandchildren to see what it was like then.' That was enough.

IN 1965, WHEN BILL BALLANTINE arrived from the United Kingdom to take the post of director at the marine laboratory, it was an unfurnished hut on a headland and, as mentioned above, he was its sole employee. Today it is a major facility, recently redeveloped as the University of Auckland's South Pacific Centre for Marine Science. It has accommodation for 16 staff and for students researching a wide range of topics, including the development of new aquaculture species. An educational hub called the 'Edith Winstone Blackwell Interpretive Centre' showcases local marine life and the centre's work, with interactive displays, tanks holding real sea creatures and video documentaries.

The Leigh Marine Laboratory with Goat Island and the marine reserve in the background.

Ballantine, who was born far from the sea in Leicester, came to New Zealand on a two-year NATO post-doctorate to pursue an academic interest in limpets (this country has many species but the UK has only one). After his appointment to the laboratory, he and his wife Dulcie moved to Goat Island Road, where he still lives.

Now retired, he nevertheless continues to promote marine reserves. Progress is slow and his frustration sometimes shows. 'If you want a post-graduate course in Idiot Politics, then marine reserves are a really good field!' he says with a laugh.

In fact, he says, you need two things to be able to argue for a marine reserve. The first is determination to hang in for the long haul and the second is a sense of humour. Being able to laugh, above all at yourself, prevents being boxed in and helps keep an open mind, he says. 'It doesn't mean you don't believe in what you are doing . . . but you can't laugh at something properly unless you do.'

And believe in it, he does. He talks with wonder of the oceans. 'Marine organisms are completely different from terrestrial organisms. Think of the starfish,' he says.

Dr Bill Ballantine at his home in Leigh; the Goat Island Marine Discovery Centre, both 2013.

There is no terrestrial equivalent of a starfish. There's nothing remotely like it! This is actually known to cartoonists — if you want to show it's a

sea shore all you have to do is draw a little starfish and everybody knows it's the seaside. It can't be a lake; it's the sea.

But starfish are amazing — they haven't got a front! They have no eyes, they have 400 legs or tube feet; they have no brain. They have a nervous system that is very simple — it's just a ring around the mouth, one nerve down each arm but, they can open mussels . . . which people can't do, without a knife!

BALLANTINE'S ULTIMATE REBUTTAL TO OBJECTIONS about the creation of marine reserves is that *children have rights* and *children come first*. He talks of a 12-year-old girl running up a beach in a marine reserve. She's shouting, ecstatic: 'I saw a fish! I saw a fish!' Says Bill,

It's not that remarkable to see a fish — on a fishmonger's slab, in an aquarium . . . Why is she so excited? It's very simple — obvious — but it needs thinking about. She didn't just see a fish, she saw a living *fish.*

Well, a goldfish in a bowl is a living fish. So it's more than that. She saw a living fish where it lived *. . . And she didn't just see a fish where it lived, she saw it* doing whatever it was that they do, *unrestrained by people.*

Outside marine reserves, fish flee from people on sight, so you don't see many, even if they're there. In a marine reserve, they have learned that people are harmless, so they react in the way they react to passing cloud shadows. They notice them, but they don't mean anything, so they don't pay any attention. Which means you can see them doing whatever it is they do there.

People watch birds — but you can't fly with them. This 12-year-old could swim with the fish in a marine reserve.

So there's a simple scene of a young girl excited about a fish, but if you think about it, it makes a lot of sense. I will go in front of any group of fishermen anywhere in the world — angry, excited fishermen — and say 'Children come first. Never mind your bloody rights. The kids've got a right to see the full works. Not just the bits you didn't catch or couldn't catch or didn't want to catch. They should see it — and we should arrange it.'

So marine reserves come first, and they get the best bits.

PRICKLY CUSTOMERS

Kina or sea urchins (*Evechinus chloroticus*) are echinoderms, from the Greek '*ekhino*' 'hedgehog' and derma 'skin'. They belong to the same phylum as starfish, brittle stars and sea cucumbers. These otherwise unassuming creatures live on the floor of rocky coastal reefs, dotted like pom-poms along crevices and in hollows, the smaller ones tucked safely under ledges and rocks beyond the reach of predators. They may live up to 15 years and in the far south can grow as large as 130 millimetres in diameter, not counting the spines.

Kina are relatively simple creatures with no brain — and no head either, come to that. They have a five-part body that is symmetrical around its central point, a stomach and sex glands that are a traditional food, eaten raw by Māori in spring when they are fat and swollen prior to spawning. Like starfish, kina have no front, sides or back, although they do have an 'up' and a 'down'. In apparent violation of the law of gravity, 'down' is the site of the mouth and jaws and 'up' is where the anus is located.

Kina have a hard shell called a 'test' — the rather lovely, hollow, pale green dome with radial lines that is sometimes found on the shore. When the animal is alive, the test is overlaid by a reddish mantle or skin that is in turn covered with defensive spines, as well as rows of extendible, hollow tubes tipped with suckers known as 'tube feet'. Kina sometimes use the feet to gather small stones and debris, which they hold up like umbrellas in an effort at concealment. They move by a combination of hydraulic action using the tube feet and rotating the spines, a bit like walking on stilts, and can cover something like five metres in a night out feeding.

Perhaps the most remarkable thing about them is their extremely efficient and complex mouthpart, known as 'Aristotle's lantern' (named by that gentleman because he thought it resembled a lamp made of horn). It consists of five teeth that are connected to 40 skeletal elements and muscles that give them horizontal and vertical movement. Armed with these teeth, kina are little eating machines that chaw and grind their way through such seaweed as comes their way. They have a fondness for common kelp but they're not fussy.

Kina barrens don't occur everywhere and no one really knows what tips the balance and causes the little creatures to, as it were, run amok and turn into a prickly tide that devours all in its path. It's likely that the presence (or absence) of predators, such as snapper and crayfish, plays a part but the ocean is a complex place and that may not be the whole picture. There's a lot to learn.

OPPOSITE: A kina barren in the making: the urchins have chewed out the kelp stipes, destroying their food source and habitat in the process.

KINA TO THE RESCUE!

The invasive opportunistic seaweed *Undaria pinnatifida* is cultivated for human consumption in Japan but is a disaster in New Zealand because, just like a terrestrial weed, it forms dense underwater thickets that exclude native marine life. Although established in this country's major ports, it had not appeared on the South Island's west coast until April 2010 when a single mature specimen was discovered in Sunday Cove in Fiordland's Breaksea Sound. An intensive seek-and-destroy programme was launched and 1887 Undaria were found and removed.

Three years later, with fingers crossed and no plants detected in the first five months of 2013, the response team (Environment Southland, DOC, MPI and the Fiordland Marine Guardians) were tentatively beginning to celebrate.

Just to be safe, though, a squad of around 3000 kina were rounded up and transferred into the Undaria-infected zone. Kina hoover up most algae, making it easier to spot any remaining pest weed, with the even better likelihood that if they encounter any Undaria, they'll chomp through that as well.

It's not clear what the kina were planning to do after that . . .

The message for boaties is clear, however: if you have a vessel, you *must* ensure that the hull is clean and clear before you enter a fragile environment such as Fiordland.

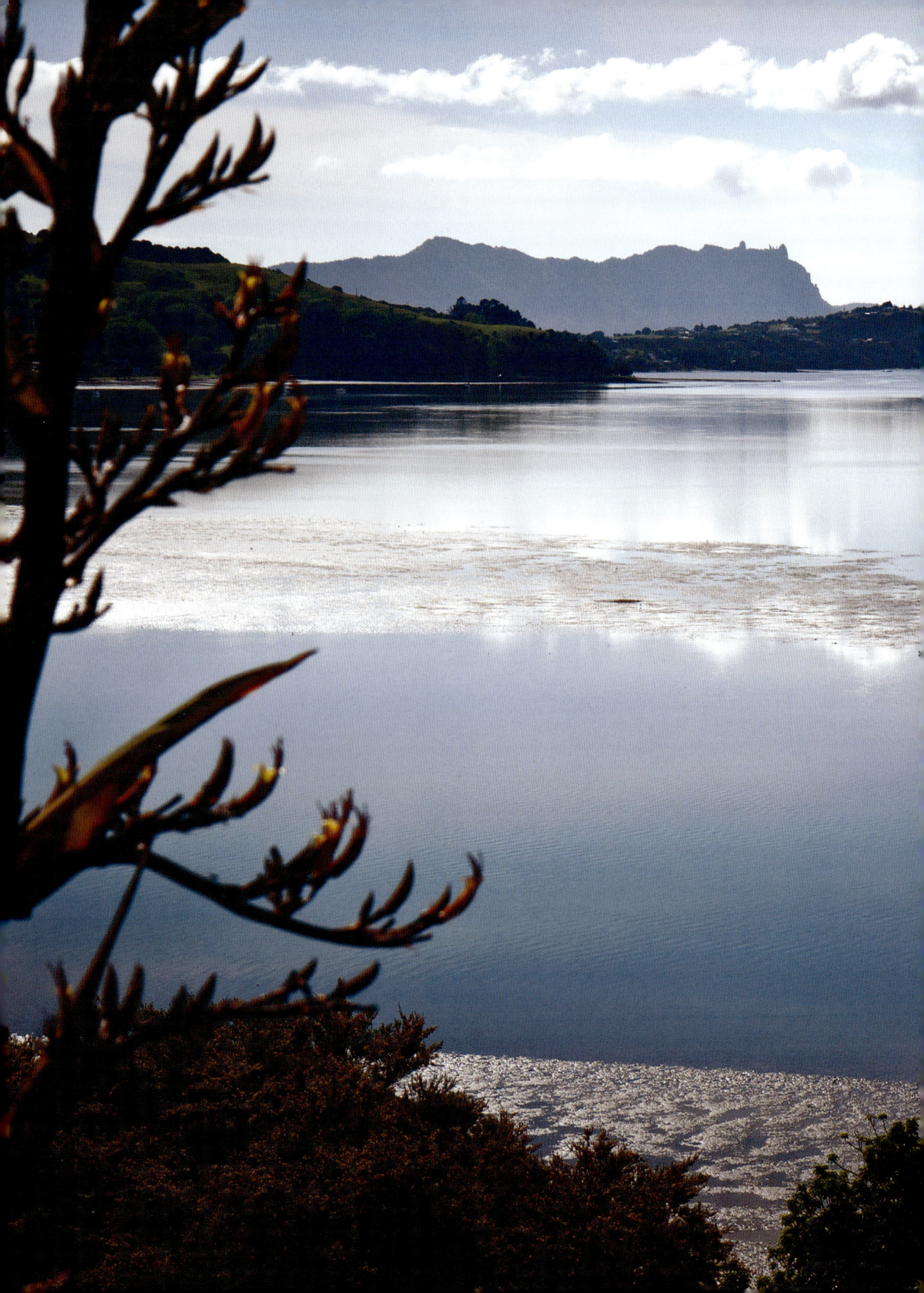

3
HARBOURS & KNIGHTS

THE FAR NORTH

If it were not for a slender neck of land separating the Manukau Harbour from the upper reaches of the Tāmaki River and the Hauraki Gulf beyond, the land north of Auckland would be a narrow island, its long, relatively straight western coastline notched and nibbled by extensive, inland-reaching harbours and its rounded eastern shore broken by a seemingly endless succession of inlets and outlets, bays, beaches and islands. All up, the Northland coastal landscape is spectacular, with a myriad of watery habitats.

The two marine reserves in this region could scarcely be more different. The first, in Whāngārei Harbour on the east coast, is a sheltered world of mangroves, sand and mud; it is utterly attuned to the daily ebb and flow of tide and typical of all Northland's harbours. The second, the Poor Knights Islands Marine Reserve, is offshore, the toothy remains of an ancient volcano, washed and sloshed by the briny; in many respects, it's representative of the islands down this coast, but is also, in many ways, one out of the box.

The gap between two islands looking towards Tawhiti Island in the Poor Knights group.

THE LITTLE SCHOOL THAT DARED

Whāngārei Harbour is a 24-kilometre-long estuarine inlet approximately 150 kilometres north of Auckland. It was once a river valley but became an inlet between 6500 and 10,000 years ago when the seas flowed in at the end of the last ice age. It's huge, approximately 100 square kilometres, with the Hātea River carving a deep channel through the upper harbour en route to the coast and many secondary tributaries and interwoven channels, sandbanks, mangrove forests and saltmarshes, as well as several small islands. At low tide, extensive mud and sand flats are exposed.

There is a substantial deep-water port on the south side of the harbour entrance at Marsden Point and another at Portland in the upper harbour that serves the Golden Bay Cement Company. Port Whāngārei, also in the upper harbour, closed in 2007. The harbour's northern skyline is dominated at the seaward end by the dramatic 490-metre-high volcanic pinnacles of Whāngārei Heads peninsula.

IT WAS A LIFE-CHANGER for Samara Nicholas, then Samara Sutherland. She was in her final year at Kamo High School in 1998, when she became part of the Whāngārei Harbour Marine Reserve project.

'It started in 1990 so it had already progressed quite a bit,' she says. 'I was always an ocean kind of person — when my dad was snorkelling, getting crayfish, I used to hold on around his neck and I learned to swim under the water before I swam on top — but it wasn't until I was involved in preparing the marine reserve proposal that I realised I could be doing something to make a difference.'

Geography teacher Warren Farrelly gently steered the project. Each year he would introduce the idea to his senior class by taking them snorkelling at Motukaroro Island, a small rocky islet west of the harbour channel on the south side of Whāngārei Heads. 'We saw seahorses and lots of bright and colourful marine life like anemones and sponges. It got me quite excited and involved from that point onwards,' Samara says. 'It was very hands-on. And the way he presented it, it was ours — it wasn't his thing that we were working on, it was the students' project and we just had to pick up where the previous group left off.'

WHĀNGĀREI HARBOUR MARINE RESERVE is the only 'no-take' conservation area in New Zealand and possibly the world that was created by schoolchildren — by the time it was signed off in 2006 by then Minister of Conservation Chris Carter, it had involved many hundreds of youngsters. It was environmental education at its widest and best: students gathered and analysed data, planned where the reserve would go, wrote press releases, sketched maps, plotted diagrams, designed logos and posters, liaised with iwi, consulted the wider community, collected signatures, gathered sponsorship and talked to experts.

Samara was hooked from that moment at Motukaroro. 'I spent a lot of time. I interviewed Wade Doak and he was very inspirational. And also Dr Bill Ballantine.' She left school at the end of the year and travelled overseas, returning to New Zealand with fresh eyes, focus and enthusiasm. 'I decided that Northland is the place where I want to be and that's where I want to put all my energy.'

While she was studying environmental management at NorthTec, she taught snorkelling to students from Whananaki Primary School. She vividly recalls their faces when they visited Goat Island Marine Reserve down the coast at Leigh. 'I was buddied up with two kids and they just about pulled me under the water when they saw this snapper! It was awesome.' She subsequently assisted with the closing stages of the marine reserve proposal, including working with some of the children who wrote letters of support.

From those first steps, Samara went on to co-found the Experiencing

'We did it!' Kamo High School students celebrate the approval of the new marine reserve, December, 2004. Samara is at centre front, and Chris Carter, then Minister of Conservation, is at rear.

Marine Reserves programme, which now occupies her full time. Her efforts have been recognised by a number of awards including Whāngārei Young Person of the Year 2004. In 2005 she was the first woman and youngest person ever to win the Sir Peter Blake Emerging Leader award. She became a member of the Sir Peter Blake Trust environmental planning group; a career highlight was being instrumental in the planning of the Young Blake Expeditions to the Kermadecs in August 2012; see chapter 13 for information about the Kermadecs and other way offshore islands.

The majority of marine reserves are on one site but the kids from Kamo planned three different but interconnected locations: Motukaroro Island, a small, lower-harbour, ocean-influenced site; Waikaraka, a larger tidal zone in the lee of Onerahi Peninsula and Motu Matakohe or Limestone Island near Waikaraka. Together, they would provide protection to a sequence of habitats and the species that depended on them. It was good too that they were accessible to 45 schools and other educational establishments.

Ultimately, only the first two became reserves.

The smallest site is Motukaroro. The waters around it are fed by harbour currents carrying nutrients from the extensive mudflats and mangrove-fringed estuaries upstream. Around 50 species of large and small reef fish such as blue maomao, snapper, John Dory, parore, spotties and other wrasses, demoiselles, butterfish, mackerels, kingfish, crested blennies, goatfish, triplefins, conger eels and octopuses live around the island and the wealth of marine life on the rocks and reefs includes anemones, sponges, kelp gardens, nudibranchs and the seahorses that first entranced Samara.

In particular, Motukaroro's southern shore boasts the most impressive zonation on a rocky shore anywhere in the world, according to Dr Ballantine. 'The rock face is so uniform and geometrically simple that the brightly coloured zones of lichens, barnacles, oysters and seaweeds appear like painted bands paralleling the water line and running up into the coastal forest that crowns the island,' he wrote in 1992.

The second site is Waikaraka, adjacent to the suburb of the same name. It forms a deep rectangle pinned to the shore at the base of an estuary with a swathe of mangroves extending from smaller plants along the land to mature trees on the harbour side. Beyond the mangroves, the floor falls away to a deeper channel then rises to a sandbar where, at low tide, wading birds pick a living on its gleaming flanks.

Mangroves (*Avicennia marina*) are one of New Zealand's more contentious plants, earning the displeasure of those who see them as oozing, people-repellent destroyers of beaches. They happily colonise harbours and estuaries where there is silt or a muddy bottom, and have been taking command of estuaries and harbours in the frost-free north since the late 1970s. Their forests are vastly underrated and highly productive: beneath their olive-green exteriors, they are important habitat for juvenile snapper, trevally, kahawai, mackerel and kingfish and for many species of shellfish such as oysters and little black mussel, as well as barnacles, mud snails, crabs, worms and shrimps. They are transit zones for migratory native freshwater fish, such as eels and banded kōkopu, and provide food and roosts for birds such as pied stilts, royal spoonbills, shags, banded rail, kingfishers and herons. The trees were important for pre-colonial Māori who harvested mullet, cat's eye, eels and oysters and used the intensely black, anaerobic mud from around the roots and the lichens from the trunks for dyes. The trees are protected but in the past were destroyed to enable activities such as farming, roading and urban and industrial development.

The waters around Motu Matakohe or Limestone Island were to have been the third component of the reserve. The island was once the site of Matakohe Pā and from 1885 was the site of New Zealand's earliest cement

OPPOSITE: Motukaroro Island at the mouth of Whāngārei Harbour, with Marsden Point across the water behind. The innocuous little island gives no hint of the world of wonder below the surface.

The Waikaraka site of the Whāngārei Marine Reserve at low tide.

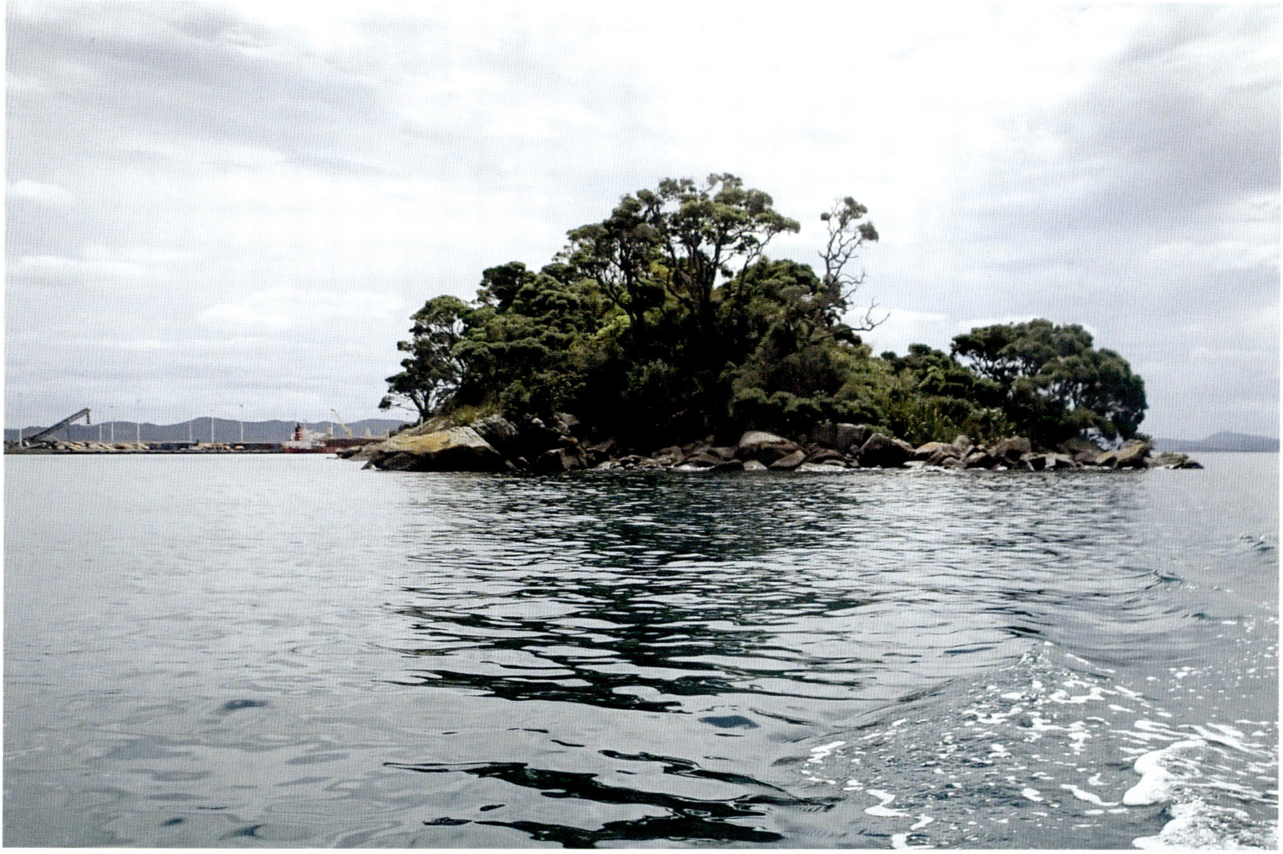

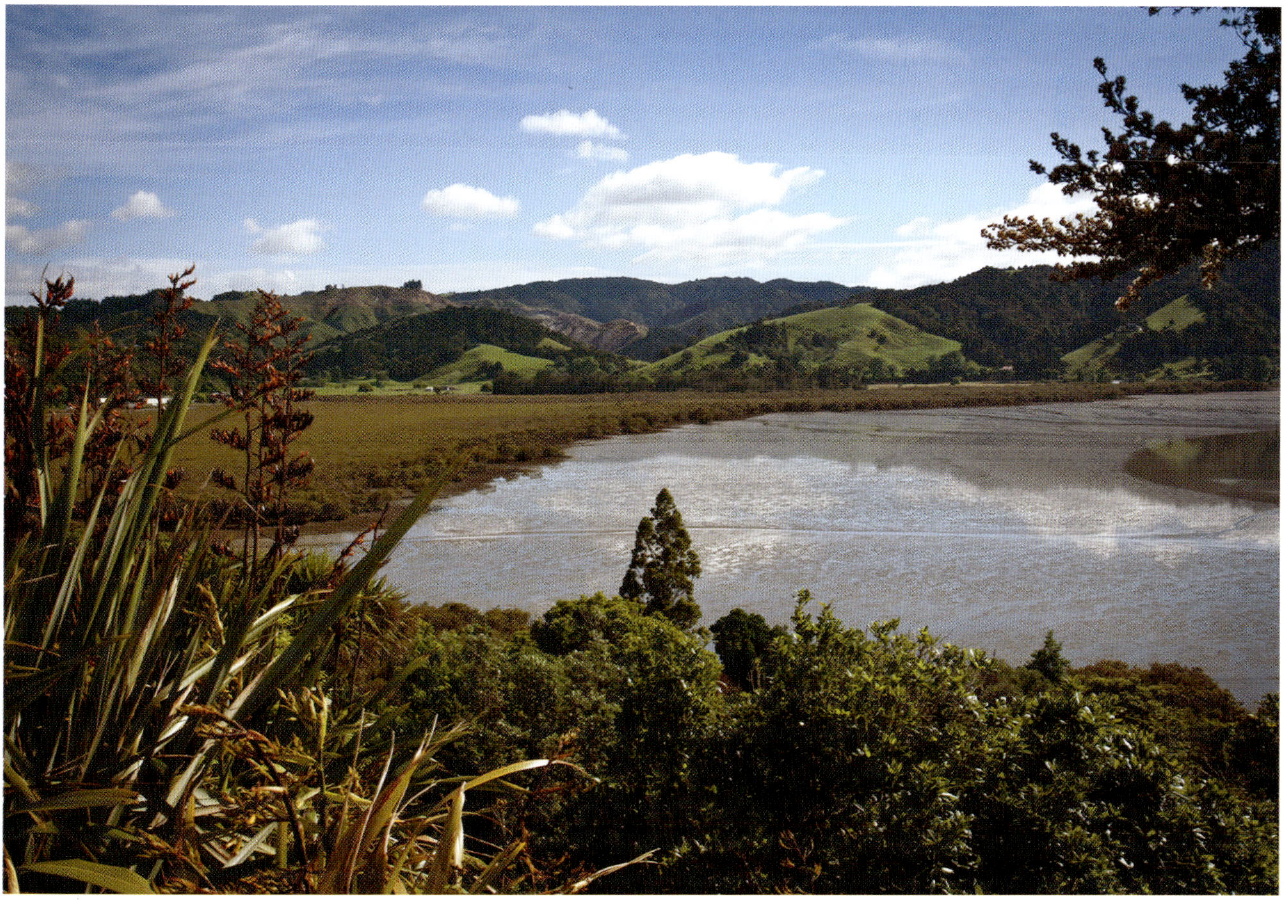

Submarine life at Motukaroro.

―

Clockwise from top left: Red moki and finger sponge; organ pipe sponge and clown sea slug; a feathery hydroid; a tiny triplefin scoots above golf ball sponges and anemones; sponges and jewel anemones.

―

works. It is now a pest-free sanctuary under the care of DOC and the Friends of Matakohe, and is home to kiwi, banded rail, New Zealand dotterel, moko skink and forest gecko. It would have been fitting for the terrestrial reserve to be partnered with a marine equivalent but when the final call was made, to the disappointment of the reserve's proposers, it was excluded, a concession to concerns of iwi and the fishing fraternity.

Motukaroro at low tide: clear species zonation from lichens at the top through to seaweeds at the bottom.

EXPERIENCING MARINE RESERVES

The Whāngārei Harbour Marine Reserve was just the beginning of Samara's story. While at NorthTec, she met biologist and environmental educator Vince Kerr, who was then employed by DOC. They saw a need and an opportunity to expand on Samara's experiences with schoolchildren, to bring the students and the marine reserves together. 'Vince and I came up with a programme,' she says, 'and he was able to get some source funding for a pilot study.'

The Experiencing Marine Reserves programme brings people and marine reserves together, mainly, but not exclusively, through schools. The key to its success is direct, hands-on experience. It's elegant in its simplicity.

After a brief classroom introduction to biodiversity, students explore an area of coast where fishing is permitted. At the same time, they learn to snorkel and to be secure in the water. Safety is paramount at all times: below year eight, there is a ratio of one adult to two students, which has the incidental benefit of involving family and friends, many of whom are as blown away by the experience as are their charges.

The programme provides the students' gear, including snorkel and mask, wetsuit and flotation board, now all brightly coloured in yellow and dark blue and clearly labelled with the programme's logo as well as a fish-ID chart on its side.

Next, the students visit a marine reserve. The comparison with the non-protected area is immediate and unforgettable. Kids and their grown-ups come back buzzing after seeing crays, stingrays, snapper and anything else that happens to swim by on the day.

The last step is perhaps the most important: the children learn to take action as Kaitiaki Tangaroa or guardians of the ocean. They write to politicians and

An EMR participant watches snapper feeding, Poor Knights Marine Reserve, 2007.

OPPOSITE: Samara and the then Whāngārei District Council Mayor, Pamela Peters, at Community Guided Snorkel Day, 2007.

local papers, clean up or monitor the shore and the ocean, make presentations to school or community, design signs, plant sand dunes — anything, in fact, that expresses their increased awareness and contributes to the greater health of the coasts and the seas. As Samara once did, 'the kids take it beyond their school environment and make a difference,' she says.

The programme started in 2002 and is so successful that it has expanded to Auckland, Gisborne, Coromandel, Taranaki, Wellington and Nelson, with Otago planning to join in 2014.

Each area has its own umbrella organisation. In Northland it is the Mountains to Sea Conservation Trust, whose seven members include youth, marine biologists and business people. DOC is a foundation sponsor and the Tindall Foundation has been 'a major, major support,' says Samara, 'especially in the expansion of the programme to other regions. We wouldn't be able to do what we do without them.'

The trust has fingers in other pies, including the Whitebait Connection (WBC) programme, a terrestrial companion to Experiencing Marine Reserves that emphasises care and restoration of freshwater streams and catchments. In addition, in Whāngārei, the trust has developed a Drains to Harbour (DTH) stormwater programme for schools, funded by the district council and aimed at strengthening awareness of the connection between drains, waterways and the sea, and ultimately reducing pollution of the harbour. The trust also runs MarineNZ, an interactive and ever-evolving website that aims to be an 'information portal' for all things marine.

Experiencing Marine Reserves runs guided snorkel days for adults and families, as well as guided kayak days in areas such as the Waikaraka Marine Reserve in the Whāngārei Harbour.

'Our most exciting thing has been like the other day,' Samara says. 'To hear parents raving about their experience is so satisfying — they were buzzing about little things, like triplefins. We do what we do because we want to get kids excited and inspired, and we do that by hands-on experiences and promoting marine conservation. It's really great.'

Indeed.

A WET LIBRARY

No librarian worthy of the badge likes to think of books and water in the same sentence! 'Wet libraries' was Wade Doak's idea, a vehicle to promote marine reserves to the nation. The passionate conservationist and eloquent advocate for the seas has been diving since the 1950s. Even then, he now realises, the ocean was overfished, especially at points that could be reached by motor vehicle.

'It was two years of diving before I ever saw a fish,' he says.

Wade believes the highest value of marine reserves, even beyond their inherent worth or importance for scientific research, is what they teach us.

'Because of the deterioration that I've witnessed in my lifetime, most people don't know what it used to be like — what abundance there used to be,' he says. He has seen the Experiencing Marine Reserves programme in action.

'There's Samara with her little parcels of kids from the Far North: they come out of the water and they're glowing, and a wee Māori boy says, "I saw the red moki!"

'A wet library is a concept that we can all tune in to because we know how important a library is . . . every parent should be asking that their kids could be within bussing distance of a wet library, right throughout the country . . .

'If we don't have them, we won't even know what we've lost and tomorrow's children will go into the sea and it will be bereft, and they'll think it's good — "I saw a rock!"'

'You need to go and stand in the mangrove mud, feel the spines of the crayfish, watch the schools of fish, touch the bull kelp and see the crusts of sponge lining the cave.'
— Dr Bill Ballantine

3 · HARBOURS & KNIGHTS | THE FAR NORTH

WHEN THE TIDE IS LOW and the mud and sand are exposed, the channels reduce to pools and trickles; it may appear to the passerby that little goes on in the open harbour, but look closer, and you'll see it teems with life — even if most of it is taking cover from the birds: kingfishers, gulls, royal spoonbills, stilts, oystercatchers, dotterels, herons and, for some of the year, migrants such as eastern bar-tailed godwits pick their way over the flats in search of the abundant worms, crustaceans, shellfish and juvenile fish that inhabit this challenging environment.

Five to six hours later, the tide turns and there's a changing of the guard. The birds retreat to roost and the flats, now blanketed in water, come to life: barnacles and tubeworms extend delicate tendrils as they strain the current for detritus, a flatfish scuds across the shallows, a stargazer hunkers in the sandy bottom until an unwary New Zealand bigeye passes,

AN UNDERWATER LIGHT SHOW

One of the most surreal sights I remember while filming in the northern harbours was a dive over fanworm beds in Whāngārei Harbour. The entire bottom for as far as we could see was a carpet of what looked like white flowers swaying in the current as they filtered out minute particles, the bright sunlight from above making them glow like some gigantic biological LED light panel. As I skimmed just above the beds with my camera rolling, red goatfish fleeing ahead of me left dark swathes through the bed as the light-sensitive fanworms retracted with each passing fish. The transformation from light to dark was so instantaneous and the effect so choreographed that it was as though we were seeing an underwater stage show with lighting technicians switching the lights off in time to the fishes' movements; very cool and hypnotic!

Dave Abbott, underwater cameraman

when *gulp*, it's all over for the bigeye; an eagle ray buries itself in sand until detected by a pod of orca, when it must fly for its life.

The film crew for the television series *Our Big Blue Backyard* had close-up views of the changing shifts with each tide. Diver Winston Cowie was entertained by chasing stingrays around the harbour. 'After the rays realised they couldn't shake us (we were doing a good job of being orca),' he said, 'they would stop and flap their wings as fast as they could, in what we believe was an attempt to muddy the water and hide themselves. They would also point their tails towards us in a threat display. The behaviour seemed to be learned and not instinctive — some of the rays in the harbour had previously escaped an orca pod . . . they got away from us too!'

IT WAS DR INGRID VISSER who first realised that the charismatic orca were hunters of stingrays around New Zealand shores. She observed them in 1994, hunting in an estuary like Whāngārei Harbour, going so far into the shallows that their dorsal fins protruded high above the water. They appeared to be digging the bay's muddy floor with their beaks, stirring clouds of sediment. She zeroed in on one female.

'After watching her digging for several more minutes, I saw a huge billowing of bubbles and then she surfaced again. This time she had something in her mouth and it was alive — a stingray. The ray was large enough that its wings stuck out each side of her mouth and they were flapping. Its tail was also sticking out of her mouth and was whipping around, trying to sting her with the barb.'

The orca tossed the ray and it landed helplessly upside down on the water, becoming as incapacitated as a cast sheep. She and a companion then tore it apart and devoured it.

TOUCHED BY MAGIC

Warren Farrelly, the teacher who initiated the marine reserve proposal, has an orca story of his own. He was using strobe lights, diving and photographing paddle crabs around the base of Motukaroro. Between shots, the lights would recharge with a shrill electronic whirr but he was becoming aware of another high-pitched sound — almost an echo. Nevertheless, he continued shooting until his film was exhausted. Wade Doak continues the story:

Warren began to worry about the sound in his ears. It would rise as the strobes recharged and reduce as they reached a full charge. It seemed to be mimicking the sound-pattern strobes make, but where was it coming from? He felt no pain in his ears. He was kneeling on the bottom, so there were no pressure changes. Slowly Warren realised it was behind him.

On turning round, I was eyeball to eyeball with four nosy, motionless orca whales. The middle pair I could have touched. In the gloom a white patch along their sides initially caught my notice. Then my focus shifted closer in, to their eyes and mouths. The blackness of their heads disguised their faces in poor light. I just gawked. With no electronic flashes recharging to challenge their powers of mimicry, they may have become bored. They departed. Those huge creatures turned away and powered off, hardly moving their tails. They didn't seem to disturb the water in the least. For some time I continued to hear their sonar squeals out in the harbour. Then silence. I left the water feeling incredibly clumsy but touched by magic.

A pod of orca filmed by the NHNZ crew in Hokianga Harbour. The spouting orca with the taller fin is a male.

OPPOSITE:
The orca were efficient and relentless in their pursuit of short-tailed stingrays.

Orca (*Orcinus orca*) belong to the order Cetacea (whales, dolphins and porpoises). The largest members of the dolphin family, they are readily identified by their striking black and white suits. As cetaceans go, they are relatively small although males have the tallest dorsal fin of any — up to 1.8 metres high.

They are found in all the world's seas and are apex predators, needing fear no creature in the ocean other than man. Like the other dolphins, they are highly sociable and communicate by clicks, whistles and pops.

Orca live in matrilineal groups, usually composed of a female, her sons and daughters and her daughters' offspring. Despite being organised killers of other species, they appear well disposed towards humans and, in the 1840s, functioned like dogs in the vicinity of whaling stations, herding and rounding up whales for the slaughter.

Orca diets include fish, sharks, jellyfish, squid, turtles, penguins, dolphins and other cetaceans but the New Zealand population of 200 or so have a special taste for rays and methodically work the coastlines in their pursuit. Dr Visser has seen rays in Whāngārei Harbour trying to escape their giant pursuers by hiding beneath wharves and has seen the orca going so far into the shallows that they beach on sandbars before rolling themselves free.

It's high-risk behaviour. Not only are the mammals at risk from the barbs of the rays, which can kill through infection or allergic reaction, but hunting in the shallows no doubt contributes to the disproportionately high number of orca strandings in New Zealand waters.

ANCIENT AND ELEGANT — RAYS

She is stateliness itself; if she had a neck, she would hold her head high, skirts swishing at her ankles, a dowager countess in full sail as she effortlessly soars over the ocean floor, passes a rocky outcrop and negotiates a stand of kelp. Her only obvious means of propulsion is a rhythmic rippling of wings. She is a long-tailed stingray (*Dasyatis thetidis*), just quietly browsing on molluscs, crustaceans and other bottom-dwelling invertebrates. Little will disturb her other than a human accidentally standing on her or snagging her in a net, or those deadly orca, with only one thing in mind: stingray supper.

The rays that are hunted by orca in Whāngārei Harbour are New Zealand's three most common ray species: the short-tailed stingray (*Dasyatis brevicaudata*), long-tailed stingray and the eagle ray (*Myliobatis tenuicaudatus*). The long-tailed has a tail twice the length of its body, while eagle rays have protruding heads and more pointy wings. It's those whip-like tails that give all of them their common name — stingray — and confer a degree of notoriety, especially since 2006 when Australian conservationist Steve Irwin was killed by the barb of a bull ray.

It's true that rays have venomous barbs at the base of the tails (and the sting they deliver is described as unbearably painful) but their name and reputation are largely unjustified. Unless threatened, whether deliberately or by accident, they are shy, solitary creatures, preferring to be left to just get on with life.

Rays are ancient creatures, going back some 200 million years. They are Elasmobranchs, belonging to the same class as sharks and skates; like them, they have no swim bladder, are relatively long-lived, slow breeding and bear live young — although these little creatures, from 400–600 millimetres long, are rarely seen. Above all, Elasmobranchs are known for having cartilage instead of bones.

Nevertheless, they *are* fish. In most fish, the pectoral fins are the smallish ones below the head beside the gills. In rays, these fins are enlarged to form the 'wings' that give them their characteristic diamond-ovoid shape. Rays are elegant swimmers: short- and long-tails ripple their wingtips as they move through the water while eagle rays flap their wings like large, graceful birds in flight.

The eyes of rays are on the tops of their heads, all the better to detect the shadow of an orca above. They never see the world below: instead, they have electro-receptors that detect signals from buried prey, as well as lateral lines that sense vibrations in the water and well-developed senses of smell and hearing. They bury themselves in the sand when threatened.

IT'S PRIVATE

It's weird, but shooting sequences of animals mating is one of the holy grails of documentary filming, so when Winston and I saw a small male eagle ray come swooping in on the large female ray I was filming on the sand and start pirouetting around her, I thought we were in for filming gold.

The little male rubbed himself alongside the female ray and looked as excited as an eagle ray is capable of looking, so Winston and I sat back rolling camera and hoping for a little 'ray on ray' action! It was all going promisingly when the female decided this little guy wasn't doing it for her, and started swimming off; he followed her like a dog chasing a bitch on heat but after it became obvious he wasn't going to get lucky, we disappointedly headed back to the boat.

A couple of weeks later I couldn't believe my luck when I saw the same thing beginning to happen again on a dive near Northern Arch in the Poor Knights Islands; this time though it was between two short-tail stingrays. Again a small male came gliding in on a large female ray lying in a rocky alcove; he circled her excitedly, and she lifted off the bottom and spun around him too, then just as I anticipated a once-in-a-lifetime sequence she again decided he wasn't the right guy and took off in a huff.

This time though, the rejected and frustrated male turned his attentions to me and came circling in amorously until he realised (luckily) that I was the wrong shape and no keener on him than the female ray had been!

Dave Abbott, underwater cameraman

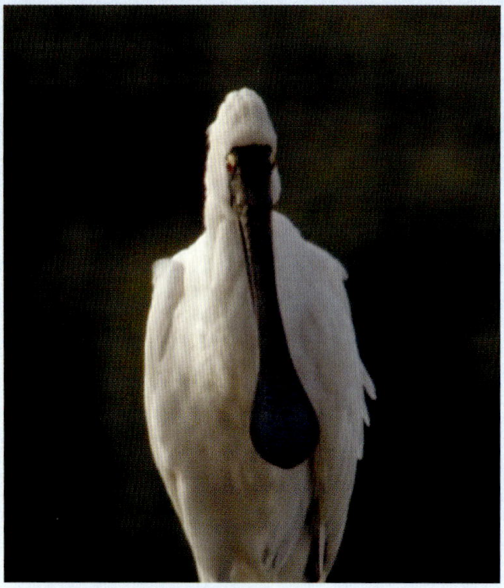
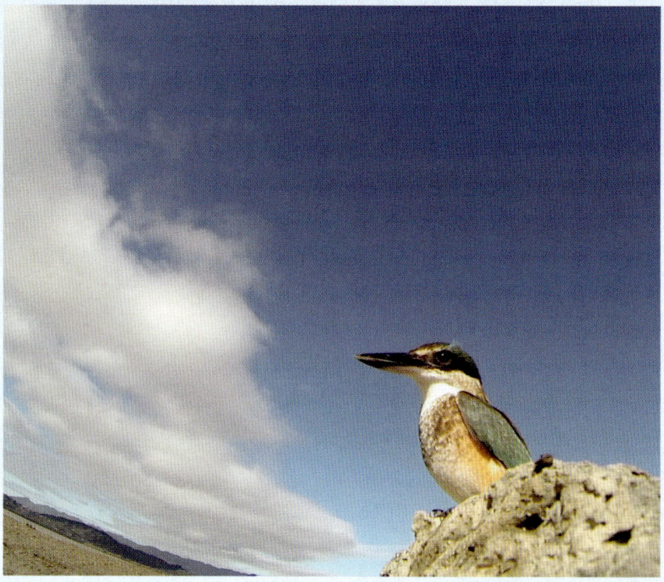
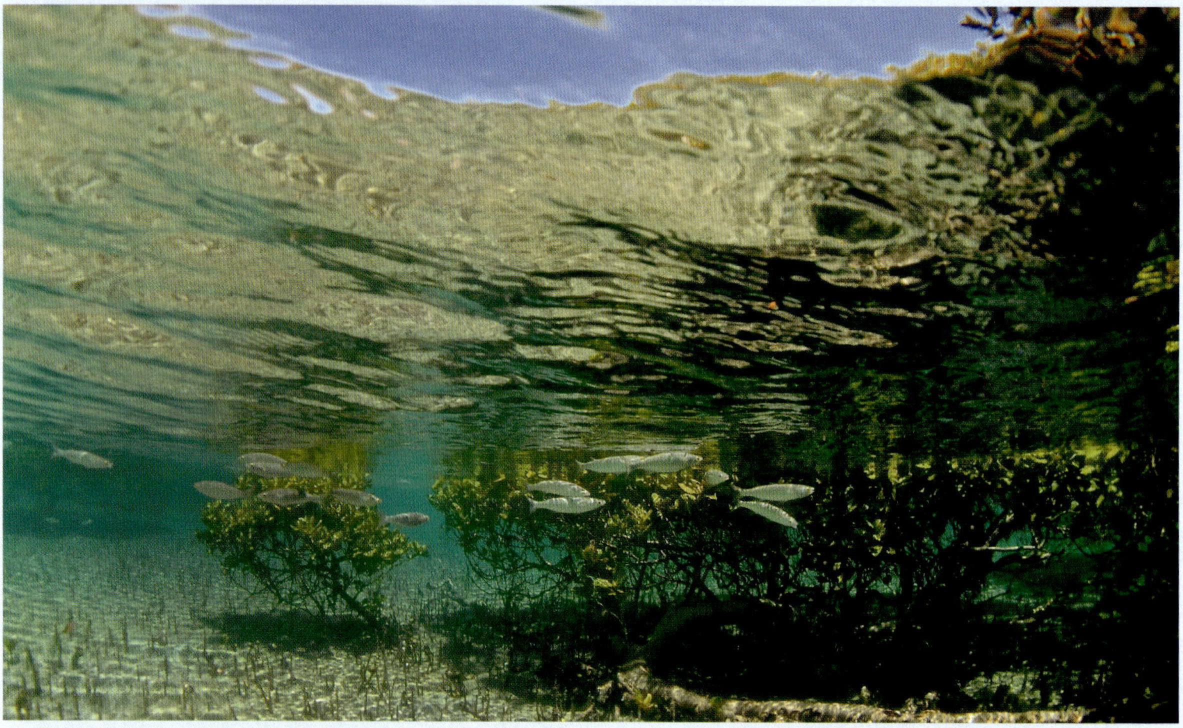
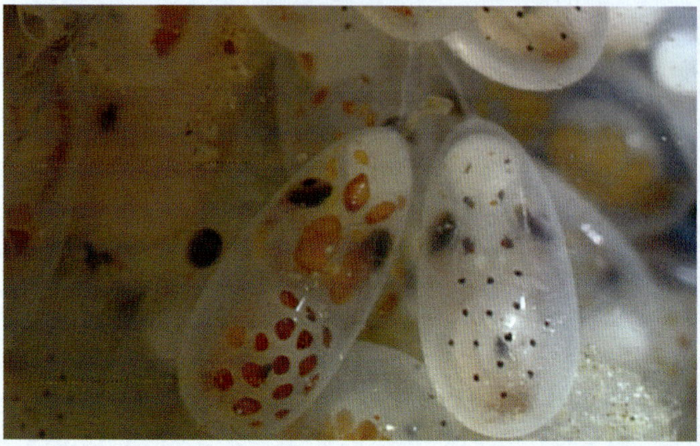
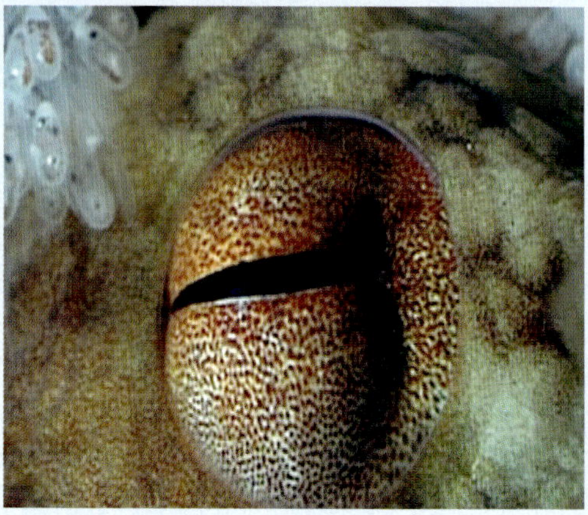

STARS IN THEIR EYES

Rangaunu Harbour is one of the most pristine harbours in the country, mostly because there is no development or runoff into its clean waters, but also because of its healthy mangrove forest, vast populations of filter-feeding life and its strong, clean tidal flow. Diving near the entrance to this beautiful harbour while filming was exhilarating when drifting with the tide but not so good when trying to go against it.

Winston and I had just been filming healthy pipi beds along the shallow sandbanks on the ebb tide, and tired after trying to hold position for several minutes in the outgoing current, I buried my hand into the sand to try and hold myself in place for a minute and get a breather, when I felt a wriggle beneath my fingers!

Quickly anchoring my other hand and camera as best I could, I brushed a few inches of sand away and saw olive mottled skin, then two goggle eyes and a wide, curved, upward facing mouth; I had flukily put my hand right on top of a spotted stargazer (Genyagnus monopterygius)! Not believing our luck I tried to hold position in the current and waved Winston over to help brace me so I could film this weird and ugly fish; I set the camera rolling and recorded a sequence of it gulping and expelling water through its gills to displace the sand while at the same time wriggling to re-submerge itself.

Once buried the stargazer was completely invisible, so I re-exposed and filmed its disappearing trick a second time before leaving it to its sandy bed and drifting on down the channel.

What is amazing to me about this ambush hunter is that for most of the time stargazers are so completely covered with sand that not even their eyes or mouth are showing, making them incredibly hard to find: this was one of those lucky filming opportunities you just can't plan for but which make your day!

Dave Abbott, underwater cameraman

OPPOSITE: Life in a Northland harbour. Clockwise from top left: A royal spoonbill, one of many wading bird species that make the most of this environment; a fish-eye view of a kingfisher; a school of yellow-eyed mullet feeds in the mangrove forest at high tide; octopus eggs and the maternal octopus eye — the female octopus finds a refuge where she lays up to 7000 eggs that she protects and nurtures for 50–60 days. She does not feed during this time and dies when her task is complete.

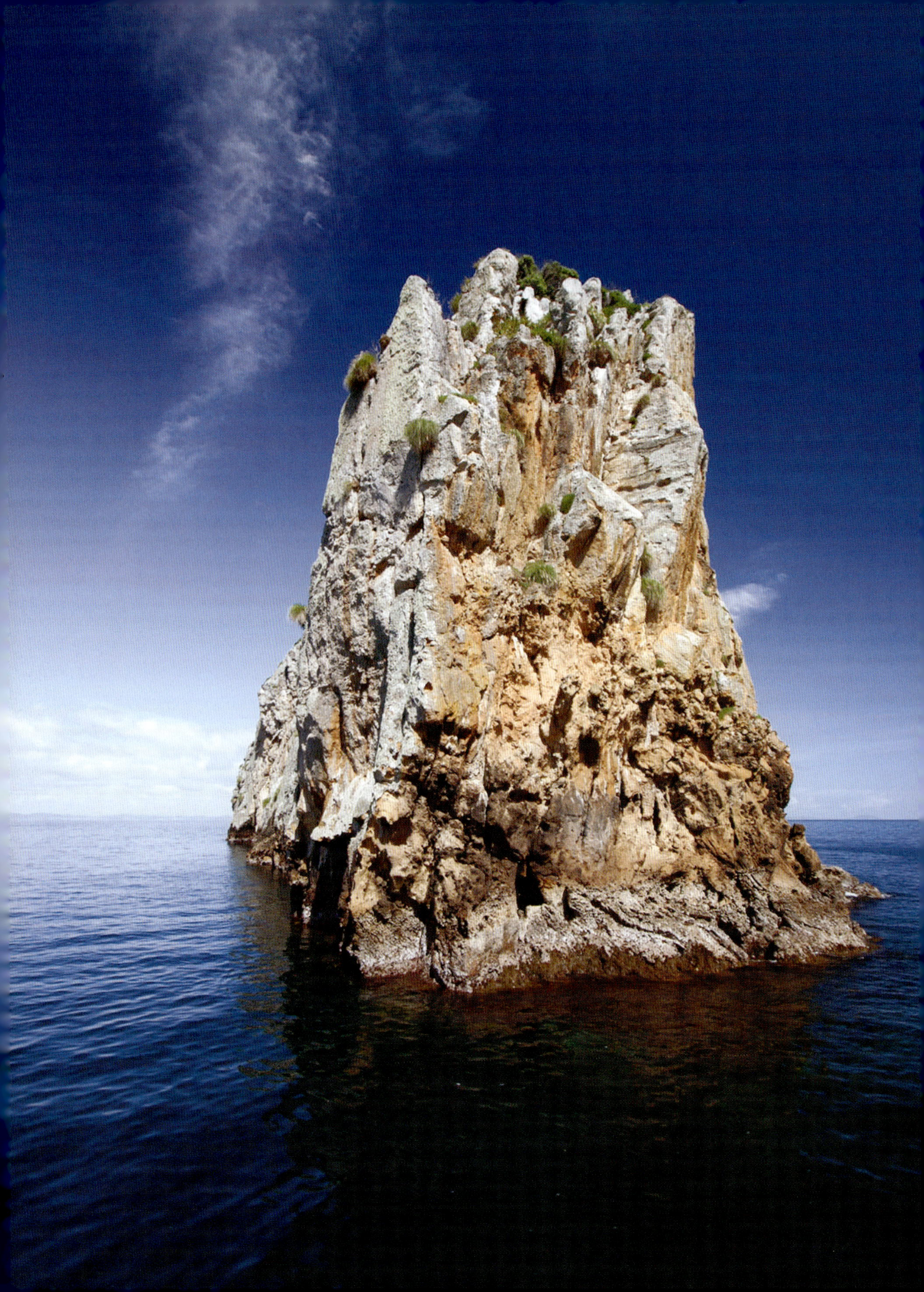

POOR KNIGHTS/ TAWHITI RAHI

Blue water coming in! That's what the folks around Tutukākā Harbour say in summer, referring to the changing water regime at the Poor Knights Islands, a group of two main islands, Tawhiti Rahi and Aorangi, and a number of smaller islets and stacks 24 kilometres off the coast, 30 kilometres northeast of Whāngārei. They are famed for their towering architecture but even more for pristine waters and rich plant and animal life. They were rated in the world's top ten by undersea explorer and researcher Jacques Cousteau when he visited in the late 1980s.

The islands are the remains of a rhyolite volcano that erupted around ten million years ago, one of many in a series along the eastern side of northern New Zealand, including the Mokohinau, Great Barrier (Aotea), Rakitū, Mercury, Ohena and Aldermen islands. Had anyone been present to witness it, the exploding Poor Knights volcano would have provided quite some fireworks display — the resulting cone peak was up to 25 kilometres in diameter and perhaps 1000 metres higher than the surrounding land. Towards the end of its life, a burst of intense heat and gaseous activity smelted much of the underlying material into hard, erosion-resistant silicon-containing rocks.

Millions of years passed. The seas rose and fell, and the land rose and fell. Soft portions of the volcano corroded, fractured and succumbed to sea, sun and wind until there were only stumps, a jumbled and dramatic assortment of pinnacles, terraces, cliffs, channels, inlets and bays. But it's what lies below that is truly exceptional: cliffs that tower 240 metres above the waterline also fall sheer over 100 metres into an underwater world of grottos, arches, caves, tunnels, domes, reefs, beaches and platforms. It's a diver's heaven and attracts visitors from all over the world.

Motu Kapiti Island on the western side in the channel between Tawhiti Rahi and Aorangi islands, looking almost directly west.

The islands are impressive in themselves, but it's their combination with the waters of the subtropical East Auckland Current, flowing from the vicinity of Lord Howe Island, that makes them really special. It not only brings slightly warmer, saltier and clearer water but also a cargo of exotic passengers normally seen only in tropical and subtropical waters.

Some of the visitors drift in as tiny plankton, settle and mature at the Poor Knights; most don't establish permanent populations but for one or occasionally several summers, an exotic and colourful complement to the islands' permanent residents. Of the approximately 187 fish species, 38 percent are subtropical.

'There's always something new cropping up,' Wade says. A NHNZ diver investigates a grotto.

Nature lovers at sea and on land. Wade and Jan Doak in a neighbour's garden overlooking Ngunguru estuary.

WADE AND JAN DOAK have spent more hours around the islands than anyone — living, exploring, probing, observing and photographing. Wade is the outspoken author of many books about the ocean and its inhabitants and Jan is an enthusiastic and skilled photographer. For them the Poor Knights have a physical form and spiritual dimension that makes them 'the cloisters and aisles of a huge cathedral'. For years, the Doaks have noted the influx of subtropical creatures with pleasure — creatures such as the small and gorgeous violet aeolid nudibranch, the paper nautilus octopus with its delicate egg case or, at the other end of the scale, an extraordinary, metres-long, jelly-like colonial animal known as a 'giant salp'.

In early 1994 they were delighted not only to see a manta ray, a turtle and a seal, but to also hear the 'strange music' of a humpback whale singing for the first time since the 1960s when, Wade says, the Navy recorded one off Great Barrier. At that very same time the last whale was being harpooned at the Whangaparapara whaling station (also on Great Barrier). The station closed in 1962 because there were no more humpbacks; members of this migratory species were being intercepted and slaughtered in the Northern Hemisphere.

Then silence.

Until 1994. Wade: 'I felt a rush of joy. Humpback songs at the Knights — *again*! . . . The longer you dive the Knights, the more wide-eyed you get. There's always something new cropping up.'

SNAPPER EAT VIRTUALLY ANY ANIMAL MATTER, including small fish, shellfish, squid, octopuses, crabs, shrimps, barnacles, crayfish, worms, starfish and kina. Cameraman Dave Abbott describes the day that he, Steve Hathaway and Brady Doak encountered a snapper feeding frenzy.

Snapper are generally a smart, cautious fish that are quick to disappear when divers are anywhere near, and although they are often less flighty within a marine reserve, they are still a difficult fish to get really close to, apart from the odd individual, usually a big old moocher.

The one time they lose most of their characteristic caution is when they are feeding hard, and at the end of one of our Poor Knights filming dives when just about to come up, we were lucky enough to encounter a large school of snapper right at the surface, gulping at a vast school of tiny red euphausiid shrimp.

They were so engrossed that I was able to get right in amongst them; they were literally bouncing off me and the camera in their haste to gorge on the shrimp, and I could barely see Steve, my dive buddy that day, through the confused mass of turning, twisting bodies! After using up the last of our air hovering just below the surface with them we swam back to the boat and Brady was also able to jump in and capture more footage of this spectacle before the last of the shrimp were consumed and the snapper dispersed back out into the blue.

A NHNZ *Our Big Blue Backyard* cameraman at the Poor Knights focuses on the elusive Sandager's wrasse.

New Zealand's rays are not extensively studied — no one knows a great deal, for instance, about their breeding habits, numbers or movements, especially in winter; but in summer months, they are an unexplained phenomenon at the Poor Knights. From January to March especially, when the water is warmest, large numbers of mainly mature females congregate in the submarine archways where they hover in layers, stacked one above the other like aircraft in a holding pattern, using the currents to maintain their positions. Some are heavily scarred, possibly as the result of mating activity, but beyond that there are no clues to this behaviour. Rays, like sharks, have no buoyancy control and must constantly move to keep afloat. It's a Poor Knights mystery.

WHAT'S IN A NAME?

What was Captain James Cook thinking when he dubbed these islands the 'Poor Knights'? No one will ever know because the name simply appears as a minor (bracketed) note in his journal.

On 25 November 1769, on his first voyage, after taking a sizeable catch of what was probably snapper but was 'bream' to him, he named Bream Bay, Bream Head and Bream Tail. He wrote: 'At Noon, our Latitude by observation was 36 degrees 36 minutes South; Bream head bore South distant 10 Miles; some small Islands (Poor Knights) at North-East by North distant 3 Leagues, and the Northernmost land in sight bore North-North-West, being at this Time 2 miles from the Shore, and in this Situation had 26 fathoms; the land here about is rather low and pretty well cover'd with wood and seems not ill inhabited.'

Seen as he'd have viewed them, from the landward side, the two main islands are not unlike a recumbent effigy of a knight in semi-relief as was customary on tombs in churches — perhaps one of the Knights Templar, also known as the 'Poor Knights of Christ and the Temple of Solomon'. Without too much imagination, the small Archway

Island in the south can be seen as the knight's head with chin raised to the heavens; Aorangi forms the chest while Tawhiti Rahi makes the rest of the body and legs.

Alternatively, Cook may have been inspired by the pōhutukawa that was likely to have been in full bloom in November when he passed by. Perhaps, some suggest, he was feeling peckish and thinking, longingly perhaps, of Poor Knight's Pudding, a fried bread dish that in some versions is spread with jam.

OPPOSITE: The poor knight — on his back on the horizon.

Pōhutukawa in blossom on the cliffs.

To make Poor Knights Pudding

Cut two penny loaves in round slices, dip them in half a pint of Cream or faire water, then lay them abroad in a dish, and beat three Eggs and grated Nutmegs and sugar, beat them with the Cream then melt some butter in a frying pan, and wet the sides of the toasts and lay them in on the wet side, then pour in the rest upon them, and so fry them, serve them in with Rosewater, sugar and butter.

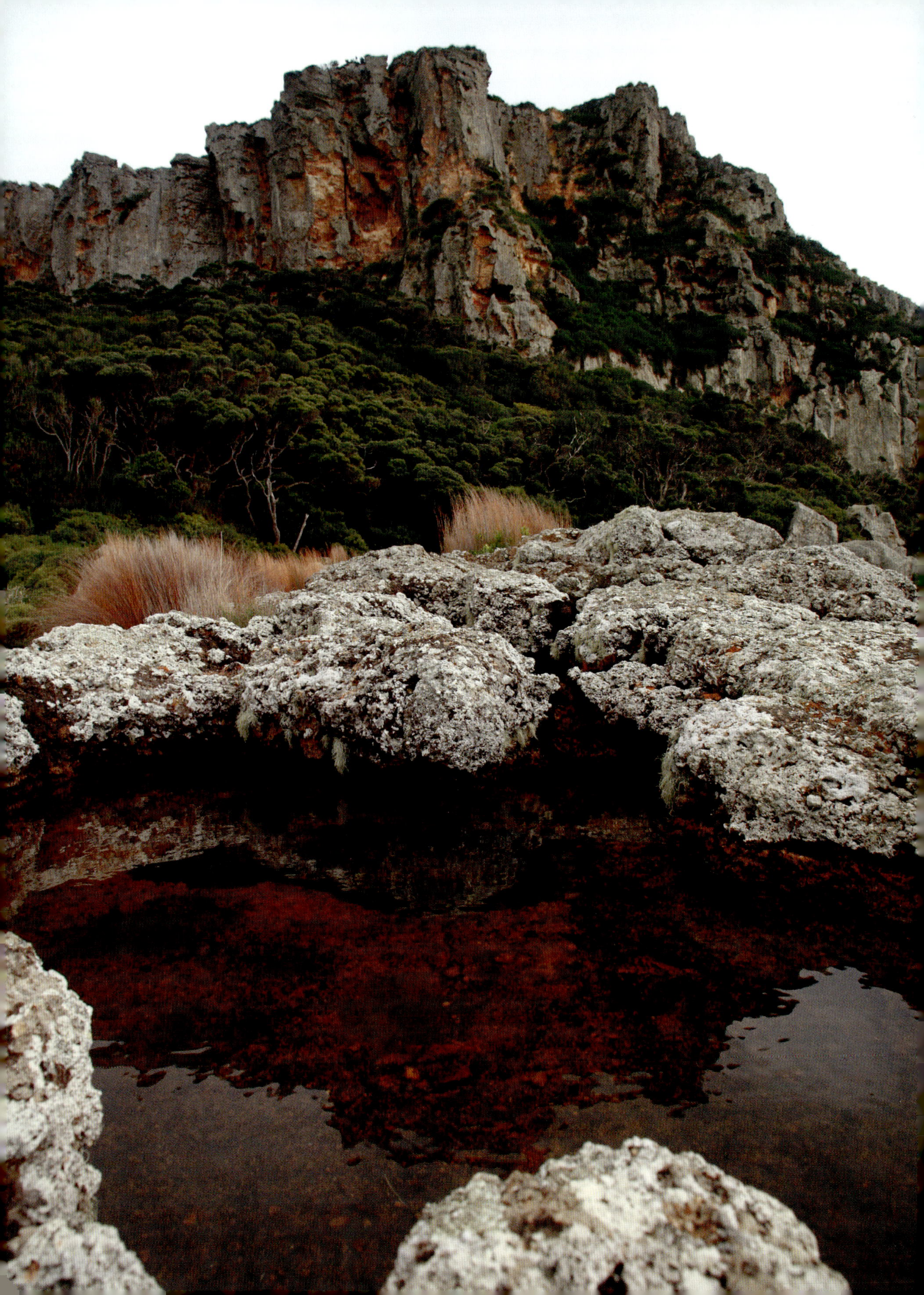

THE POOR KNIGHTS are a tūrangawaewae and taonga of Ngāti Wai. By name and by tradition 'people of the sea', Ngāti Wai inhabited the coast and offshore islands from Great Barrier north. By the early 1800s, as many as 400 lived most of the year in pā on Tawhiti Rahi, Aorangi and on one of the smaller islands, Aorangaia. They cleared land on both islands to build whare and create gardens, and were largely self-sufficient, fishing the seas, hunting the birds and growing kūmara. In the late 1700s, they brought pigs to Aorangi, to supplement their own diets and to trade with mainland iwi.

The swine proved a disaster, in more ways than one. Around 1808 a party from the Hokianga was seriously offended at not being allowed to land or buy any of the animals: they nursed their grievance and returned seeking revenge in 1822. In the absence of the then chief, Tatua, they slaughtered and enslaved all but ten of the population. Grief-stricken, Tatua withdrew his people from the islands and placed a tapu on the Poor Knights that prohibited further residence.

The buildings and walls decayed and toppled, the gardens became overgrown and, had it not been for the pigs, both islands would have begun a slow return to their natural state. By 1936 when the porkers were finally eradicated, the Buller's shearwater, a seabird endemic to the Poor Knights, was reduced to a mere 100 breeding pairs on Aorangi compared with approximately 500,000 birds on neighbouring, swine-free Tawhiti Rahi. Aorangi's forests and the insect, bird and reptile life within immediately began to recover and by 1981 the shearwater population had rebuilt to 200,000 pairs.

IN 1845 THE POOR KNIGHTS ISLANDS were purchased by a private buyer and in 1882 were on-sold to the Crown for the purpose of a lighthouse that was eventually constructed on northern Tawhiti Rahi in the late 1950s. In 1967 the islands became part of the then Hauraki Gulf Maritime Park, and in 1977 they were designated a 'nature reserve' with the highest degree of protection.

Much of the vegetation today is regenerated coastal forest that includes several unique plant species, the most well known being the popular and brilliant-flowering Poor Knights' rengarenga or lily, which grows high on

The escarpment above Urupā Point at the northern tip of Aorangi.

OPPOSITE:
Southern Archway on Archway Island off Aorangi.

—

Kawiti Waetford of Ngāti Wai is filmed by Max Quinn as he offers a karakia to the early morning, prior to the start of shooting for *Our Big Blue Backyard*.

—

the cliffs and in the branch joints of pōhutukawa. It is perfectly adapted to its island home, pollinated by the islands' lizards and nourished by seabird droppings.

A range of animals flourish on the island sanctuary including the tuatara, Duvaucel's gecko, flax snail and flax weevil, a couple of giants — the giant centipede and giant wētā — as well as cave wētā. There are terrestrial birds such as bellbirds, fantails and red-crowned parakeets or kākāriki, banded rail and spotless crakes, kingfishers, harrier hawks and pipits.

And, of course, there are seabirds, millions of them, some breeding and some there just for the fishing. They include three species of petrel, fairy prions, five species of shearwater, pied and little shags, white-faced heron and Australasian gannets, which nest on the Pinnacles and the Sugarloaf, and are a regular sight, hunting the waters around the islands' coasts.

As with other offshore reserves such as Hauturu/Little Barrier, landing is strictly controlled.

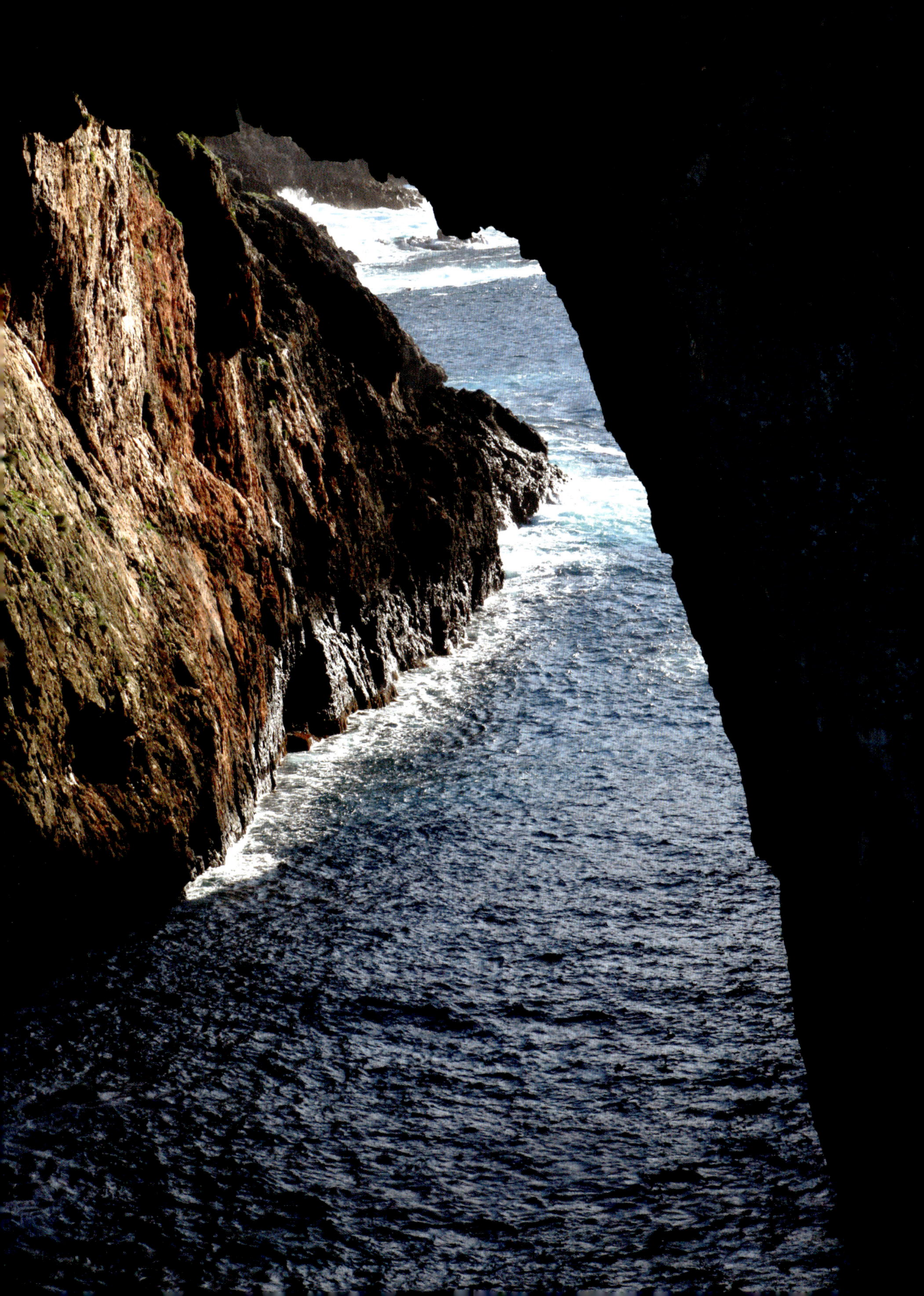

OPPOSITE: The submarine walls of Poor Knights Islands are vibrant with the colour of encrusting sponges, anemones, nudibranchs, different seaweeds and kelp.

The islands are a top destination for national and international visitors and are served by several tourism operators who offer diving and snorkelling experiences, including Dive! Tutukaka.

IN FEBRUARY 1981 THE WATERS around the islands were granted a similar protection when the Poor Knights became New Zealand's second marine reserve. Commercial fishing was prohibited up to 800 metres off all the islands, including the Pinnacles and Sugarloaf Rock eight kilometres to the south.

But there was a concession that had unanticipated consequences: prior to the reserve's creation, the islands were a popular game-fishing destination so, despite protests from conservationists, limited recreational fishing was allowed on the assumption that its impact would be negligible. That proved not to be the case, however, inadvertently providing evidence of the impact of even a small amount of extraction on a marine ecosystem, especially of larger fish. It was not until 17 years later, in October 1998, that the reserve was granted full 'no-take' status and really took off.

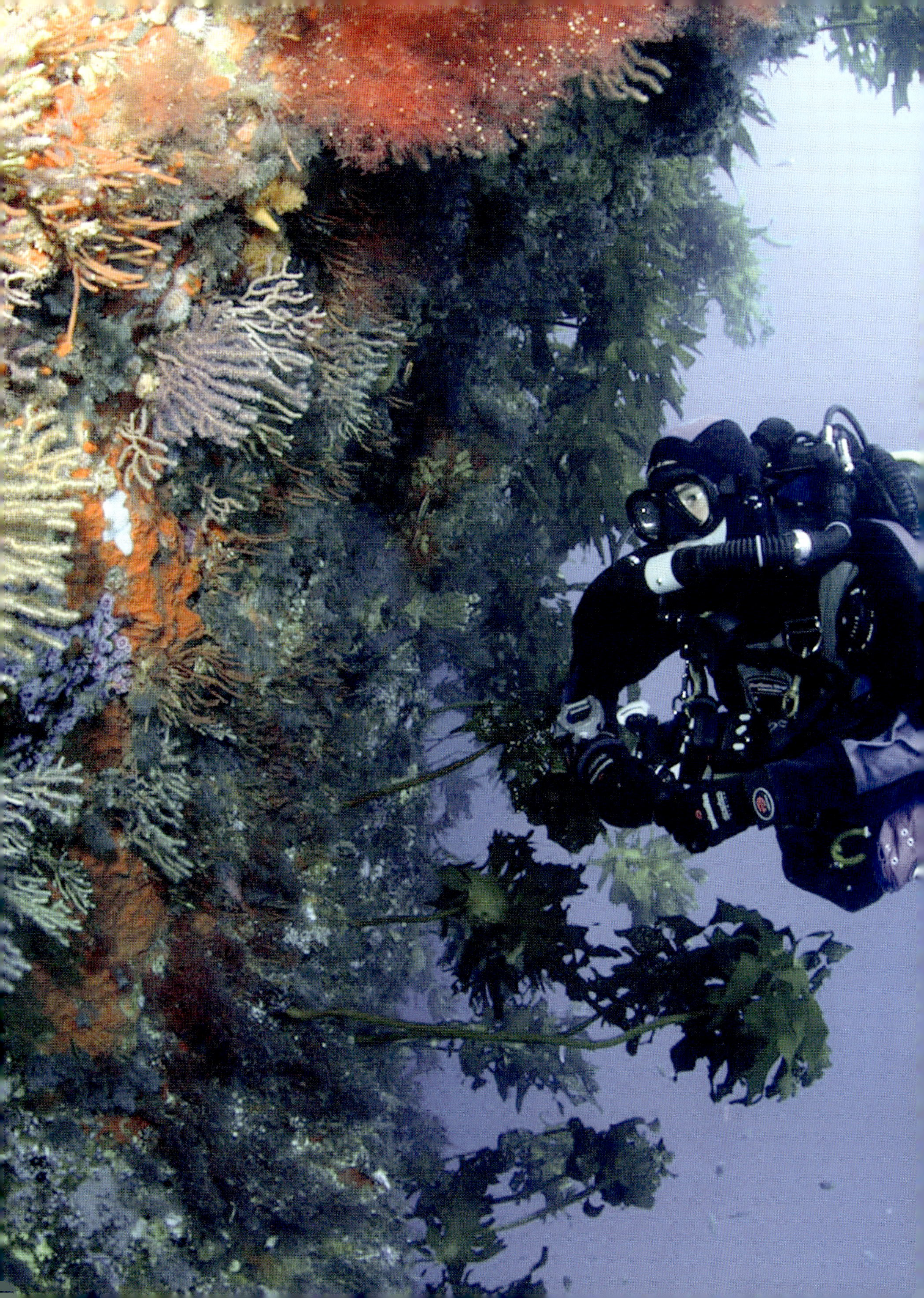

BULLER'S SHEARWATER

Calypso, the boat from Dive! Tutukaka, is suspended in blue. The sky is clear, the waters lustrous, glassy; there's the barest swell and the Poor Knights Islands are a long silhouette on the horizon. Nevertheless, there's a cloud up ahead, casting a darkness on the water like a stain. As the boat approaches, the skipper, Luke Howe, throttles back, leaving the vessel to glide quietly.

It's chow time for a raft of Buller's shearwaters (*Puffinus bulleri*) and a minor troupe of smaller fluttering shearwaters. There's turmoil below where unknown fishes are feeding, driving small crustaceans to the upper layers where they are scooped up by the birds. The shearwaters are surface feeders, scything the water to take small fish, salps, jellyfish and krill. Periodically the prey escapes and the birds wait placidly. When the next boil-up begins, they take off, running so rapidly on the water's surface that for a brief moment, they leave a trail of prints, a white arrow to show where they have gone.

Buller's shearwaters belong to the large seabird family of Procellariidae (shearwaters, fulmar prions and petrels), sometimes known as tubenoses because of the distinctive, tube-encased external nostrils that assist in the removal of salt from the birds' bodies. They are soft grey and darkish brown with white undersides and measure 460 millimetres long. The Poor Knights are their only breeding site in the world. They nest in long tunnels that they share with tuatara and fluttering shearwaters. Skilled athletes in air and sea, they are downright clumsy out of the water — like most of their kin — and crash-land in the foliage when they return to their burrows after sunset.

TWO LARGE, FRAMED WATERCOLOUR PANELS have pride of place in a corner of the Doaks' lounge, a gift from a friend retiring from NHNZ. Each shows a series of five adult Sandager's wrasses, beginning with a female but morphing with each successive image to the last, a male. It was once used to make an animation.

Sandager's wrasses (*Coris sandeyeri*) are, Doak confesses, a favourite — 'the most intriguing of all fishes at Poor Knights Islands'. They not only have a complex social structure, but they also were the source of considerable head-scratching in the days when the Doaks were studying the Poor Knights fishes.

The wrasses are a brilliantly coloured family of some 450 species of reef fishes, at least ten of which are resident at the islands. They are mostly solitary fossickers around the reefs and seafloor, with rat-like front teeth, thick lips, flexible bodies and stubby tails; they swim largely by sculling their pectoral fins. They eat a range of invertebrates including crabs, shrimps, shellfish and other molluscs, worms and barnacles, with each species dining on a slightly different menu from the others, thereby reducing competition across the whole food web.

Like all fish, a juvenile Sandager's wrasse begins life as one of hundreds if not thousands of fertilised eggs, hatches into a tiny larva and disperses, drifting on the ocean's currents. In time, if not eaten, it becomes a tiny, gold-striped white juvenile with a job: it's a cleaner fish whose customers are relieved of dead skin and irritating passengers such as lice. The little fish has a ready source of food . . . until, around 150 millimetres long, it accidentally bites a little too much and custom dries up.

As a juvenile, the wrasse sports the badge of a cleaner fish, a black spot at the base of its tail: now the spot fades and its yellow band slowly dims to two salmon-coloured patches on a white body. The juvenile is now a young female and joins between ten and 20 other females and juveniles that are presided over by the golden eye of one male. There are no young males and there's a strict pecking order among the females.

The male patrols his territory, warding off competing males, keeping his females in place and spawning with them between December and March. If — when — he dies, the dominant female undergoes a sex change; within a couple of weeks, her pale colouring is replaced, she has grown male gonads, is a fully functional male and has taken his place.

The male Sandager's wrasse is a handsome creature, about 400 millimetres long. A purple–maroon flash on his cheek extends like a vivid birthmark from the corner of his lips, passing below his eye, as far as his pectoral fin. Four stripes encircle his body, as bold as any rugby strip: black, white with a slash of pure yellow, black and then white again. The rest of his body is a paler version of the blotch on his cheek (see also p.161).

THE SANDAGER'S WRASSE IS NAMED after Andreas Sandager, the lighthouse keeper who first described them in 1888. It just happens, however, that they also have an affinity with sand and like to tuck themselves into it for the night, small ones first, then large females, and lastly the male. But they are Houdinis, present one moment, gone the next. It took great patience, a bonfire on a Tutukākā beach and a nocturnal underwater stakeout before the Doaks solved the mystery of where the Sandager's slept at night and they only ever managed to film it by remote, using their home-built camera.

So it was never going to be easy for the NHNZ crew of Brady Doak, Dave Abbott, Steve Hathaway, Steve Hudson and Winston Cowie to do the same. It happens at dusk when underwater visibility is at its worst, and, as Dave says, 'the wrasses are understandably cautious about letting any potential predator see where they are bedding down for the night.' Many dusk, night and dawn dives ensued, with the divers in teams of Dave on camera with Winston assisting and Brady on the other, with Steve helping. Eventually, after much hand-sifting of sand, they narrowed down some specific sites for a night dive. Winston describes what happened next.

> *Both teams came back to the surface perplexed; we had been surrounded by them, then just as the light was fading, they disappeared! Two further night dives sifting through the sand felt a bit like trying to find the proverbial needle in a haystack and produced no further clues on the Sandager's secret sleeping spot. Two huge packhorse crayfish scuttling across the bottom and a cool carpet shark were compensations though.*
>
> *Diving at dawn the next day, we noticed a number of northern scorpionfish sitting motionless on the sand, just out from rock overhangs with a sandy bottom. Dave and I finned over to investigate. Dave was setting up his camera when one of the scorpions mistook his glove for a small fish and had a go at him! At that moment, one of the enigmatic Sandager's popped up from underneath the overhang. Confusion, surprised faces, fish and human, all around!*

The team planned yet another evening dive. Again, they failed. They held an underwater council of war and decided they only had one choice; to go a step further and nail a world first, a Sandager's wrasse waking up! Dave continues the story.

Winston and I slipped into the dark water, dropped down and made our way to the spot we had identified as a potential Sandager's bed, crossing our fingers that we were in the ballpark and that it wasn't a moray eel!

I got in position with my camera, flicked the lights on and gave Winston the nod; he pulled out our secret weapon, a long thin nylon rod. He began easing it under the sand in the general direction of the buried wrasse. Even knowing it was there, neither of us were prepared for just how quickly it erupted from the seafloor. Suddenly it was in front of us, a big male Sandager's wrasse looking bleary-eyed, tired and confused, and despite the elation I actually felt guilty for a minute! Looking across to Winston I could see he felt the same way!

Unbelievably, we were lucky enough to film this a second time at a different dive site; again it happened incredibly quickly, and again it was another male. However, this one seemed angry at being woken (fair enough too!) and charged us several times as if to say 'what did you do that for?' (Ten minutes later he had reburied himself.)

Despite a concerted effort over several nights, including an epic set-up with two locked-off cameras on tripods, surface-supplied cable lights on stands and a remote camera/boat monitor, capturing the Sandager's wrasse actually 'going to bed' under the sand evaded us and remains a challenge for next time around!

Another time and place: a Poor Knights resident, a mosaic moray eel, is surprised by divers south of an area known as Middle Arch.

GONE, ALL GONE! ALAS!

Two-spot demoiselles (*Chromis dispilus*) are common around the reefs, rock walls, headlands and archways at the Poor Knights. They are a pretty fish, around 200 millimetres at full size, half the size of a mature Sandager's wrasse. They have large eyes, oval bodies and deeply indented tails, like open scissors. They range in colour from the emerald and olive-green juveniles to blue adults. Their name comes from two small, white spots along the spine below the dorsal fin.

Demoiselles are plankton feeders, spending their days in schools of up to 500, high in the water column, where they swoop and dart like swallows in pursuit of minute crustaceans called 'copepods' (see p.30). In large numbers, their spots create a moving, dappled pattern that is thought to act as protective camouflage.

Much of the burden of reproduction, which is never going to be easy in this eat-and-be-eaten world, falls on the male. The film crew of *Our Big Blue Backyard* captured a snapshot of the action.

It began when our hero, a typical male demoiselle, swam away from the school and selected a nest site, a shallow bowl about the size of a large dinner plate, carpeted with a lawn of short algae on the end of a reef. It was clearly special to him and he protected it jealously, rolling over it like a cat in nip, fluttering, spinning and pivoting to all points of the compass, a one-fish crime watch, vigilant against burglars.

From this base, he enticed and courted a series of females, encouraging each to lay her eggs by kissing, nuzzling and smooching his body against hers. Once the eggs were released into the nest area, he fertilised them with his sperm and commenced the next stage of his self-appointed vigil. For her part, she was off, to perform the same elaborate ritual with other males over the breeding period.

For the next five and a half days, the time it would take their microscopic spawn to hatch, he would not leave his post. He rarely ate and was on the go full time, tidying, pattering his fins against the turf, removing anything that fell onto it and ceaselessly repelling all comers.

Alas for him, while he was seeing one invader off, a female Sandager's wrasse swooped in, nosing and gobbling his unprotected offspring. It was a lolly scramble. A feeding frenzy followed, with wrasses, other demoiselles and even two normally vegetarian black angelfish joining the free-for-all.

He was swamped. Within minutes it was over and the raiders departed, leaving him quivering, alone in his empty nest. He was going to have to start all over again.

Two-spot demoiselles browsing on the walls of Tawhiti Rahi.

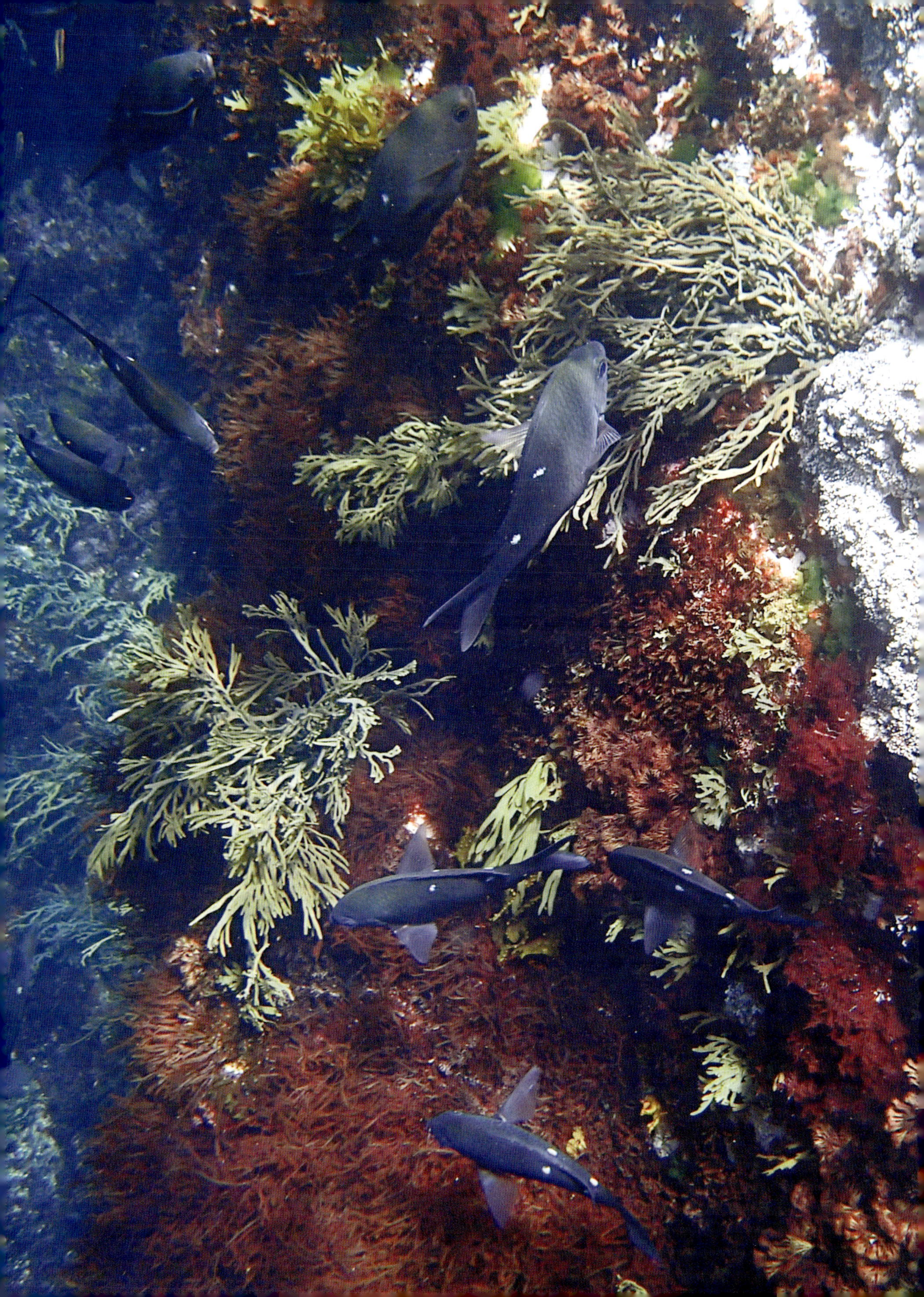

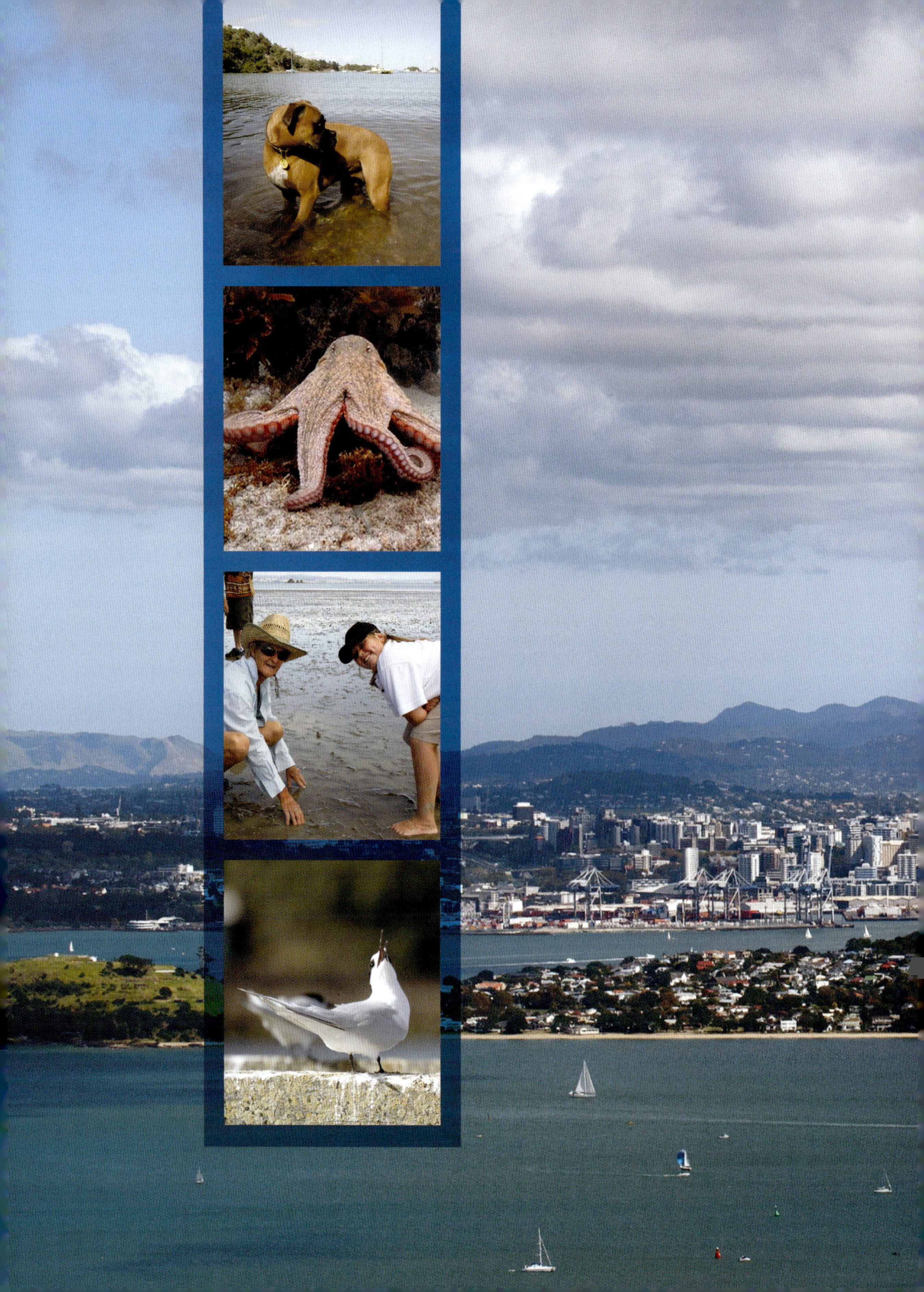

4
HAURAKI GULF MARINE PARK

TĪKAPA MOANA

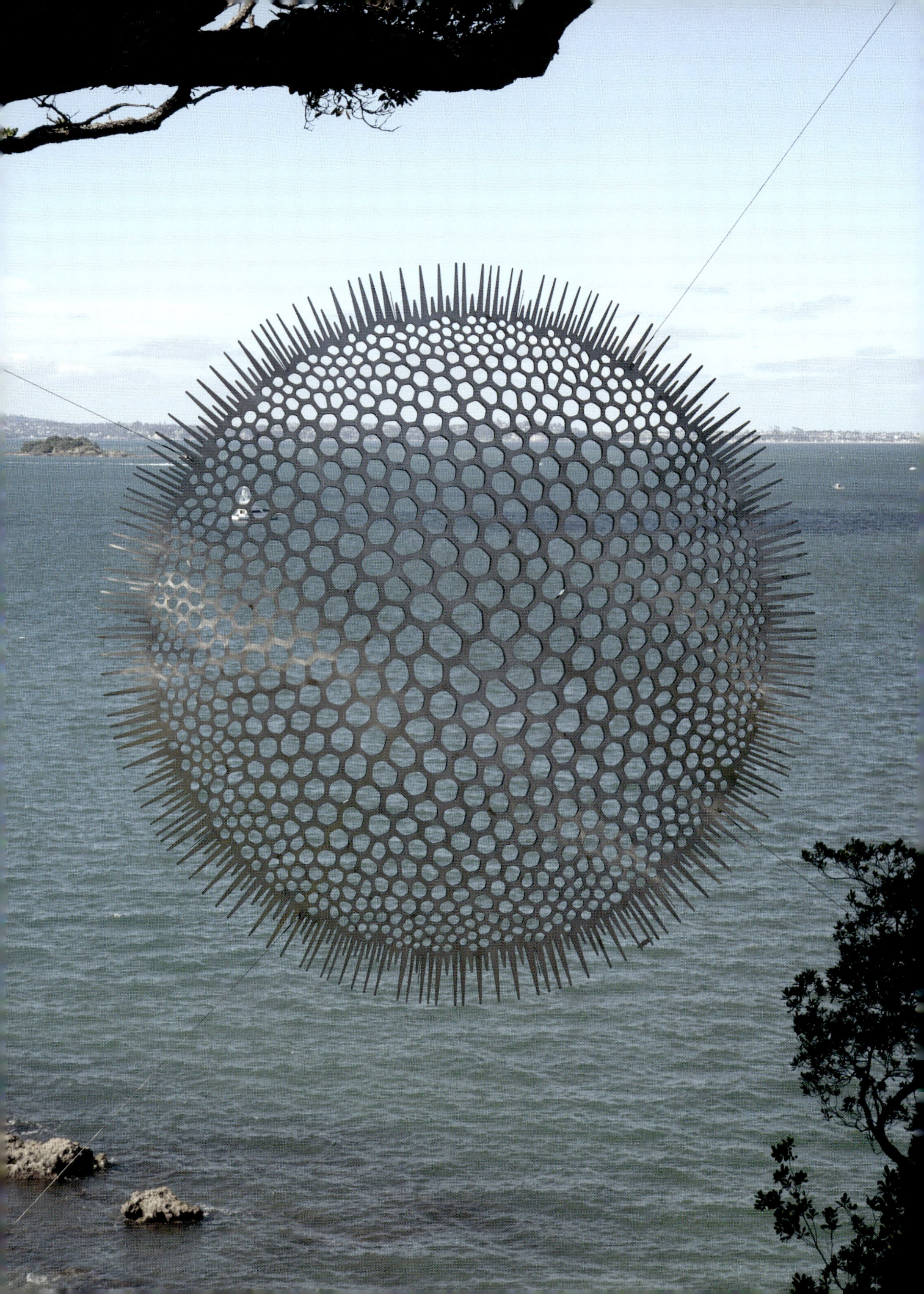

The Hauraki Gulf Marine Park/Tīkapa Moana is huge: 12,000 square kilometres of beaches, bays, estuaries, headlands, peninsulas and islands and, of course, their enclosing waters. On the landward side, it stretches south from just below Mangawhai estuary and skirts the protective islands of Great (Aotea) and Hauturu/Little Barrier islands before entering the broad mouth of the inner gulf. There, it detours into and around the Waitematā Harbour before sloping southeast into the Firth of Thames and finally, back up, over and around the Coromandel Peninsula as far as Waihī Beach. Its seaward boundary is the outer limit of the territorial sea — 12 nautical miles (22 kilometres) from mean high water springs. The park encloses more than 50 islands and island groups including the Mokohinau, Barrier, Cuvier, Mercury and Aldermen islands. Each varies greatly in size, geology, history, vegetation and animal life.

The park was designated in 2000 in recognition of its importance both to conservation and to the 1.4 million people living around its shores in the city of Auckland. For them, it is an unquestioned and defining presence — a sheet of blue on the horizon, an expanse to cross by bridge or ferry, a companionable stretch of water beside which to walk or cycle at evening, the weekend destination for swimming, fishing, kayaking and boating. Its port delivers container vessels and cruise liners direct to the heart of the city. It is as elementary to daily life as the air above.

THE PARK'S OUTER ISLANDS ARE less accessible and therefore less modified than its inner ones, and have long been havens for rare and endangered species. All are special but Hauturu/Little Barrier ('the resting place of the wind') stands out. Twenty-two kilometres from the mainland, the near circular, 3083-hectare, forest-clad extinct volcano was purchased by the Crown in 1894 to create New Zealand's first bird sanctuary. It is a

PREVIOUS:
Waitematā Harbour and Auckland city from the top of Rangitoto Island.

OPPOSITE:
Sculptor Virginia King's 'Lookout/ Pacific Radiolaria' (2011) is an expression of concern at the effect of ocean acidification on marine protozoa and everything that depends on them. The sculpture was shown in the biennial 'Headland Sculpture on the Gulf' exhibition held on Waiheke Island's western coast.

refuge and breeding site of international standing. In order to maintain the highest level of biosecurity, it can be visited only by permit and even then, under the most stringent of conditions.

By contrast, the inner islands serve multiple roles: Waiheke Island, Great Barrier and, to a lesser degree, smaller islands such as Rākino and Kawau have significant residential populations and are used for farming and horticultural enterprises such as wine-growing, for extractive activities such as quarrying and for recreation, an important part of the region's tourism industry. Many have increasing areas of regenerating native forest. A number, such as Motutapu, are being actively replanted and with threatened species such as kiwi reintroduced.

The shining example is undoubtedly the 254-hectare island of Tiritiri Matangi. Once inhabited by Māori, it was purchased by the New Zealand government as a lighthouse reserve in 1841 and leased for grazing for almost 100 years. In 1970 a portion was designated a 'recreation reserve' and in 1971 the farm lease was not renewed, leaving the bush to regenerate. At the time, a mere six percent of original forest remained, little more than skeletal canopy in the bottom of gullies. The cattle and all other introduced mammals were removed and for ten years from 1984 over 280,000 trees were planted by parties of volunteers, preparing the island for birds, insects and lizards to return, some of them under their own power and some with help.

Today, the island teems with life: kōkako, tīeke (North Island saddleback), hihi (stitchbird) and toutouwai (North Island robin) flit through the trees, kākāriki chatter in the flax heads, takahē stalk the grassy patch by the lighthouse, pāteke (brown teal) swim on the dam and kororā (little blue penguins) seek nesting boxes concealed under pōhutukawa roots around the coast. At night, kiwi call. There are tuatara, geckos and skinks; invertebrates flourish and giant wētā have been reintroduced. Some species are so successful that they are source populations for translocations to other sites in New Zealand. It's the nearest thing to pre-human Aotearoa/New Zealand close to Auckland.

Unlike Hauturu, Tiritiri Matangi is an open sanctuary and welcomes visitors.

A BEACON IN MORE WAYS THAN ONE

From 1956 Tiritiri Matangi Island claimed the most powerful lighthouse in the Southern Hemisphere, an 11-million candlepower xenon light that was theoretically visible for 58 nautical miles (in practice, its reach was limited by the curvature of the earth, the height of the tower and the height of the observer to 22 nautical miles). In 2002 that light was replaced by a state-of-the-art solar-powered 50-watt 12-volt lamp with a range of 18 nautical miles.

Tiri is, however, now best known as a refuge for rare and endangered creatures, including the takahē on the island that are so tame it's easy to overlook the fact that they are one of the world's most endangered birds, with around only 230 individuals alive today.

One of the big blue birds on the lawn below the ranger's house.

WHITE FACE? BLACK BELLY? GREY BACK? THE RETURN OF A VERY SMALL BIRD

They were presumed extinct. Three specimens were collected in New Zealand waters in the 1800s, the first two in 1827 during the first voyage of the *Astrolabe* under the command of Dumont d'Urville. The birds were duly preserved, their skins deposited in the Natural History Museum in Paris, where they remain. The third was one of 18 birds presented to the British Natural History Museum at Tring in 1895.

After that brief moment in the spotlight, the birds were not reliably recorded again, casualties, it was presumed, of the combined onslaught of humans and their mammal entourage. They belonged to the family of storm petrels, the smallest of seabirds. New Zealand's seven species are for the most part named prosaically, for the colours of their faces, backs or bellies or the place where they are found; the three hapless specimens were simply designated 'New Zealand storm petrels'.

In January 2003, Wrybill Birding Tours NZ was escorting a boatload of bird watchers towards the Mercury Islands, off the east coast of the Coromandel Peninsula, when they encountered a large number of white-faced storm petrels (*Pelagodroma marina*). That was not unusual or unexpected, but there was a stranger among them, darker, smaller than its companions, with a white rump and, it turned out, unusual dark streaks around the edges of its white belly. Its legs were so long they trailed behind its tail in flight.

Brent Stephenson, co-owner of the tour company, took six photographs of the stranger as it crossed the vessel. He and his business partner Sav Saville surmised that it was a black-bellied storm petrel (*Fregetta tropica*), but the images, when examined later, said otherwise. There were no known matches.

A small tempest blew up in the seabirder world.

'Maybe,' suggested Alan Tennyson, palaeontologist at the Museum of New Zealand Te Papa Tongarewa, 'it's *Oceanites maoriana*, the extinct New Zealand storm petrel?'

But then nothing. No more of the mystery birds were sighted until November of the same year when two ornithologists from the United Kingdom, Bob Flood and Bryan Thomas, chartered a fishing boat out of Warkworth to observe white-faced storm petrels. A few kilometres north of Hauturu/Little Barrier they trailed chum, onion bags filled with mashed and ground fish flesh and oil to attract birds, and were intrigued to be visited by up to 20 small dark petrels with white rumps, big heads and long legs that projected beyond the tail. They photographed them, thinking the birds were black-bellied storm petrels — until, as Stephenson had done, they later examined the images and realised with mounting excitement that they had inadvertently verified the existence of New Zealand storm petrels.

There was publicity, of course, and celebration. Subsequent expeditions found and captured a number of birds — the first conveniently flew into the fishing boat cabin of former wildlife officer Geordie Murman. Feather comparisons and DNA analysis confirmed the ID. The New Zealand storm petrel was no longer 'extinct'!

It is likely that the birds had been present, unnoticed, all along. They are, after all, very small at 17–20 centimetres long and not easily seen against the open sea; had it not been for the detail revealed by today's superb cameras, they may never have been outed.

The final search was for nest sites. In 2011 one of the birds was photographed with a stalk caught in a loop of plant material around its leg; approximate identification of the stalk strongly indicated that it came from northern New Zealand, probably somewhere in the Hauraki Gulf. As the birds come ashore only to breed, it had snagged the stalk as it waddled to its burrow.

The final spectacular discovery came in 2012, when nests were found in the forested interior of Hauturu. Somehow the birds had survived the predations of the island's cats (removed in 1980) and kiore (all gone by 2004).

Lucky.

Two New Zealand storm petrels in the company of a white-faced cousin. 'Petrel' is thought to refer to Saint Peter, who could walk on water as long as he had faith in Jesus. Storm petrels appear to do the same, fluttering and hovering, their pattering feet barely indenting the water's surface as they pick at crustaceans and small fish.

THE FIRST PEOPLE

The sun is not yet above the horizon; it's early summer and cool at this hour. The forest stretching behind the young Māori man to the other side of the peninsula is alive with birdsong. It's almost low tide and the sea is flat, reflecting a cloudless sky; small waves lap at the outcrop in the middle of a long beach and just beyond, a reef barely ruffles the surface of the clear waters. There's a rocky headland at the eastern end of the peninsula. A low row of dunes rises from the high-tide line and beyond it, a thread of smoke drifts and dissipates in the blue. There's a faint murmur of voices. He crosses the dunes and walks purposefully in the direction of the reef leaving prints in the soft sand. He is carrying a kete. Two oystercatchers on the reef chatter in alarm. The picture dims . . .

WE DON'T KNOW PRECISELY when this happened but it was likely to have been several centuries ago. It was just an ordinary day in a small coastal settlement, and it faded and passed without record, as did the young man and his people, long before Europeans set foot on this shore.

All we do know is that when he departed, the young man left an implement in four metres of water about 300 metres offshore, wedged in a cleft in the reef where he was fishing, perhaps, or gathering shellfish. Did he miss it? No tool that has taken time to make is lightly discarded. Did he drop it or did something happen that caused him to overlook it or prevent him from returning to retrieve it?

The implement remained jammed between two boulders; over the centuries the exposed parts became encrusted with marine plants,

Winston Cowie and Ngāti Manuhiri kaumātua Mook Hohneck with the mysterious artefact on Tāwharanui beach.

lichens and algae. Although the occasional diver passed, at that depth it went unnoticed until April 2013 when marine scientist Winston Cowie was diving and filming in the area.

Tāwharanui, where the tool was lost, is special to him.

'I grew up on the peninsula, learning to dive as a nipper on the Kawau Bay side and learning to surf on the ocean side. As I flippered around looking for a crayfish nest to film, I noticed the unusual shape and thought it was too large to be a mussel. And what do you know; there was this taonga close to where I had spent a lot of my childhood in the water!'

When he tugged it clear, he was astonished to find that it was man-made and clearly very old. It is fashioned from a hard grey stone, about 270 millimetres long, flat and sharp on one side and curved to take the grip of a hand on the other. One end tapers to a small hole for tying a rope or noose, and, whether purposely or by accident, it is notched along one edge.

Winston surmises that it was a multipurpose fishing tool. 'Ngāti Manuhiri kaumātua Mook Hohneck and I had a good kōrero about it. We concluded that it was very unusual and likely to be 200–300 years old.'

Winston reported his find to DOC and subsequently met with Ngāti Manuhiri, the local iwi and tangata whenua, about it. Ngāti Manuhiri are the likely descendants of whoever lost the implement, and are therefore its current owners. The mysterious object was returned to them after a karakia cleared the way. It has come full circle.

DESCRIBING SOME 800 YEARS of habitation in a few paragraphs is, of course, a massive simplification. However, to omit mention of those years is to fail to acknowledge the importance of the many, many people who spent their days in the gulf, the subtleties, nuances and realities of lives now largely unknown and unremembered but underlying our present reality, nevertheless. Today's landscape is so thoroughly made over to contemporary purposes that it is easy to forget those whose interaction with the physical world was so much more immediate, so closely interwoven with plenty and with paucity, with the rhythms of the tides and the year.

Recent findings indicate that immigrants from Polynesia to Aotearoa/New Zealand made initial landfall and settlement in the northeast corner of the South Island around eight centuries ago in a locality now known as Wairau Bar. They didn't stay long: for most, it was a transit camp from

Charles Heaphy's ink and watercolour painting, ca. 1850, records a Māori fishing camp either on the shores of Rangitoto or on neighbouring Motutapu.

which they dispersed to points afield, especially to the temperate north.

The Auckland isthmus and gulf islands are, and always have been, a desirable address. The region is relatively warm, largely frost-free and initially was a giant kete kai, a basket brimming with food. In the first centuries, archaeological sites tell us, it was a place of great bounty, perhaps one reason that it is known by Māori as 'Tāmaki makaurau', or 'Tāmaki: loved by many.'

Prior to the arrival of Europeans, iwi and hapū in Tāmaki makaurau

An unknown Māori woman with her catch, in Northland, ca. 1910.

were family-based groups who identified with a senior member or ancestral head after whom they were often named. They did not think of themselves as 'Māori', this term gaining currency only in the mid-1800s when it became useful to make a distinction between themselves and the incoming Europeans — Pākehā.

The people mostly lived in small, undefended kāinga on or near the coast in places where they could grow good crops in the region's fertile soils, harvest birds and plants from onshore forests and had ready access to the waters of the gulf — not only the source of the greatest quantity and variety of kai but also the easiest way to get around.

They moved according to need to seasonal camps to gather food and in response to inter-group dynamics. Relationships over the centuries were complex, fluid and occasionally volatile, with periods of peace periodically fractured by feuds or outright war. In times of conflict, they retreated to pā, fortified villages often on headlands, hills, the slopes of volcanic cones or islands. Alliances were formed on the basis of friendship and intermarriage but were liable to change; there was love, fighting, peace and more fighting.

By the early 1700s, Tāmaki makaurau and the Hauraki Gulf were occupied by four main iwi groups who, with their hapū, remain central to the region today: Ngāti Whātua, Ngāti Paoa, Ngā Puhi and Waikato.

VISITORS TO THE GULF who pass Motutapu by sea observe a pretty but unprepossessing island of relatively low, rolling, grassed hills divided by bush-clad gullies, with a coast of small bays, headlands and deeply striated cliffs. Despite its innocuous appearance, it is one of the more remarkable of the gulf islands and was attractive to Māori from the beginning.

Around 600 years ago, at the time of neighbouring Rangitoto's first eruption, an adult, a child and their dog stood on a Motutapu promontory overlooking the newly formed volcano: when they walked away, their prints were preserved in the ash, an extraordinary testament to their presence in that now-distant time. We can only wonder at what they saw and what happened to them.

Although we do not know the fate of individuals, we do know the island was occupied by a succession of iwi and hapū. The 1510-hectare island is of unparalleled importance to archaeologists because of its record of how and where those people lived: 372 sites have been documented, including 13 pā, and there are likely to have been others that have never been found, or been destroyed and overlaid by the actions of later times.

When Europeans arrived, the island was occupied by Ngāi Tai, descendants of people of the *Tainui* waka. They called it Te Motu-tapu-a-Taikehu, meaning 'the sacred island of Taikehu', a tohunga. The island is also special to the people of the *Arawa* waka, who know it as

The peak of Rangitoto Island looms above Motutapu, January 2014.

An unknown artist's ink rendition of the 'Pah of Motutapu — Tipari chief', 1842. The pā, which might hold from six to as many as 800 men, is shown in plan view and in several cross-sections.

Te Motutapu-a-Tinirau, 'the sacred island of Tinirau', son of Tangaroa. Just as Europeans travelled the world investing their new homes with names of the old, these people carried with them the link to their former Polynesian home.

The island has been farmed since Europeans purchased it in the 1840s. Today all introduced animals other than sheep and cattle have been removed: the island is still farmed in part and is managed in partnership with the Motutapu Restoration Trust, who, with the assistance of the citizens of Auckland, are transforming the remainder of the island into a wildlife haven that includes archaeological and historic sites as well as replanted forests and restored wetlands. Ngāti Tai remain actively involved in the island's management.

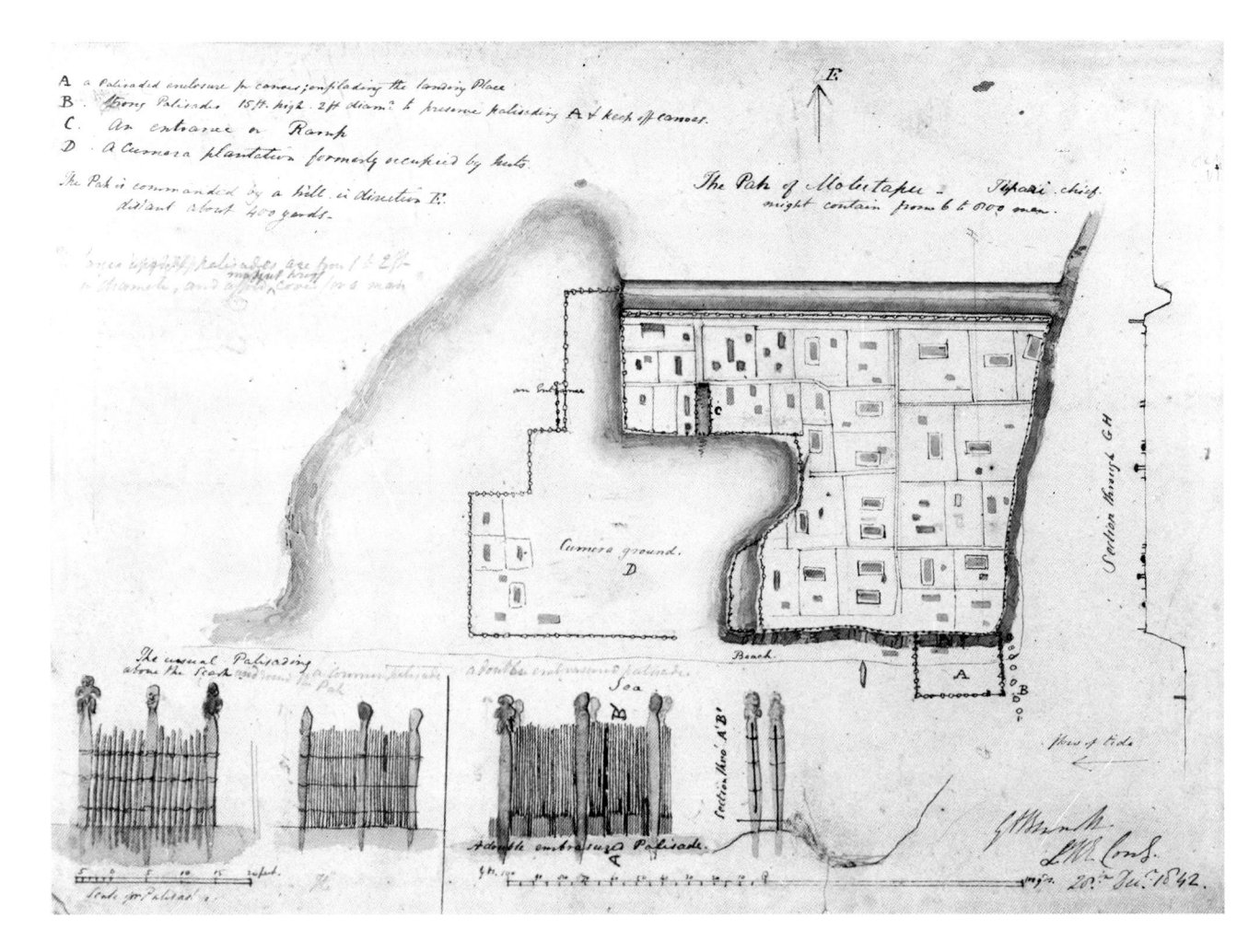

THE WATERS OF HAURAKI were worth defending. Pipi, cockles and scallops were gathered from the region's estuaries and beaches, tuatua from sandy shores and rock oysters, mussels and marine snails from reefs. Snapper, likely to have been netted in fishing expeditions from waka, was by far the most common deep-water catch. Other species on the menu included trevally, kahawai, barracouta, pōrae, rays, sharks, kingfish, wrasses, porcupine fish, rock cod, John Dory, perch, tarakihi, crayfish and crabs.

Seabirds and shorebirds were also harvested — eggs, juveniles and adults. The bones of shags (spotted and black), penguins (little blue), ducks (especially grey), petrels (fluttering and sooty shearwaters), rails, gulls, albatrosses, terns, swans, geese and oystercatchers have all been found in middens. Some, such as fledgling petrels or tītī in their burrows, were collected seasonally from near- and offshore islands as they still are in the south. Seals and sea lions were plentiful and dolphins and whales were killed when the opportunity arose.

Some of the bounty was dried for later use or to trade for items for tool making such as obsidian from Tūhua (Mayor Island). Little was wasted: flesh, bones, feathers and skins were all used, for practical, ceremonial or ornamental purposes.

It must have seemed the party would last forever but a century or so after arrival, the cumulative impacts of gathering, hunting and harvesting combined with the havoc wrought by dogs and kiore meant fewer birds in the forests, deserted seal rookeries, no sea lions and a somewhat depleted inshore fishery.

Whether a direct response to that situation or a strengthening and continuation of values from earlier times, a number of tikanga or customary protocols evolved to collectively slow the loss of the resource. Many continue to be practised in some form in modern times, such as placating Tangaroa, the turbulent ocean god and father of the fish, by the offer of karakia before and sometimes following fishing. Tangaroa is further acknowledged by the return of the first of the catch. Cleaning or eating the haul in the place where it is taken, whether boat or shore, is a no-no and food-gathering areas are not to be contaminated by human waste.

In the event of a death, particularly at sea, a rāhui such as that placed on the Poor Knights renders an area tapu or sacred and forbidden, prohibiting or limiting the quantity, size and season of gathering, depending on the circumstance. Rāhui may also be imposed at other times to conserve a fragile resource.

Other tikanga protect the seafloor, such as a prohibition against towing nets or lines, and for the same reason, containers should be lifted and carried rather than dragged to and from shellfish beds. Rocks that are turned over in the gathering of shellfish must be turned back again. Seasonal calendars that set optimum times of year and day for fishing each species are observed.

TODAY, THOSE TIKANGA ARE AUGMENTED by legal mechanisms that officially maintain the traditional relationship of Māori to the sea under provisions of the Treaty of Waitangi. They function as a cultural and spiritual complement to the science-based regimes of government departments such as DOC, the Ministry of Primary Industries (MPI) and the Ministry of Fisheries.

Rāhui, as described above, is one, a direct continuation of traditional practice. Another that recognises traditional maritime associations operates under the Fisheries (Kaimoana Customary Fishing) Regulations 1998, and allows the gathering of kai beyond usual limits within an iwi or hapū's rohe moana for special occasions. Tangata kaitiaki are appointed to prepare management plans for their areas and to authorise the harvest.

Beyond those, there are two more formal mechanisms, mātaitai reserves and taiāpure.

Mātaitai reserves strengthen connections of local groups to traditional fishing grounds. Tangata whenua may apply to MPI under the Kaimoana Customary Fishing Regulations 1998 to establish a mātaitai, which is administered by a nominated kaitiaki or guardian. On the whole, in a mātaitai reserve, commercial fishing is excluded (there is provision for exceptions) but recreational activity is allowed as of right to all. In order to maintain sustainability in the mātaitai, the kaitiaki may recommend bylaws to the minister.

As of August 2013, ten mātaitai reserves were defined, mapped and gazetted by MPI in the North Island, and 20 in the South Island.

Taiāpure are marine areas of customary importance to an iwi or hapū that are administered by a committee under provisions of the Fisheries Act 1996. Because they embrace both commercial and non-commercial activity, they are a broader option than mātaitai. Communities must go through a thorough and lengthy application process that includes opportunity for public submissions. Taiāpure give coastal people considerable say over management of the resource: as with mātaitai, they can recommend and shape regulations to govern the harvest of species and their quantities, size limits, dates and seasons, methods and area.

As of 2014, there were eight taiāpure, five in the North Island and three in the South.

Gathering cockles at low tide from Pāuatahanui Inlet in the Wellington region.

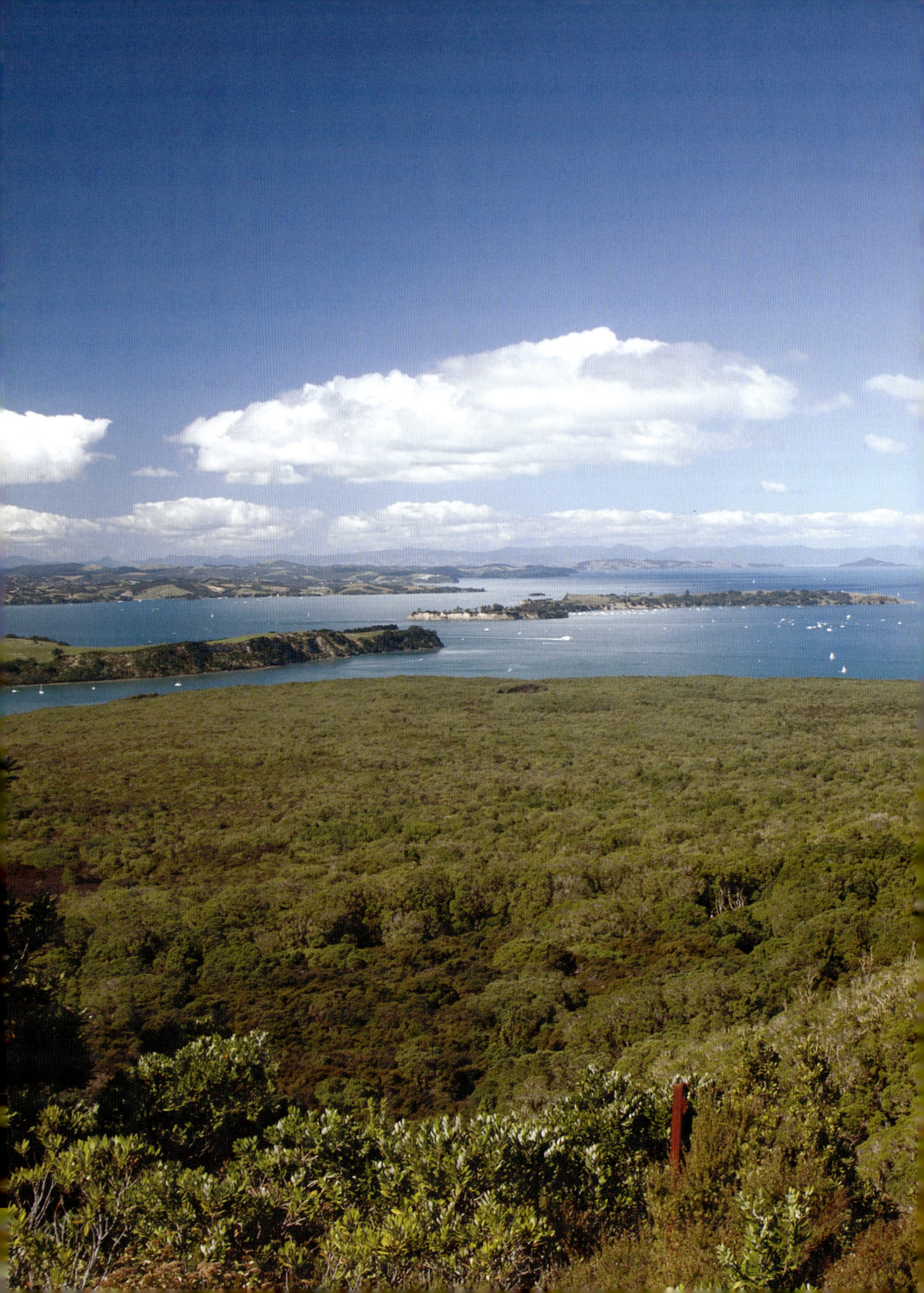

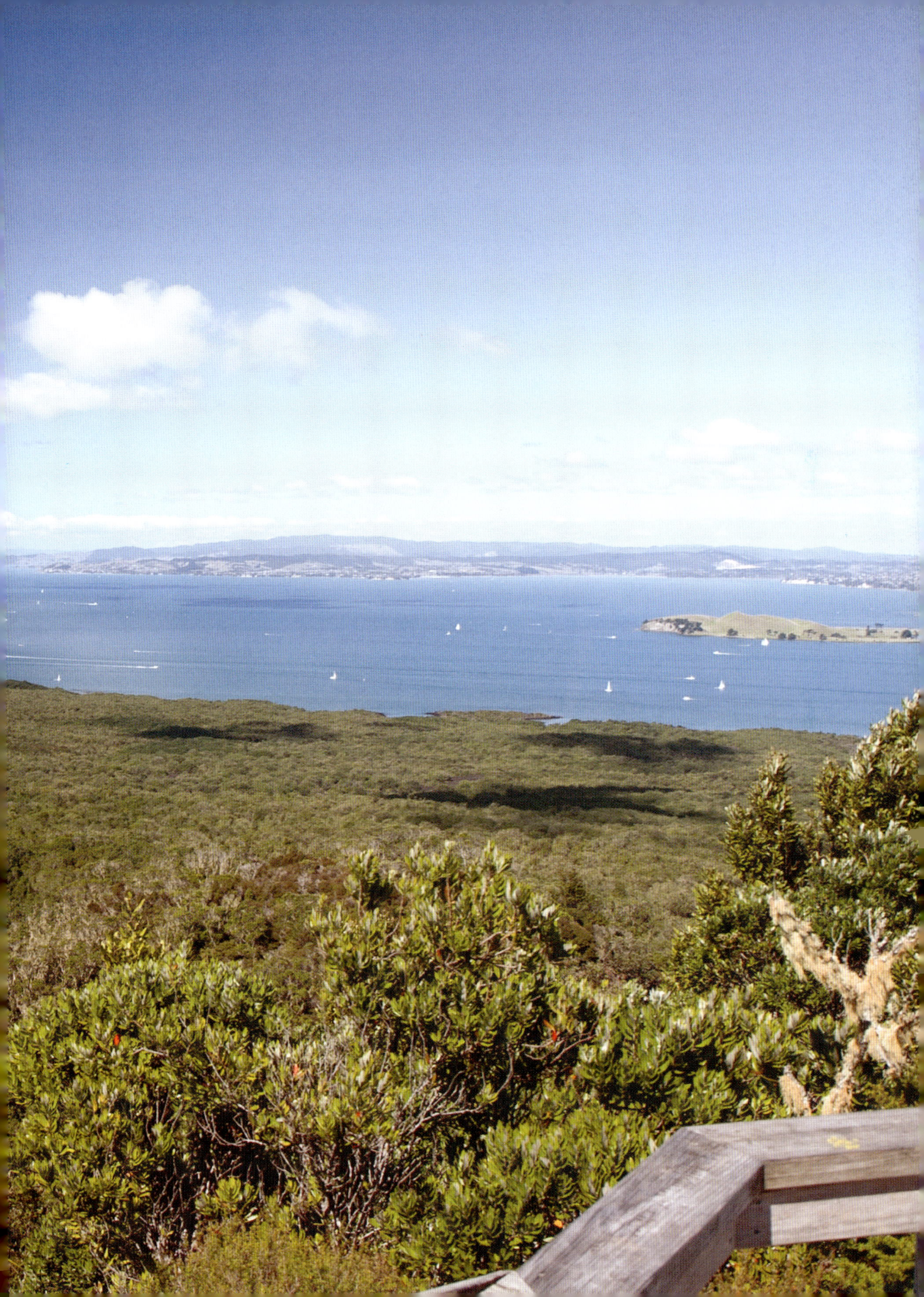

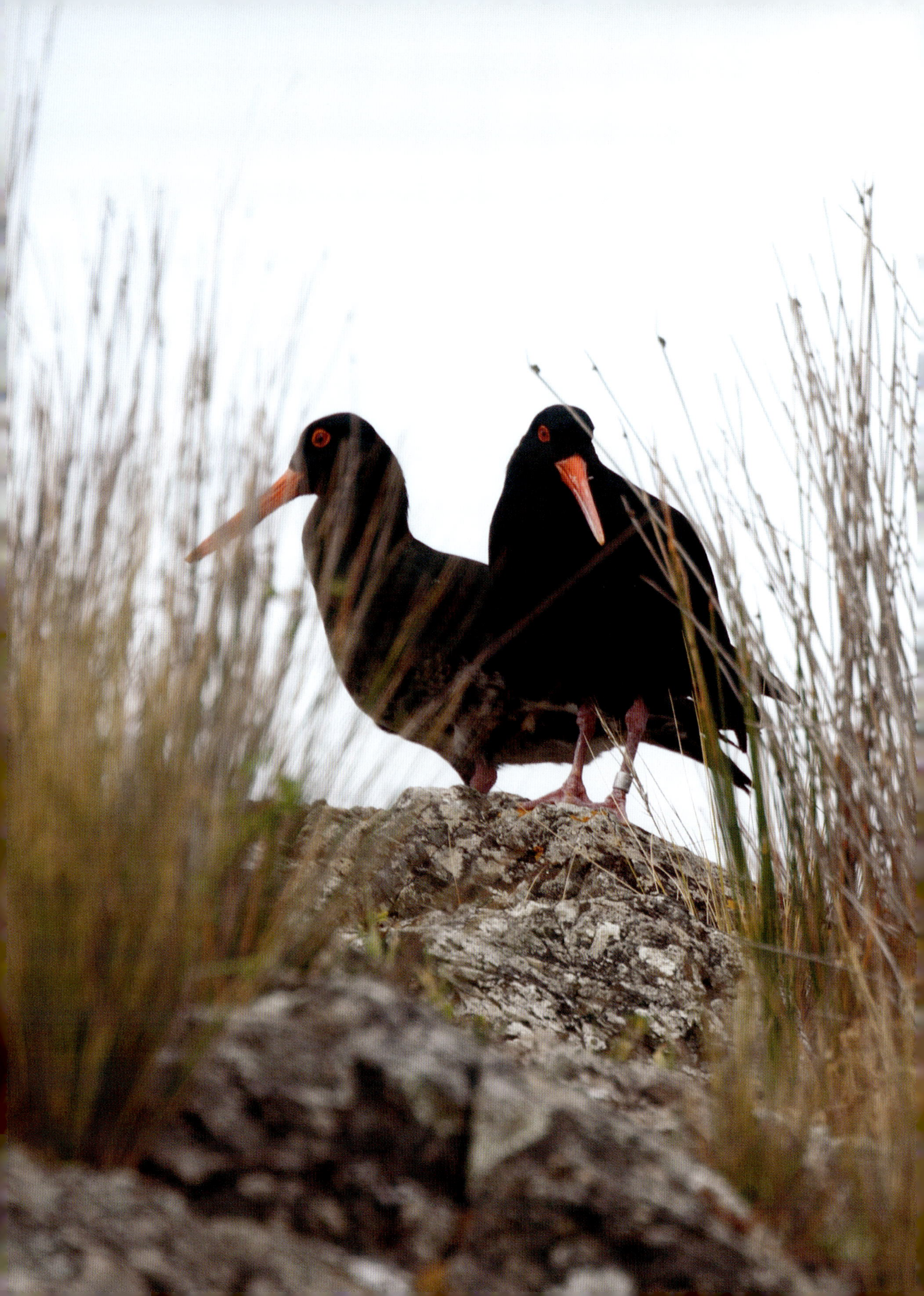

TREASURES OF THE NORTH WIND: MARINE RESERVES OF THE HAURAKI

MARINE RESERVES IN & AROUND THE HAURAKI GULF MARINE PARK

- Poor Knights Islands
- Whāngārei Harbour (2 sites)
- Cape Rodney–Ōkakari Pt (Goat Island)
- Tāwharanui
- Long Bay–Ōkura
- Motu Manawa (Pollen Island)
- Te Matuku
- Whanganui-a-Hei (Cathedral Cove)
- Tūhua (Mayor Island)

Marine Park

The Hauraki Gulf Forum, representing government departments, local authorities and tangata whenua, is the statutory body responsible for the park. Its 2011 *State of the Gulf* report makes dismal reading because almost every environmental indicator shows continuing degradation. There is, chairman John Tregidga says, 'a collective failure to halt or reverse decline in the gulf's natural resources'.

The list of woes is extensive, and includes sedimentation of the coastal zone, destruction of important habitats such as mussel beds, fallen and falling populations of fish and shellfish, the presence of toxic metals, nitrogen pollution, beach closures because of harmful algae and pathogens, litter, whale strike and death, dwindling numbers of wading birds, and biosecurity breaches from alien organisms that have hitch-hiked on visiting ships.

The causes include overfishing and ruinous extraction practices such as dredging and bottom trawling, as well as a range of impacts from the land — inefficient use of fertilisers, effluent runoff, stormwater contamination and the flow-on effects of ever-expanding urban areas. There's little to celebrate, it seems, except the wonderful conservation efforts on the islands and the park's marine reserves.

Five marine reserves are both inside the boundaries of the Hauraki Gulf

PREVIOUS: Looking east over the Hauraki Gulf from the summit of Rangitoto. Motutapu extends a headland to the left; Waiheke is in the distance with the Coromandel Range beyond; the Waiheke ferry crosses Motuihe towards the centre and Browns Island (Motukorea) is to the right.

—

OPPOSITE: A nesting pair of variable oystercatchers check things out from the security of their little island above the beach at Tāwharanui, 2014.

—

Marine Park and in the Auckland region: Cape Rodney–Ōkakari Point or Goat Island, which as we have seen, introduced no-compromise 'no-take' zones to the world and in time became the poster child of marine reserves; the recently created Tāwharanui, where Winston found the taonga; Long Bay–Ōkura, on the fringe of metropolitan Auckland 22 kilometres north of the central business district; Te Matuku, on the southern shores of Waiheke Island; and Motu Manawa/Pollen Island, on the inner shores of the upper Waitematā Harbour. A sixth, Te Whanganui-a-Hei (Cathedral Cove), is inside the Hauraki Gulf Marine Park but is otherwise considered part of the Bay of Plenty.

MUSSELS OF THE GULF

The mussel beds of the Hauraki Gulf were once so extensive that it's thought they filtered the waters of the gulf every day. Most mussels require hard substrates such as rocks or reefs but those in the Rangitoto Channel, Tāmaki Strait, Firth of Thames and along the Coromandel coast rafted together to create their own reefs, which then became habitat for a range of other organisms. Dredging up to the early 1970s not only destroyed the mussel beds but also deprived the gulf of that enormous filtering machine. The reefs have never recovered and the waters are cloudier as a consequence.

However, a team called 'Revive Our Gulf' are attempting to re-create the mussel beds off eastern Waiheke by seeding the seafloor with farmed mussels: it's early days yet but first trials appear promising.

Sweep, spotty and parore swim above mussel beds at low tide on Waiheke's north coast.

TĀWHARANUI

The northern side of Tāwharanui Peninsula was New Zealand's first marine park, designated in 1981 after the realisation that its mix of open beaches, rocky headlands, kelp-covered sandstone reefs, underwater tunnels, caves, sandy seabed and rich array of fish, shellfish and bird life was something special. The area is home to over 50 fish species, its rock pools brim with oysters, mussels, kina and other shellfish, and whales and bottlenose dolphins pass through its waters. The marine park neatly partnered with the adjacent regional park and (since 2004) the predator-fenced Tāwharanui Open Sanctuary.

Being a park meant no fishing for three kilometres along the coast, up to half a nautical mile (926 metres) offshore. It was always potentially confusing for the public, however, especially as the Cape Rodney–Ōkakari Point Marine Reserve is just up the coast, not far away. The park also lacked permanence and the absolute security of a reserve so in 1994 Mike Lee, of the then Auckland Regional Council, suggested that it be 'upgraded'.

White sands, sandstone reefs and rocky headlands at the eastern end of Tāwharanui Marine Reserve.

The process was nowhere near as simple as he thought it would be and it was not until 2011 that it did, in fact, become a reserve. At the same time, the boundary was adjusted, increasing the protected area by another 16 hectares to just under 400.

ROGER GRACE IS A MARINE BIOLOGIST, professional photographer, writer and campaigner for marine conservation. He received the Queen's Service Medal for public service in 2005. He lives in the Ōmaha area on a sandspit with the estuarine Whangateau Harbour on one side and the white-sand ocean beach on the other. He casually mentions that a group of eight orca recently spent two or three hours in the harbour chasing stingrays in the shallows and there was a pod of 30 bottlenose dolphins here a couple of months ago. The sea is his life.

Like Wade Doak and Bill Ballantine, Roger has been going down to the sea for many decades, especially to Tāwharanui. Like them, he has witnessed many changes. He is equally passionate about his subject and frustrated by our collective inability to act on evidence that is only too clear.

Former Minister of Conservation, Kate Wilkinson, and then chair of the Auckland Regional Council, Mike Lee, shake hands over the dedicatory plaque at the opening of Tāwharanui Marine Reserve on 28 August 2011.

He talks of hāpuku. Hāpuku or groper (*Polyprion oxygeneios*) are a slow-growing, silver-grey fish with large eyes and a protruding lower jaw. They use those large eyes and biting jaw to eat a wide range of other fish species including crayfish. Like humans, hāpuku mature when they are teenagers and can live to around 60 years: at their largest, they may be up to 1.8 metres long and weigh as much as 100 kilograms. They are sometimes described as 'wreck fish' because, although they were also once found in surface waters, they are primarily deep-water fish (to 400 metres) and often shelter in shipwrecks and caves. They are gregarious and used to be found in places like the Poor Knights and the Three Kings in schools of 30 to 100 individuals. Wade Doak describes 'a huge herd of hāpuku, that came whirling up from the deeps like a maelstrom and caromed around me for 10 minutes before vanishing again into the dark blue', when he was diving at the Three Kings in the 1960s.

Roger saw them in smaller numbers at the Poor Knights in 1969:

> I was out at the Pinnacles with a dive group from Pukekohe Underwater Club. After the first dive, these two guys came back raving about this whole heap of hāpuku they'd found. There was a place probably 200 metres off one of the islands with deep water between and this little hump, still fairly deep water, around 30 metres, and on the top there was a school of about 30 hāpuku swimming around.
>
> They took us back there for the afternoon dive and at that point all the hāpuku had gone down into what we term the 'hāpuku slot', a great big rock, a slab that leans against the underwater cliff, and forms a sloping tunnel that tapers to nothing at the top. And there were these same hāpuku milling about. This was quite deep, almost 60 metres, getting down a bit deep for diving. I remember peering into this hole and this HUGE hāpuku, it would have been five and a half feet long and weighed about 90 kilos,

Roger Grace counts cockles in the Whangateau Harbour.

A Wade Doak image of the now-scarce hāpuku. 'Like trying to photograph a dodo,' said Roger.

came whizzing out and stopped about half a metre away and waved his jaw up and down. And of course, I had my close-up camera gear on!

No more. Hāpuku were fished out and are now locally extinct at the Poor Knights. 'About five years ago, three juvenile hāpuku stayed in Maroro Bay on the western side for about a month and then disappeared,' Roger says.

WE HAVE NO HISTORICAL NUMBERS for this species but we do know that hāpuku used to be common inshore fish, caught around the reefs and off the rocks. Roger estimates the population is now less than five percent of its pre-fishing size.

Hāpuku are still sold in supermarkets but commercial boats have had to move into deeper waters further offshore to catch them; recreational fishers continue to haul them aboard from places like the Mokohinaus. Unfortunately, as Wade points out, once these denizens of the deep are hauled to the surface, they cannot be returned because their swim bladders expand irreversibly and even those returned to the sea will die.

For Roger, one answer for this species is 'a total rest for years and see what happens, a total allowable catch of zero. I think people would be surprised at what might happen.'

Marine reserves are another, especially if they are of substantial size. In the early 1990s, DOC began talks with locals and tangata whenua about some form of protection in the coastal waters of Great Barrier (Aotea) Island. Nothing eventuated until 2003 when a substantial reserve was proposed off the island's northeast coast. At 49,500 hectares, it included 22 kilometres of coast and extended to the 12-nautical-mile limit. It excluded an estuarine area in deference to local needs for shellfish gathering but otherwise protected a wide range of habitats; it would have been New Zealand's third-largest after the far-offshore Kermadec and Auckland islands reserves.

Early feedback appeared positive. A call for submissions in 2003 was followed several years later by sign-off from the Ministers of Conservation and Transport but the proposal collapsed at the final hurdle in May 2008, when then Minister of Fisheries, Jim Anderton, turned it down.

Hāpuku were among the casualties: they might have stood a chance, given that the proposed area included three deep reefs. 'It would have been wonderful!' says Roger.

All is not lost — although seriously ponderous and slowed by red tape and the democratic process. In 2013 the Great Barrier Environment Strategy Planning Committee convened hearings to consider afresh the question of marine protection areas. A new proposal has been floated, to ban commercial fishing, allow a certain amount of fishing by locals, as well as smaller 'no-take' areas or marine reserves. Will this be sufficient to save the hāpuku? Will it happen in time?

THE CONTRIBUTION MADE TO THE DEBATE by Roger and his colleagues is invaluable. Through sheer persistence, dogged patience and long-term commitment, they paint a picture that is hard to deny. For 36 years, he has been methodically sampling three major locations, two at Tāwharanui (inside and outside the park) and at Mimiwhangata Marine Park up the coast.

Mimiwhangata is about an hour's drive north of Whāngārei on the coast. Its varied reefs, boulder fields, turf flats and sandy spots were scientifically assessed in the early 1970s as exceptionally biodiverse despite past heavy commercial fishing. In 1984, after ten years of consultation and discussion, 2000 hectares was designated a 'marine park'. Like Tāwharanui and New Zealand's other then marine park, Sugar Loaf Islands in Taranaki, it was a compromise, a weighing of the needs of existing users against the protection of reef fish, pāua and rock oysters.

It resulted in a total ban on commercial fishing with the exception of a 'grandfather clause' that allowed commercial fishers who used long-lines and craypots to continue another nine years. Recreational fishing was limited to unweighted single-hook lines, trolling, spearing and hand picking of a restricted list of species. Only species that were thought to be open-sea rather than resident reef fish were permitted to be taken and cray-potting was to be 'only one pot per person, party, or boat'.

It didn't work. Ironically, the publicity associated with the park's establishment drew an increased number of visitors, the waters were

'If you look at aerial photographs of Mimiwhangata, you can see most of the reef there is shallow rock and we know that's kina barren. You can see the black dark around low tide and a little bit of kelp forest way down here and all the rest is kina barren and that's in a marine park, where there's no commercial fishing. In the partial protection area the end result was the same as if it was fished, pretty well. It's shocking. And Fisheries seem to think this is OK! It's not! It's terrible!' — Roger Grace

cleaned out and accessible large kina were stripped from the rock pools along the shore. The area became a tragic example of the failure of partial protection.

IN 2007 ROGER FOUND ONLY seven legal-sized crayfish at Mimiwhangata over 320 sampling sites, when once they were so plentiful and so large that local kaumātua Puke Haika recalls a 50-pound (22-kilogram) specimen as big as a small child when he was a diver in the 1950s. 'That represents 1.75 legal crays per hectare,' Roger says, 'compared with 1000 inside the reserve at Tāwharanui. And if you consider 1000 to be probably the natural population level, that means that the Northland coast is fished down to less than 0.2 percent of its original size. The only thing that has worked is total "no take", where it's gone up and up and up.'

In a healthy marine ecosystem, crayfish are among the largest, most abundant predators on New Zealand coasts, which is why they, along with snapper, are used by Roger as indicator species. They're called 'spiny lobsters' in the rest of the world, as distinct from 'clawed lobsters', which have fearsome, crab-like pincers for front legs. There are four species in New Zealand waters but only two are common: the most numerous, the red crayfish (*Jasus edwardsii*) and the largest in the world, the green or packhorse crayfish (*Sagmariasus verrearuxi*). Red crayfish are found on reefs from the Three Kings Islands to the Auckland Islands and the Chathams, and on shallower seamounts throughout the country's EEZ.

Tāwharanui has been protected for approximately 30 years — the lifespan of a crayfish — which explains some of the very large animals Roger has seen. 'They're big crayfish! Like small dogs — HUGE crays!'

THERE MAY YET BE HOPE for Mimiwhangata. Ngāti Wai, who are tangata whenua/tangata moana, are leading an initiative with the support of the Royal Forest & Bird Protection Society to restore the reserve via rāhui tapu, a 'no-take' zone that in this instance would be flanked either side by customary fishing areas. Governance would be shared by hapū and community trustees and although subject to 25-year review — and therefore a notch less secure than a marine reserve — it is thought unlikely that anything would change because of the involvement and investment in the project by local people.

A cluster of crays: they flourish in marine reserves.

NEK TIME, NEKTON! THE EXTRAORDINARY JOURNEY OF THE CRAYFISH

Armour-plating. It's all very well to have a strong, rigid exoskeleton for protection but just like school shoes, it pinches when your feet get bigger. Like all arthropods, crayfish increase in size by growing a complete new shell — including eyes, mouthparts, hairs, feelers and legs — and shedding the old one in a rather astonishing process called 'ecdysis'. A split appears like a zip across the back; the front tips forward and the crayfish hunches up and wriggles out backwards. It's perilous because until the new shell hardens, the crayfish not only does not feed but is also vulnerable to attack. Young crayfish moult several times a year but adults only once, the females in autumn, and males in spring.

Crayfish are relatively anonymous characters — if indeed, you can call them characters at all — but these large crustaceans have complex and interesting lives and travel hundreds of kilometres in their various incarnations. Those that attain adulthood may live to 30 years.

A female crayfish reaches sexual maturity between three and eight years, depending on whether she lives in the north or the south. She breeds in autumn, a month after moulting. Large females seek similar-sized partners and produce higher numbers of eggs proportionate to their size — up to half a million — a fact that matters when you consider that the bigger crayfish are the ones taken by fishers.

Courtship, which lasts up to three days, involves the face-to-face touching of the small antennae above the mouth. When the pair is ready to mate, they rear up in a tight frontal embrace and the male deposits a packet of sperm onto her belly. She immediately releases eggs, which, after being fertilised, attach to long hairs on the swimmerets on the underside of her tail to be incubated for 100 to 150 days.

At sunrise of the day the eggs hatch, the female stands on her leg-tips, lifts her tail and violently beats the swimmerets. Her brood rise to the surface in the dawn light and spend up to 30 minutes in the first of their many larval forms. They then undergo their first moult, into tiny transparent, spider-like creatures called phyllosoma.

Each fragile little animal is now on its own, a member of the vast community of oceanic plankton. For two years it is at the mercy of current and tide, and may drift as far as 1000 kilometres. It spends its days at the very edge of the photic zone around 200 metres below the surface, and each night ventures to the surface to feed on other plankton — small jellyfish, fish larvae and shrimps.

If it is not eaten itself, it undergoes many cycles of moulting and growth until it is no longer plankton but nekton, meaning that it can move independently; it is only 25 millimetres long and still transparent but is now identifiably a juvenile crayfish, a puerulus, and about to commence the next phase of its journey. The puerulus has no mouthparts — it has no time to waste on eating: its imperative is to return to coastal waters. Incredibly, this little creature, a 'strong swimmer', lives on its stores of fat (it's only tiny, remember) as it makes its way, up to 150 kilometres from wherever the sea has carried it, back to the nearest shore. Any further, and it is unlikely to make it.

Once there, it finds a chink or crevice in a shallow reef and resumes life, eating, growing and moulting. It's not yet necessarily in the ideal place, however. More travel! In spring and early summer, it joins its cohort in undertaking a further migration but this time, it's on foot, so to speak. If it has ended up on the coasts of the lower South Island, it makes its way northward against the current, bouncing on the tips of its legs along the seafloor. One juvenile packhorse crayfish has been recorded as travelling 1070 kilometres.

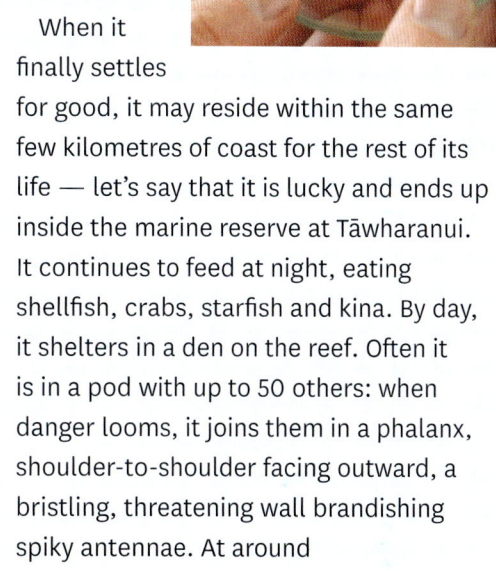

When it finally settles for good, it may reside within the same few kilometres of coast for the rest of its life — let's say that it is lucky and ends up inside the marine reserve at Tāwharanui. It continues to feed at night, eating shellfish, crabs, starfish and kina. By day, it shelters in a den on the reef. Often it is in a pod with up to 50 others: when danger looms, it joins them in a phalanx, shoulder-to-shoulder facing outward, a bristling, threatening wall brandishing spiky antennae. At around age five, it is ready to breed and set another generation on its long journey.

CLOCKWISE FROM TOP: Two final-stage phyllosoma larvae of the red rock lobster *Jasus edwardsii*; a final stage phyllosoma; a juvenile.

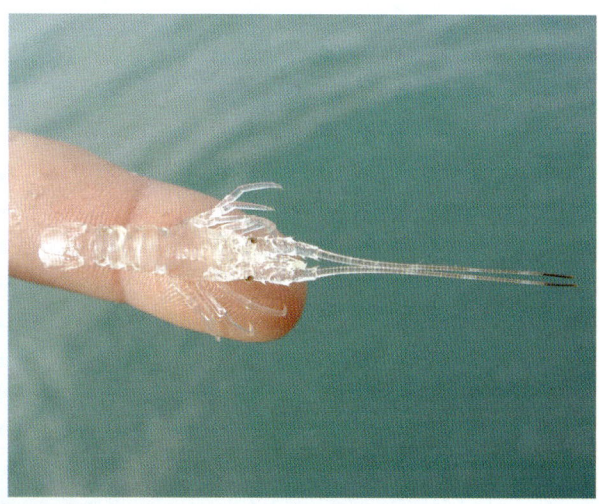

LONG BAY-ŌKURA

Long Bay is one of the most publicly accessible marine reserves. It is a typical stretch of north Auckland east coast — a long, flat, sandy beach with layered sandstone and siltstone cliffs rising sharply from eroded and potholed sandstone platforms at either end. On a typical early spring morning, the sea is flat and tinged with gold and Tiritiri Matangi Island floats in faint outline above the horizon. The kilometre-long expanse that Māori knew as Oneroa, or 'long beach', is dotted with walkers exercising dogs or just strolling quietly. A child crouches to examine a find; a lone southern black-backed gull cruises the waveline with an eye, perhaps, on winkling a feed of tuatua or a sand dollar urchin from the sands close to shore. An oystercatcher picks among seaweed on a reef.

A pothole below the cliffs is a small reservoir at low tide, a tiny world brimming with life. Its lip is edged with a necklace of barnacles and its sides are thick with a lawn of the red seaweed *Corallina officinalis*. This amazing plant extracts calcium from the sea and uses it to build lime-reinforced cell walls. The base of the pool is scoured clean by the churning action of waves on a small pile of stones in the bottom. Nevertheless, there are tiny black snails, mussels, small anemones, worms, oysters and large olive anemones — the closer you look, the more you see.

There's even more in the reserve beyond the waves: sponges, other anemones, bryozoans and ascidians or sea squirts, kelp, spotties, snapper, parore, mullet and crayfish. It is the reverse of what might have been — and very different from less protected parts of this coast.

The beauty and tranquillity of the view out to Tiritiri Matangi belies the wealth of life beneath the sands and water of Long Bay.

THE RESERVE WAS INITIATED by the Sir Peter Blake Marine Education & Recreation Centre. The centre is a complex of unremarkable wooden buildings tucked against the hillside on Auckland Council land at the south end of the beach. The Awaruku Stream flows along the turning circle on the road outside and curves around the front of the building before flowing away across the sands. The complex has a marae-style entrance, painted red with a carved head at the apex of the gable.

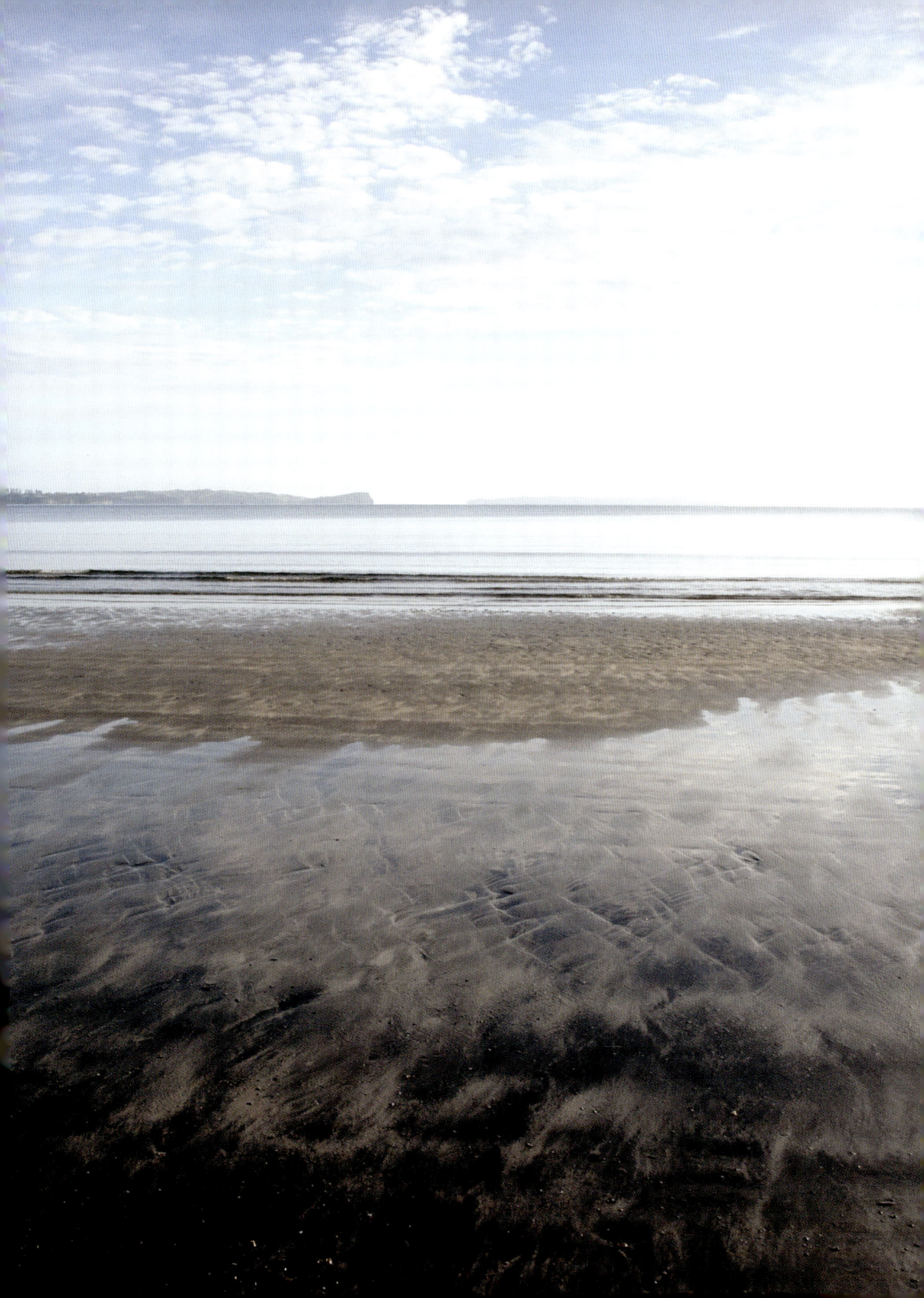

Tī kouka or cabbage trees and a ponga fence complete the picture.

The centre has been in operation since 1990, the result of 12 years' hard work by a group of yachtsmen and teachers who saw the need for marine education in Auckland schools — large numbers of children, up to 50 percent of junior classes in some areas, had never been to the beach.

It was built on sponsorships, donations, grants and by the sweat of volunteers; it offers a variety of programmes for schools and the general public, and has facilities for overnight stays and for conferences. Sir Peter Blake was the centre's patron although he played no part in its formation.

Once it was up and running, a marine reserve was almost inevitable. One of the group, Ross Garrett, wrote a series of articles on the subject for the centre's newsletter. Then another of the team, John Maxted, found juvenile shellfish plundered from the beach in his seafood chowder; he realised with horror that the bay was on the verge of being cleaned out and called a public meeting. The East Coast Bays Coastal Protection Society Inc was formed, leading to the reserve's ultimate establishment in 1995.

At first glance, it's just one of many tiny tide pools on the shelves below the cliffs but look more closely and each is a world in miniature.

A high school group and their teacher taking transepts on the rock platforms in 2011. The centre complements the reserve, introducing a wide range of groups and children to activities around, in and on the water.

—

The Sir Peter Blake Marine Education & Recreation Centre in the light of early morning.

—

MOTU MANAWA (POLLEN ISLAND)

The thousands of commuters who stream over Auckland's northwestern motorway across the upper reaches of the Waitematā Harbour, as they travel to and from West Auckland to the central city every weekday, are possibly not aware that they are passing through the heart of a marine reserve — although those who leave the car in the garage and cycle the same route are perhaps more knowledgeable.

    The first clue on their way home is the mangrove thicket and saltmarsh on their left beside Oakley Creek; they then roll onto a bridge over the tidal channel before passing onto a causeway. If they have time to look, they are surrounded by shining water at high tide and gleaming mudflats at low ebb. By the time they reach the exit at the far side, they are again looking at expanses of mangrove and saltmarsh with larger wetland trees

The characteristic yellow triangle that signals the reserve's boundary is actually attached to the side of the motorway.

A wide view of the upper harbour shellbank and mangrove forest of Pollen Island with Rangitoto, the harbour bridge and the city in the distance.

The Forest & Bird Motu Manawa Restoration Group conducts guided educational walks in the reserve: the spoils from a rubbish clean-up in March 2014.

The very rare New Zealand dotterel nests on Pollen Island, a scientific reserve.

Evidence of Pleistocene ice-age sea-level changes: a fossilised shrimp burrow preserved in marine mud deposited on top of 170,000-year-old peat remains from an ancient freshwater rush marsh.

such as tī kouka or cabbage tree on their left.

Away from the motorway, the reserve is a place of reflected light and beauty, heaped white cockle-shellbanks, soft gold wetland rushes and small plants of the saltmarsh; it encloses two low-lying tracts of land that merge so seamlessly with the tidal flats that you are barely aware of them, Pollen Island and Traherne Island.

Paradoxically, the presence of the motorway means relative isolation and freedom from disturbance for the reserve and its creatures. The many different habitats support a diverse bird community, from the reclusive fernbird, banded rail and spotless crake populations of the wetlands to waders such as New Zealand dotterels and flocks of seasonally migrating eastern bar-tailed godwits; and to the locals — Caspian terns, southern black-backed gulls, oystercatchers and the occasional passing royal spoonbill. The area is a vital nursery for juvenile fish.

A RARE MOTH

Bill Ballantine uses the Pollen Island reserve as an example of how to 'dodge the silliness of concentrating on the least important' and focus attention on what really matters. A Bactra moth, allegedly found nowhere else in the world, lives on the island but that is not why the reserve is important, he says.

For Pollen Island we should say 'Let's keep at least one really natural bit of mangrove forest right in the middle of the metropolis of Auckland. Much of the original harbour edge has been developed out of existence or completely altered but this piece is still typical. It contains representative shellbanks, bird roosts, saltmarsh, sediment flats and creeks, and these habitats contain their typical flora and fauna. It will serve as a benchmark, so we can judge the rest. It will remind us of our natural heritage. It will help keep us sane, healthy and informed.'

When we have said a lot to that effect, we could add 'and it has a rare moth'.

The moth is so rare, there is no photograph of it!

A wide range of bird species including the rare fernbird (above) and the endangered migrant eastern bar-tailed godwits (below) hang out in the reserve in full view of the city; the locally uncommon plant *Mimulus repens* grows on Traherne Island.

4 • HAURAKI GULF MARINE PARK | TĪKAPA MOANA   139

TE MATUKU

Waiheke Island's Te Matuku Marine Reserve lies on its relatively sheltered south coast. The area is named after the Australasian bittern or matuku that is now rare in the reserve's wetlands — if, indeed, it is still there at all. It is not far from the small community of Orapiu and its boundaries include a cluster of predominantly holiday homes in Pearl Bay but it is otherwise in a more sparsely settled area of the island.

The reserve is a long, narrow inlet surrounded by steep hills clad in mature and regenerating native forest, much of which is either protected reserve or covenanted, creating a seamless transition from land to sea and clear, unpolluted freshwater entering the reserve.

From north to south, this reserve is special for its uninterrupted sequence of plant communities, beginning with coastal forest and passing through saltmarsh, mangrove forest, tidal flats and shellbanks before finally entering deeper waters in the Waiheke Channel in Tāmaki Strait.

At the top of the bay, several small streams feed two substantial channels

From coastal forest to open sea, Te Matuku Marine Reserve is a sequence of protected ecosystems. At half-tide the saltmarsh behind the sandspit in the upper inlet is exposed.

that flow like long arms down either side of a 50-hectare mangrove-fringed saltmarsh; in time-honoured fashion, as wetlands do, this wetland is slowly becoming dryland, with a small island forming in the middle. In colonial times the upper estuary was sufficiently clear that boats could travel from the coast to one of the island's first villages at the top of the bay. The island's first school, which also doubled as a hall and a church, was built in 1882 but closed 50 years later because the island's population centres had developed further to the west. All that remains of those people and their times is a pioneer cemetery overlooking the reserve; it's a quietly pretty spot, overtopped by native trees, with dappled light falling on moss-covered graves and picket fences.

The middle portion of the reserve is 150 hectares of mud–shell–sand flats that are so level they are almost completely drained at low tide. They have a complement of residents that is typical of the middle and upper Waitematā Harbour, among them crabs, whelks, cockles, pipi, wedge shells, snails, barnacles, trough shells and tiny nut shells. There is an unusual abundance of the spiny tubeworm *Pomatoceros caeruleus*. Tubeworms anchor themselves to hard surfaces such as cockle shells and build fragile clumps of tubular structures that resemble worm casts on a lawn. They are up to five centimetres high and are easily overlooked or trodden on.

The flats are rich pickings across the spectrum of the tide: wading birds take their fill when it is falling or low, and juvenile flounder and mullet take their place when it returns.

The reserve is notable for a scimitar-shaped spit parallel to a forested peninsula, itself a scenic reserve, that juts like an elbow from the eastern shore into the middle of the bay. The spit has accumulated over time as coarse sediments and the shells of dead cockles have been pushed across the flats by small waves and deposited in a low ridge. Between the spit and the forest, a further flat of fine mud is a safe, high-tide roost for a range of seabirds including the endangered New Zealand dotterels that congregate in winter, with some staying on to breed in spring. They are in the company of a flock of around 200 eastern bar-tailed godwits that summer here from October to March. Caspian terns, oystercatchers and reef herons also feed or breed in the reserve.

Tubeworm casts in the mudflats at Te Matuku.

A GATHERING PLACE FOR TŪTURIWHATU

Waihekeans are fond of their New Zealand dotterels (tūturiwhatu) and go to considerable lengths to eliminate predators such as rats, cats and hedgehogs from the vicinity of nesting sites. They even appoint human guardians to patrol the beach at Whakanewha Regional Park, west of Te Matuku, and deflect human and canine disturbance. Te Matuku is a significant site for the birds, not only for breeding in spring but also later in the year when they flock from all over the island, and birds that have lost mates find new ones and young birds pair for the first time.

New Zealand dotterels (*Charadrius obscurus*) are small-to-medium wading birds with two distinct subspecies, North and South. The northern birds are found mainly on east coast beaches between North Cape and East Cape, where they feed on small invertebrates and fish found when the tide recedes. Their flecked, pale greyish-brownish plumage makes them almost invisible against sand, shell and pebbles — their biggest giveaway is their typical darting and running as they hunt down a meal.

Like most of their kin, they are most vulnerable when breeding. They are territorial, spreading in pairs along the coast to nest from August to September, laying three eggs that hatch within about a month. The chicks are tiny, defenceless balls of fluff, with long, delicate legs, that feed themselves from the word go; if danger looms, their only protection is to crouch and freeze or, once they are older, to scarper and hide.

Breeding can fail for a number of reasons including the aforementioned predators as well as avian burglars such as gulls. The nests are simple scrapes in the sand with well-camouflaged eggs that are easily destroyed by walkers or riders who may not even be aware what they have done. The birds also sometimes lose nests to natural events such as storms and tides. They will re-lay if a clutch of eggs is lost but usually raise only one brood of chicks.

This vulnerability has caused the northern subspecies to be classed as 'threatened' — there were around 2000 in 2011 — but the southern subspecies is 'critically endangered' and has disappeared from the South Island mainland altogether. They are found only on Stewart Island/Rakiura where they number around 300. Both groups are described as 'conservation dependent': they decline without ongoing human assistance.

OPPOSITE: A New Zealand dotterel in Whakanewha Regional Park, west of Te Matuku.

The godwit guardian sculpture in the park.

They are small and plain but these snoozy birds are very special: they are New Zealand dotterels flocking in winter to the sandspit area in Te Matuku Marine Reserve.

4 · HAURAKI GULF MARINE PARK | TĪKAPA MOANA   143

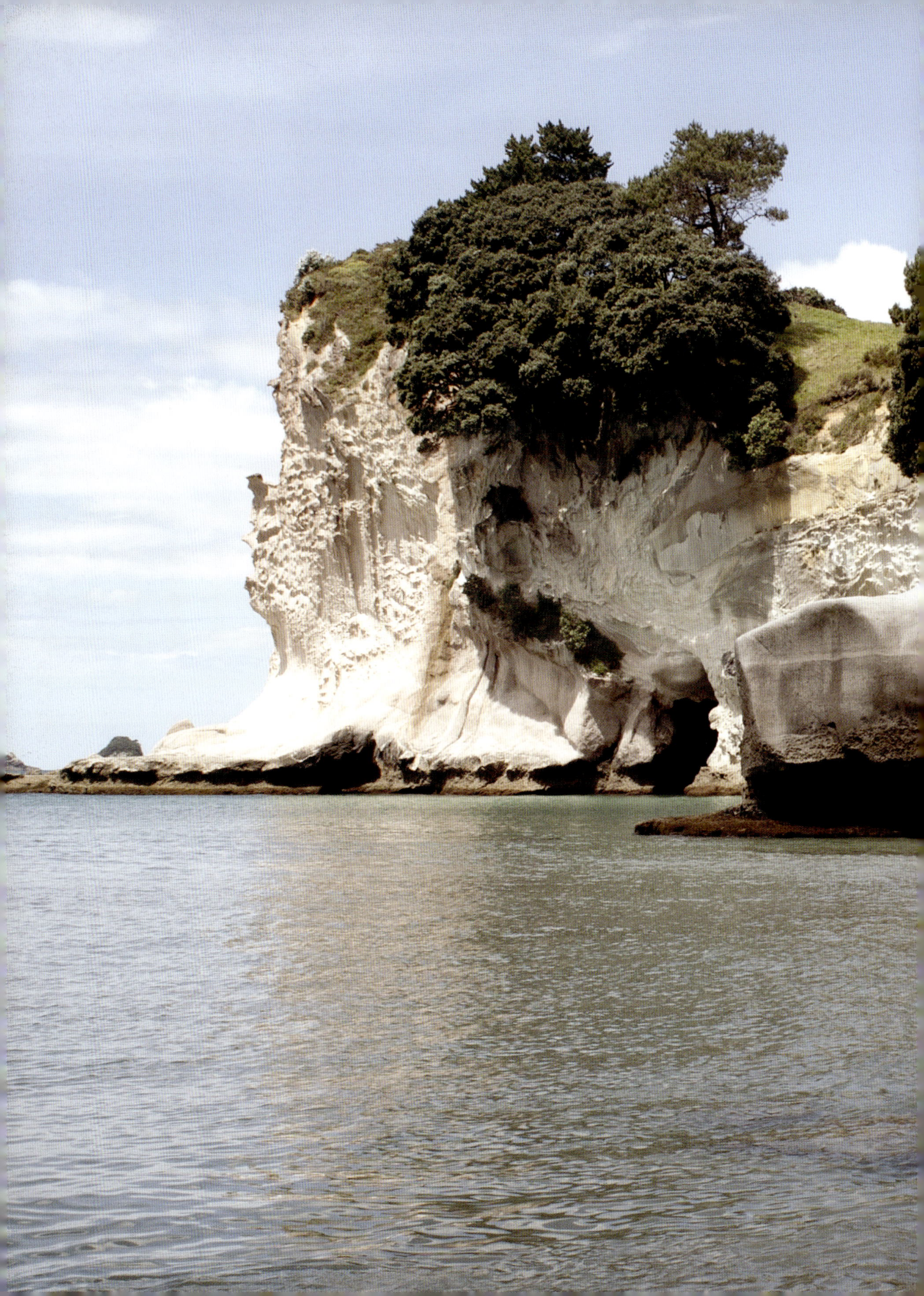

5
ROCKS & ISLANDS

THE BAY OF PLENTY

The Bay of Plenty forms a large bowl with the east coast of the Coromandel Peninsula on one side and East Cape on the other, and a long southeast-trending swoop of bay between. It contains three marine reserves: Te Whanganui-a-Hei, Tūhua (Mayor Island) and Te Paepae-o-Aotea (Volkner Rocks). Each is a product of volcanic activity and, like the waters of the Hauraki Gulf and the North, continues to fall under the influence of the East Auckland Current.

TE WHANGANUI-A-HEI

The castle of Cair Paravel on its little hill towered up above them; before them were the sands, with rocks and little pools of salt water, and seaweed, and the smell of the sea and long miles of bluish-green waves breaking for ever and ever on the beach. And oh, the cry of the seagulls! Have you heard it? Can you remember?

— The Lion, the Witch and the Wardrobe

Sometime in the 1300s, the *Arawa* waka sailed along the east coast of the Coromandel Peninsula and its people, under the leadership of a tohunga named Hei, settled in the vicinity of what is now known as Mercury Bay. That he was a person of great mana is evident from the number of places that bear his name, including the bay itself — Whanga-nui-a-Hei or 'large bay of Hei' — and the village of Hāhei, down the coast. The area was rich in seafood and bird life and the climate was benign.

Over six centuries later, Hei's descendants, Ngāti Hei, continue to have strong connections to the area's historic pā sites and to value and protect its spiritual and physical qualities.

PREVIOUS: The iconic white cliffs, pearly sands and blue-green waters of Te Whanganui-a-Hei.

TE WHANGANUI-A-HEI (CATHEDRAL COVE) is the sixth marine reserve in the Hauraki Gulf Marine Park. It is just south of Mercury Bay and is subject to two administrative authorities, being outside the Auckland area, in the Waikato region, but at the same time being within the Hauraki Gulf Marine Park.

Unlike the estuarine and sheltered Te Matuku, the waters of Te Whanganui-a-Hei Marine Reserve are oceanic, washed by the same current as the Poor Knights. Its boundary encloses an 840-hectare rectangle, running south from Cook's Bluff through a succession of headlands and coves: Cathedral Cove, Mare's Leg Cove, Stingray Bay and Gemstone Bay to the northern tip of Hāhei beach. Its seaward boundary tips the north side of Mahurangi Island before crossing to the southern point of Motukorure Island. It completely encloses several smaller islands: Moturoa, Motueka, Poikeke, Waiharanga and Okorotere.

It's a postcard-perfect coast, its deep blue sky offsetting translucent blue-green waters that in turn contrast with white-gold sands, white-grey ignimbrite cliffs and dark green pōhutukawa. A medley of spectacular columns, arches, caves, coves, reefs and islands rise dramatically from the sea or cast reflections of themselves at low tide. They are the weathered and eroded leftovers of the chain of the Coromandel's 40-or-so ancient volcanoes. The Hereherataura headland just south of Hāhei is so stunning that it was used as the set for the ruins of the castle Cair Paravel in the 2005 film *The Lion, the Witch and the Wardrobe*, which is based on C.S. Lewis's *The Chronicles of Narnia* novels.

Cathedral Cove itself is a crescent of white sand famed for an arch drilled by the sea through the rock beneath its southern headland. It is much loved by photographers, a natural frame for high or low water, the rock stack along the beach or the silhouettes of visitors.

The rocky landscape continues beneath the waves, with underwater reefs, caves, platforms, more arches and sand flats, each with unique and complex plant, crustacean, mollusc and fish communities. There are lush kelp forests, sponges, anemones, corals, crayfish and starfish and a huge variety of fish including snapper, marblefish, butterfish, red moki and black angelfish. As with other marine reserves in these northern waters, once the area was designated 'no take', there was a remarkable recovery of snapper, which are 18 times more numerous inside than out, and crayfish, which are eight times more numerous.

A leatherjacket and two scarlet wrasses cruise through an underwater garden off the coast north of Te Whanganui-a-Hei.

The reserve is a popular tourist destination, with over 200,000 annual visits from locals and travellers from overseas. There is no road access but visitors trek across the cliffs, kayak or take boat tours to it, and those who want to dive or swim have the option of learning about its enchanted undersea world by following a snorkel trail in Gemstone Bay where marker buoys with handles and information panels are anchored.

TŪHUA (MAYOR ISLAND)

Tūhua (Mayor Island) is an astounding place. It's not just an island, of course, but also the upper portion of what has been described by GNS Science as 'the most unusual of New Zealand volcanoes'. Like the Coromandel Peninsula with its abraded peaks, it derives from weaknesses in the earth's crust associated with the colliding Pacific and Australian plates.

Specifically, Tūhua is the result of over 130,000 years of volcanic activity. It began with an undersea lava flow that eventually formed a shield volcano, a vast dome shaped like a primitive burial mound. That volcano was subsequently destroyed by a more explosive eruption that formed a collapsed crater or caldera, which in turn was partially filled by another dome that was later destroyed by a further massive eruption and so it goes... According to GNS Science, there have been at least 52 volcanic episodes, with a full suite of eruption styles, among them the aforementioned domes, fire fountains, Strombolian explosions and highly volatile steam eruptions. It's not clear when the last event occurred but some of the lava is dated between 500 and 1000 years, meaning that although Tūhua is not currently active, there are no guarantees that it won't flex muscle again in the future.

At the present time, the island is sweetly cloaked in pōhutukawa forest and apparently snoozing. It is roughly circular, approximately four kilometres across and dominated by a sunken crater that is walled by a ring of cliffs and contains two lakes almost at sea level, one black (Te Paritō) and one green (Aroaro-tamāhine). Hot springs are a gentle reminder of the mighty forces below ground. The coast is rocky, with small white-sand beaches, headlands and cliffs.

Tūhua's volcanism made it immensely attractive to early Māori. The eruptions left an abundance of obsidian rock or matā tūhua; formed by rapidly cooling silica-rich lava, obsidian is black, glassy and sharp, and was without equal for the manufacture of tools. Although there were other sources around the country, Tūhua was by far the most important and the controllers of this resource were powerful people.

However, the island was often raided and was the scene of many bloody battles. Its inhabitants lived in the relative safety of pā on headlands and when things were really bad, took refuge in the ultimate citadel, Taumou, on the eastern cliffs. It was virtually impregnable, with seven massive hand-hewn terraces descending to the sea and a single approach up a steep gully that was easily defended by a pile of rocks at the top.

But you can't eat obsidian, and island life was isolated and often harsh: there were fewer edible birds than on the mainland and most arable land was at Opo (Southeast Bay) where, in 1884, surveyor Eric Goldsmith found only nine inhabitants, members of Te Whānau-a-Tauwhao hapū of Ngāi Te Rangi. They were, he said, growing a range of fruit including bananas, figs, grapes and peaches, and cultivating large gardens of potatoes, corn, kūmara and tobacco. They also had cats and pigs.

The introduction of metal implements by Europeans eventually rendered obsidian obsolete and by the early 20th century, even those hardy people had departed. The cats and pigs had run riot and caused mayhem in the forest but were ultimately removed and in 1953 Tūhua became a wildlife sanctuary, operating under the same exacting conditions as apply to Hauturu/Little Barrier. It is administered on behalf of the people of Te Whānau-a-Tauwhao by the Tūhua Board of Trustees.

TŪHUA IS 26 KILOMETRES FROM WAIHĪ BEACH, 35 kilometres north of Tauranga; it is on the edge of the continental shelf and far enough from the mainland to be pollution-free. Its blue-black waters are known for their clarity and in summer, migratory ocean fish such as marlin and tuna are found around its shores. From the early 1920s, Southeast Bay on the island was a base for the then Tauranga Big Game Fishing Club, hauling in kingfish, marlin, tuna, broadbill swordfish and many species of shark — 85 marlin and 37 mako sharks are recorded for the summer of

1929. Although the club is now the Tauranga Fishing Club and no longer headquartered on Tūhua, its members still fish the island's southern waters. The area is designated 'restricted fishing', meaning no commercial fishing, set nets or longlines are permitted.

The marine reserve is in the island's north. A stretch of coast five kilometres from Tūmutu Point in the west to Tūranganui Point in the east fans out for one nautical mile, creating a 'no-take' zone of approximately ten square kilometres. The submarine landscape is spectacular, with its volcanic forms including lava columns, stacks, caves, boulders and hot springs. Reefs and shallower waters near the island drop away to 50 metres on the outer boundary on the edge of the continental shelf. It's a diver's paradise, with forests of kelp and other seaweeds and a wide mix of fish species including open-water and subtropical species. There are schools of kingfish, blue and pink maomao as well as big game fish in summer, and dolphins, seals and whales pass through.

Tūhua (Mayor Island), showing the massive crater, the two lakes and the marine reserve area in the lower portion of the photograph.

THE UNTHINKABLE

She is the poster child of an oil spill. She stares without comprehension at the camera, firmly held by hands clad in thick, red rubber gloves. She and the gloves are white with detergent: there are suds all over her head, in her eyes, her nostrils, her open bill. She's what New Zealanders call a little blue penguin or kororā (known elsewhere as a 'little penguin' or 'fairy penguin'). Beneath the lather, however, she's more black than blue. She is covered in a layer of sticky oil.

How has this happened? It's not hard to imagine.

It was around 2.00 am on the night of 5 October 2011. The little blue penguin was feeding along the northern coast of Mōtītī Island, east of Mount Maunganui. She was sleek and healthy, a juvenile from this year's crop. The sky was clear and hung with stars: the moon, which would be full in five days, was sinking below the horizon.

Not far to her north there was a rocky outcrop known as Astrolabe Reef or Otaiti. It's a popular diving spot, renowned for clear water and a spectacular drop-off to 37 metres. The area was alive with fish and even the occasional seal. It was an hour after full tide and the summit of the reef was below water.

At 2.20 am, the MV *Rena*, a 236-metre cargo vessel carrying 1386 containers, 1700 tonnes of heavy fuel oil, 200 tonnes of marine diesel and with a crew of 20, drove onto the reef. Her front half stuck fast but the stern end was almost immediately under unsustainable pressure, wagging and sagging above the drop-off.

Towards dawn, the penguin returned to shore and hunkered down as she did every day, in a hollow beneath a log.

It was not until the evening of the 10th that she encountered the first oil from the stricken vessel; it was a dirty brown slick, a stain that she did not even see. Within minutes, she was coated and in trouble.

As soon as the scale of the disaster became apparent, volunteers turned out to help, aware that there might be hundreds and maybe thousands of birds like our penguin. Many, of course, were never found. However, this bird was in luck: a day later, against the odds, she was picked up on shore and taken to a wildlife rescue facility on the mainland where she was washed and rested. She was returned to the sea six weeks later, complete with microchip to assist in further monitoring.

5 · ROCKS & ISLANDS | THE BAY OF PLENTY

22 October: dead, dying and oiled birds were collected off the shore.

19 January: the clean-up under way on Mōtītī Island.

OPPOSITE: 10 January: the stern section has fallen off and the bridge is almost totally submerged.

Of course, it's no accident that our girl was the poster child: the penguins are loved by all — so cute, so *human*, with their upright stance and toddler-like gait. Less seen and known were the casualties of the open sea — the unnumbered individuals of ocean-going species such as petrels, shearwaters, Australasian gannets and terns. Some washed ashore, blackened and lifeless, and were collected and laid in rows. Dr Brett Gartrell from the National Oiled Wildlife Response Centre, based at Massey University, identified 2000 birds as having died as a direct result of the disaster but no one will ever know the true figure.

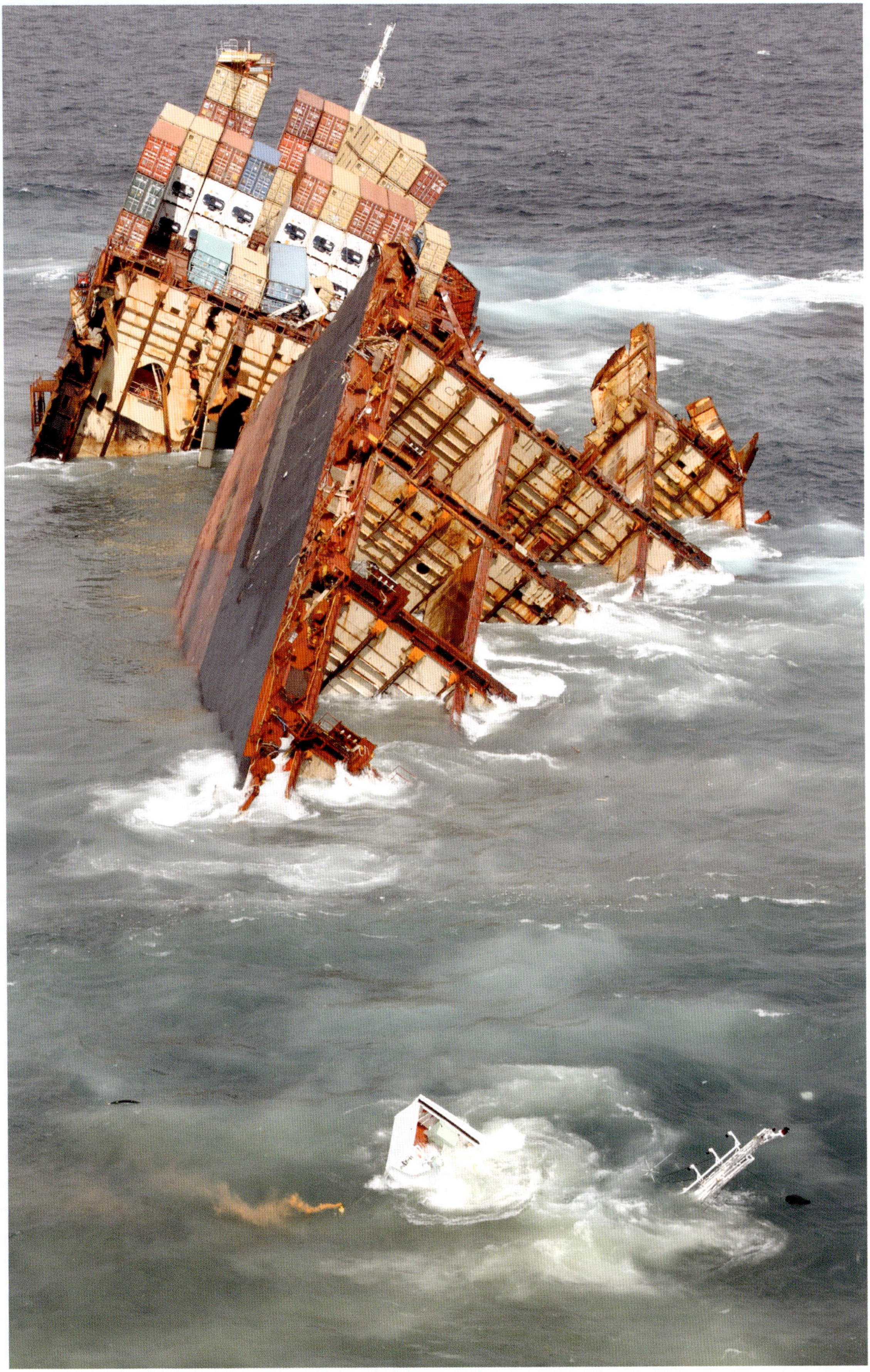

The sinking of the *Rena* was New Zealand's worst maritime environmental disaster for many reasons.

First, there was the oil and diesel. Fortunately, the vessel did not break up immediately and much of its fuel was able to be pumped off. Nevertheless, about 350 tonnes escaped and washed onto Bay of Plenty beaches. Booms were laid where feasible, especially around sensitive places such as Maketū estuary and peninsula on the mainland south of Pāpāmoa, as well as Tūhua (Mayor Island) and Whangamatā, but they were a small gesture compared with the scale of the accident. The chemical dispersant Corexit was used for a brief period but is considered by many to be as harmful as the oil it displaced.

On shore, teams painstakingly removed over 1000 tonnes of thickened, tarry, biscuit-sized blobs of oil-contaminated sand from the beaches. More than 4500 tonnes of containers and debris were picked up. Nearly three years on, most of the fuel is gone from sand and sea, broken down by microbe activity and dispersed by wind and wave.

Then there were the containers. When she hit, *Rena* was loaded high above deck level like a giant child's Lego construction. As she toppled, 88 containers washed overboard and others followed weeks later when the ship broke apart. Some sank, some floated dangerously and some were smashed, releasing potentially toxic contents. Over the next year, most were either removed from the boat or retrieved from beaches and waters around the Bay of Plenty — 999 of them by September 2012.

Debris was a third problem. Smashed wood, pieces of timber, insulation foam, milk powder, meat and tiny polymer beads drifted on the waters and washed up on beaches as far away as the Coromandel and even Great Barrier (Aotea) Island. The polymer beads were of particular concern — 3.5 tonnes were picked up as late as August 2012. Ngāi Te Hapū, the people

13 October: containers disgorge polystyrene and packets of milk onto the beach south of Mount Maunganui.

of Mōtītī Island, watched in horror and despair as their shores became clogged with wreckage.

The wreck itself was and is, of course, the largest chunk of debris. The massive structure snapped in two on 10 January 2012 and progressively disintegrated thereafter. Portions were removed for scrap but dealing with the sunken sections was difficult and dangerous. As of early 2014, parts of the stern remain on the deep seabed and the owners are signalling their desire to leave it there, despite the opposition of Māori and the local council. Three years on, that outcome is yet to be determined.

ASTROLABE REEF

Louis Auguste de Sainson's 1833 depiction of 'The Corvette *Astrolabe* falling suddenly on reefs in the Bay of Plenty, New Zealand'.

Dumont d'Urville named the rocks in February 1827 after his corvette, the *Astrolabe*, very nearly had its own *Rena* event. D'Urville was following Captain James Cook's chart, but aware that it was imprecise. As the *Astrolabe* entered the Bay of Plenty on 16 February, the expedition encountered thick fog and a furious storm from the northeast. It was, d'Urville said, 'a frightful disorder of nature'.

He was unaware of his position and certain of only one thing: that the ship was in great danger. Shortly before noon, the fog lifted to reveal that they were about to collide with a reef that was being lashed by huge waves, with spray rising high in the air. All hands were called to the deck and all sails were hoisted immediately; although the corvette heeled so perilously that the upper deck was under water and her keel was exposed, they safely rounded the rocks and sailed away to the north.

If there was anything positive to come out of this terrible event, it was the unprecedented community response. On one hand it involved an extensive range of official agencies, too many to list in detail, including local and regional authorities, government departments, harbour boards, the armed forces, the police, zoos, universities and corporate organisations.

They were matched by 8000 registered volunteers, including iwi and members of community groups such as the Ornithological Society of New Zealand and the Royal Forest & Bird Protection Society. People came from all over New Zealand and from overseas, and in turn were supported by voluntary caterers and those who offered accommodation, vehicles and equipment. Over 240,000 hours of volunteer effort were logged — and those are just the ones that were counted.

The financial cost is another matter again and kicks in at every point and at every level including, in the long term, the cost of monitoring into the future. It's *huge*.

Release day. It was a big occasion for all concerned.

In the days following the wreck, it was important to capture unscathed New Zealand dotterels before they too fell foul of the spill. They were not released until November, one year later. Kaumātua Huriwaka Rewa and dotterel expert John Dowding with one of the birds.

17 February 2012: penguins return to Mōtītī Island. Catarina Cruz (left) of Tauranga, Marco Cruz of Tauranga, Carlijn Bouwman from the wildlife centre and Zeta Schuler from Waihī — and maybe that's our little penguin.

TE PAEPAE-O-AOTEA (VOLKNER ROCKS)

It's not surprising that the three pinnacles known as Volkner Rocks, or Te Paepae-o-Aotea, or the 'speaking place for the clouds', are sacred to Ngāti Awa, the people of the *Mātaatua* waka. They are awe-inspiring, rising steeply from the water to point heavenward like dramatic spires: this is where the spirits of the dead of Ngāti Awa pause before departure from this world.

WHITE ISLAND, OR TE PUIA-O-WHAKAARI, lies east and south of Tūhua, 55 kilometres from Whakatāne. It is New Zealand's most continuously active volcano, with plumes of smoke, ash and steam regularly rising from its crater. Nevertheless, it is a tourist destination and was mined for sulphur in the early 1900s, with ultimately disastrous consequences: two firemen were killed in separate incidents early in 1914, and in September of that year a lahar swept ten miners to their deaths. That put an end to the operation until 1923 when mining again commenced only to be finally halted forever by the Great Depression of the 1930s.

Volkner Rocks are part of the same geologic formation as the island. They lie five kilometres to its northwest and are connected to it by an underwater ridge known as the Whakaari High. Three pinnacles rise steeply from the ocean floor and there is a spectacular submarine landscape with a wide range of habitats including boulder banks, archways and walls covered in encrusting organisms.

This is the southern end of the influence of the East Auckland Current: as with most reserves further north, this not only delivers water of great clarity, it also imports an exotic crew of subtropical organisms, including yellow-banded perch, red- and white-banded coral shrimps, blue knifefish and toadstool grouper as well as blue moki, golden snapper, northern scorpionfish and moray eels. There are schools of blue maomao, kōheru, demoiselles and many types of kelp, nudibranchs, gorgonians, sponges and an unusual little crustacean called 'the Spanish lobster'. Oceanic or pelagic visitors include yellowfin tuna and blue sharks. Kingfish, which would otherwise travel widely, appear to like their rocks address and don't move far at all.

In recognition of these outstanding natural and ecological features, the area around the rocks to a radius of one nautical mile (1.8 kilometres) was declared a 1267-hectare marine reserve in 2006. As elsewhere, there was opposition from some charter boat operators and some fishers, who were not convinced that anyone would travel so far just to snorkel and dive. On the other hand, Ngāti Awa were delighted.

Male and female Sandager's wrasses at South Rock, White Island.

SHARK BLUES

Blue sharks (*Prionace glauca*) are nomads of the world's tropical and temperate oceans. They are sometimes called the 'wolves of the sea' because they are known to school according to age and size, and on occasion, to hunt collectively. They are the widest-ranging of all their kind, and individuals tagged in the vicinity of Volkner Rocks Marine Reserve have been tracked across the Tasman, in the Indian Ocean and as far across the Pacific as Chile.

They are beautiful creatures, with slender, streamlined bodies shaded vibrant blue on the upper surface and silver-white below. They have wide, wing-like pectoral fins, a long, conical snout and large, round eyes. They hunt in the dark at depths of around 300 metres using ampullae of Lorenzini, the same electro-sensory organs as stingrays, to detect small fish and squid that rise each night through the water column to feed. Their teeth are small because they eat their prey whole.

Once full, they move to the surface where the warmth assists with digestion: being cold-blooded, they use the ocean's temperature to manage and conserve their energy. They spend the day in the surface layers, cruising, taking the odd snack before descending again for the evening meal. They are not considered dangerous to humans.

Blue sharks bear live young, up to 135 pups per litter, and are slow growing, living for perhaps 20 years. Mature males may reach almost 3 metres in length and females close to 3.5 metres.

Researchers tracked the sharks using fisheries tags (seen to the right of the dorsal fin). Satellite tags are now used instead.

As apex predators, sharks are essential to the health of ocean ecosystems, removing old or unwell members from populations below them in the food web and keeping numbers in balance. However, they are in decline around the world, with (some believe) potentially disastrous consequences for the oceans.

It is likely that blue sharks are no exception but because they are migratory, it is impossible to know precisely. It is estimated that between 50,000 and 150,000 are taken per year in New Zealand fisheries primarily for their fins, a delicacy in Asian markets. Some are targeted under the Quota Management System and some are bycatch of the fisheries of other species — some 20,000 were taken by the tuna fishery in the 2011–2012 year, for example. Wastefully, the bulk of these were killed, finned and their bodies thrown away — it has been illegal since 2009 to fin live sharks in New Zealand waters.

That is all about to change. A *National Plan of Action for the Conservation and Management of Sharks* released in 2013 announced an end to finning, requiring fishers to either release sharks alive or bring them ashore with fins attached for processing. Blue sharks are most likely to be released because they have little commercial value and the space their bodies will occupy on board will not be economically justified.

Initially, blue sharks were excluded from the ban until 2016 but that decision has been reversed in response to widespread concern from the public and conservation groups, including the New Zealand Shark Alliance. All sharks will be protected by the new regime, from October 2014.

Finning is illegal in over 100 countries including Australia, the European Union and the United States.

THE FIERY URCHIN

One of the reefs around the pinnacles, Diadema Rock, is named after the subtropical sea urchin, *Diadema palmeri*, that grazes its walls. One of six species of diadema urchins, it is found in the northern waters of New Zealand, on Australia's southeast coast, at Lord Howe Island and off the Norfolk Island Ridge.

The urchin was first found at 40 metres at the Poor Knights Islands by Bill Palmer, who noticed an unusual dark sea urchin with luminescent, blue lights between its spines. Wade Doak describes the moment: 'He lifted it up on his steel cray hook and balancing it there, rose to the surface. To his astonishment, the sombre colour began to lighten as the surface light increased, from black to ruddy brown and, bursting through to the sunlight, a brilliant ruby red.'

The luminescence comes from tiny organs in the skin that are thought to enhance sensitivity to shadows of potential predators passing above. What appears to be a single protuberant eye is actually an anal sack where faecal matter is stored until it is ejected at pressure to move it clear of the animal's spines.

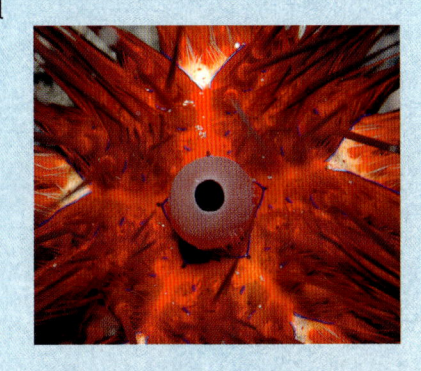

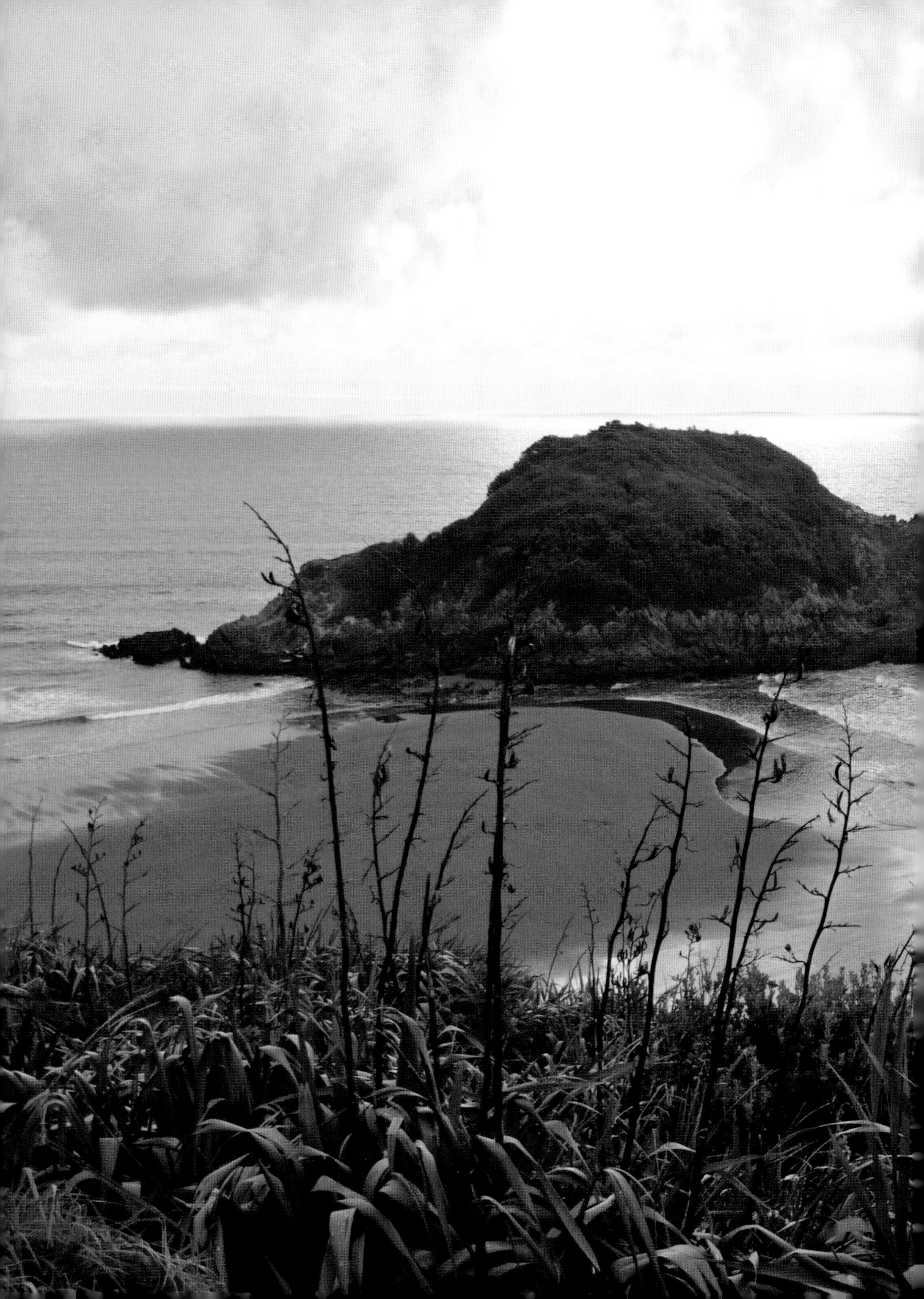

6
BLACK SANDS & VERY SMALL DOLPHINS

TARANAKI

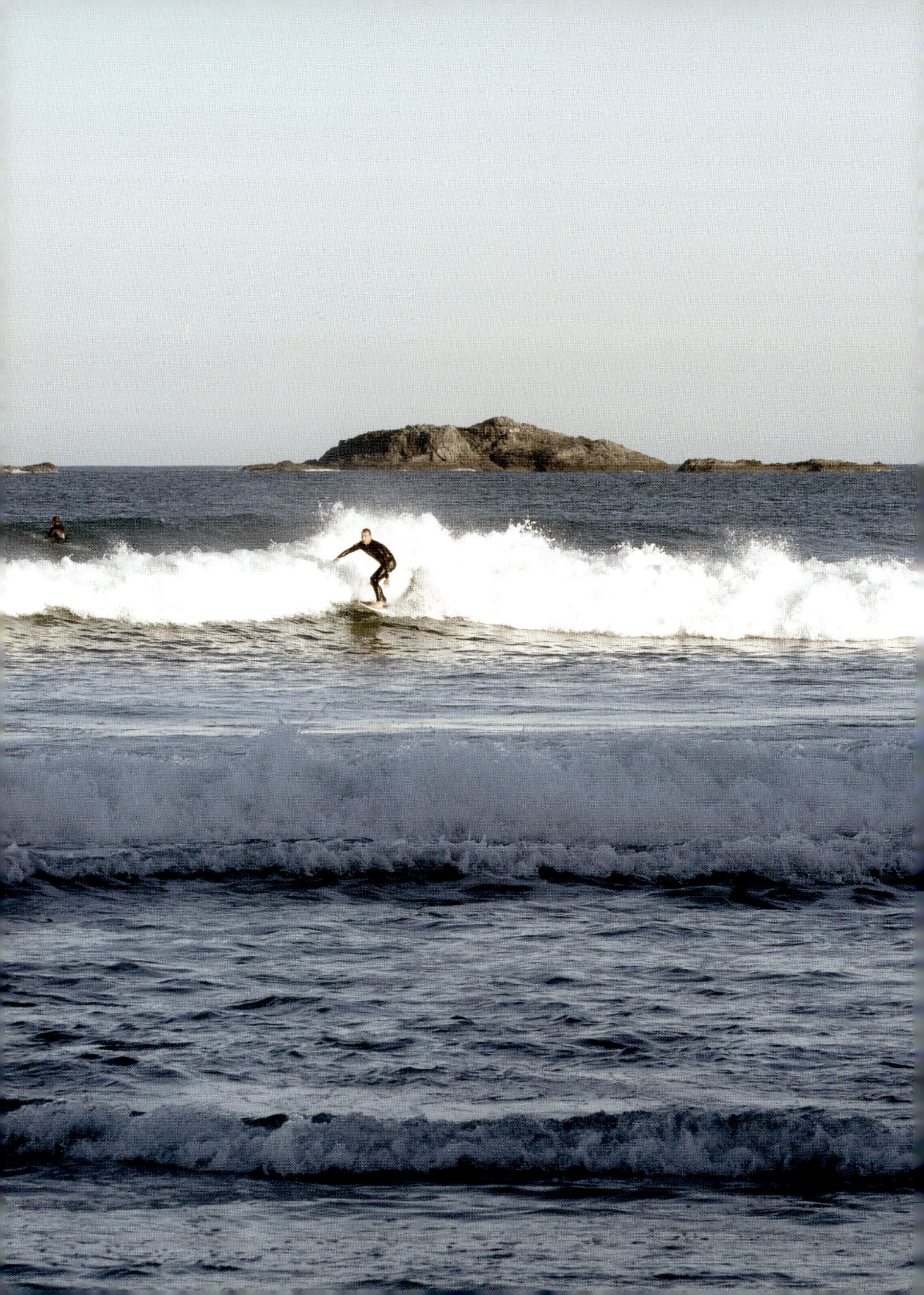

They don't call it the Wild West for nothing! The east coast — with its relatively benign sheltered waters, many islands and population centres — is not far from the North Island's western shores as the seagull flies, but there could be a continent between them.

The waves roll across the Tasman in row after serried row of white caps. South from Cape Rēinga, there is the empty expanse of Ninety Mile Beach and the vast sand dunes of Northland before an extended sweep of rugged coastline stretches to the Taranaki region and the first major population centre on this coast, New Plymouth. It's a shore of rocky cliffs and hills, crumbling and falling before the weather's onslaught, with low-tide sandy beaches at their feet. There are few islands. A series of harbours and estuaries where rivers disgorge to the sea are the only interruptions in this long arc: Herekino, Whāngāpē, Hokianga, Kaipara, Manukau, Port Waikato, Raglan, Aotea and Kāwhia.

Two currents affect this coast, both weaker and more variable than their eastern counterpart. The West Auckland Current, twin of the East Auckland Current and on average one to two degrees cooler, flows south from North Cape to Raglan, while the Tasman Current tracks from the west to strike the jutting nose of Cape Taranaki before splitting and heading north into the Taranaki Bight and south to join the D'Urville Current. Prevailing winds are moisture-laden westerlies, also from across the Tasman.

PREVIOUS:
Looking across the black sands towards the Sugar Loaf Islands.

OPPOSITE:
Surfers catch the first sun and the first waves at New Plymouth's Back Beach adjacent to the Ngā Motu Marine Protected Area.

NGĀ MOTU/SUGAR LOAF ISLANDS MARINE PROTECTED AREA

As elsewhere, volcanoes underlie the Taranaki maritime story. Beginning at what is now the coast, much of the region was formed by a succession of south-trending eruptions culminating in Mount Taranaki and a secondary cone, Fantham's Peak. The first volcano, existing around 1.7 million years ago, has long since eroded to a group of seven islands and a number of rock platforms just off the city's port: Ngā Motu, 'the islands' or, as Captain Cook called them (feeling peckish again), the 'Sugar Loaf Islands'. Unlike the pinnacles and spires of the Poor Knights, they are relatively low and helmet-shaped, with stunted vegetation on their crowns and blackened, bare rock in the intertidal zone.

The islands are a comparatively sheltered spot on an otherwise exposed coast, and an important roosting and nesting site for 19 species of seabird. They are also the site of the small, northernmost breeding colony of kekeno or New Zealand fur seals. Beneath the waves a diverse mix of underwater habitats: canyons, pinnacles, caves, boulder fields and sand flats are home to 89 species of ocean and reef fish, 33 species of sponges, 28 species of bryozoans and nine species of nudibranchs.

The island group was first designated a 'marine park' in 1986, with additional protection conferred by its own Act of Parliament in 1991 when it became the 749-hectare Ngā Motu/Sugar Loaf Islands Marine Protected Area. The legislation was directed in the first instance at protecting the area from petroleum prospecting but also prohibits commercial fishing, set nets and longlining (apart from trolling for kingfish and kahawai). Recreational fishers are restricted to one line with a maximum of three hooks. Species commonly taken include kingfish, kahawai, snapper, blue cod, trevally, blue moki, sweep, red gurnard and tarakihi.

Low tide around the islands: the island in the left foreground is Mataora, with Pararaki to its rear. Motumahanga/Saddleback Island is in the distance.

TAPUAE

Barbara Hammonds and Anne Scott from Ngā Motu Marine Reserve Society with film-maker Peter Crabb, on top of Paritutu Rock with Tapuae behind.
—

In 2008 the 1404-hectare Tapuae Marine Reserve was added to the southwest boundary of the Sugar Loaf Islands Marine Protected Area. It forms a rough rectangle stretching from Herekawe Stream in the north to Tapuae Stream in the south. The northern portion of the reserve shares the volcanic features unique to the Sugar Loaf area, especially around Seal Rock where the fish life is rich and diverse. The southern portion, on the other hand, is more typical of exposed Taranaki coast, with underwater reefs and boulder platforms interspersed with stretches of sand and mud and black-sand beaches on the shore.

The initial proposal for the reserve, which was put forward by the Ngā Motu Marine Reserve Society, was ultimately reduced in deference to Ngāti Te Whiti and fishers keen to continue surfcasting in the Sugar Loaf area. Both Ngā Motu and Tapuae have easy land access from both Tapuae Stream and popular nearby Back Beach, which is a good spot for walking as well as fishing, and is rarely without a contingent of surfers making the most of the high-energy environment (but is not recommended for novices for that reason).

The marine reserve society continues to promote activities in the marine protected areas and along the coast. This includes the establishment of an educational display centre on the New Plymouth foreshore in 2012, as well as supporting ongoing research into the lives and care of the little blue penguins that frequent this coastline.

FROM LEFT: Brayden Thompson, Jessica Berntsen and Nikita Taiapa from Moturoa School, who spoke at the opening of the educational display centre in 2012 and presented plants they had grown in the school nursery for the gardens outside.

WHAT DO YOU SEE IN SEAWEEK?

It's a scene that repeats all around the country every year during SeaWeek: snorkellers of all ages don wetsuits, flippers and masks, and take to the water to experience the wonders of the ocean.

SeaWeek is the flagship event of the New Zealand Association for Environmental Education (NZAEE), a national non-profit organisation that promotes and supports lifelong learning and encourages behaviour that leads to sustainability for Aotearoa/New Zealand. It began in 1987 in Australia, when it was a marine-themed art competition; the first New Zealand event was held in 1992. It is run by regional coordinators who are either volunteers or work for an organisation that supports the event, and is aimed at all sectors of the community.

Each year has a theme, beyond which there are a number of constant and underlying messages: kaitiakitanga or shared responsibility; awareness of actions in the present and their effect on the future; the importance of oceans in our stories and lives; and — last and best — loving, enjoying and celebrating the sea. The 2014 theme emphasised the fragility and finite nature of the marine environment.

SeaWeek volunteer Abbie Bates prepares to accompany Eli Hancock to the reef at Ngāmotu Beach, New Plymouth, 2014. Abbie, a committee member of Ngā Motu Marine Reserve Society, grew up in Taranaki and works in marine and environmental management.

MARINE MAMMAL PROTECTION

They are called 'right whales' because, in whaling days, they were the *right ones* to catch: slow-swimming, easy targets that yielded plenty of oil and even — obligingly — floated when killed. There were so many southern right whales, it's said, that colonists in coastal cities such as New Plymouth and Wellington were kept awake by the noise the great creatures made off the coast, slapping the water with their tails, singing whale songs and having whale conversations (. . . a whale of a time).

The hunting ceased only because, in the end, so few right whales remained that it was no longer economic: the species was on the verge of extinction. The waters around New Zealand fell silent and folks could sleep at night. *Whew*!

The recovery of right whales, like that of the similarly hounded humpback, has been slow. However, both species are now occasionally seen in the waters around Taranaki, along with pilot whales, orca and astonishingly, blue whales.

THE SEAS OFF THE COASTLINE between Auckland and Taranaki have the dubious distinction of being the setting for another, modern, near-extinction — that of one of the world's smallest and rarest cetaceans, the Māui's dolphin.

Māui's dolphins (*Cephalorhynchus hectori Māui*) are a subspecies of Hector's dolphins (*Cephalorhynchus hectori*), a species found mainly in the vicinity of Banks Peninsula off the east coast of the South Island. Until

2002 it was thought Māui's and Hector's were one and the same because they are outwardly identical but advances in scientific techniques revealed significant genetic variation as well as differences in skulls and jawbones. It now appears likely that Māui's dolphins have been a separate population for thousands of years.

Dolphins are toothed whales, members of the same sub-order as porpoises, beaked whales, orca and sperm whales. Hector's (and Māui's) are the smallest of those. Females grow to 1.7 metres long and may weigh up to 50 kilograms; males are a little smaller. They are smartly coloured with light grey backs, white bellies, black facial markings and black fins. Unlike the distinctly beaked dolphins such as the common dolphin, the Hector's and Māui's belong to a group with heads that slope continuously from blowhole to pointed snout. They are especially known for rounded dorsal fins and flippers — compared to the more triangular or crescent-shaped fins and flippers of common dolphins.

All of which gives them a very cute, teddy-bear appearance.

Not Māui's: these Hector's dolphins are stand-ins, surfing (one below the water) in just the same way as the Māui's used to surf along the western coast of the North Island.

'ONLY 55!' The people of Whāingaroa/Raglan have a long and special bond with Māui's dolphins: large pods used to surf and play in the waves with the locals within living memory. At the March 2014 Māui's Dolphin Day everyone turned out to make a point.

NUMBERS HAVE BEEN INEXORABLY FALLING and a 2010–2011 survey of Māui's dolphins pointed to a continuing and unsustainable decline. The population was estimated, with 95 percent confidence, to be around only 55 individuals over one year old — confirming their continued status as 'critically endangered' or, in other words, 'perilously close to wipe-out'.

There are a number of causes. Both the Hector's and Māui's frequent harbours and estuaries less than 20 metres deep. Unfortunately, this inshore area is also a human high-use zone, so the dolphins become entangled in and drowned by fishing gear, are hit by boats, may fall foul of pollution and are perhaps affected by marine mining activity such as seismic survey. To make a bad situation worse, when numbers tumble so low, natural happenings such as predation by sharks and orca, disease and extreme weather events have a disproportionately negative impact.

And because, like some of our endangered birds, these dolphins are long living and slow breeding, recovery — if it happens — will take a very long time. Females don't mature until between seven and nine years old and may bear a calf only every two to four years. As they live to around 20 years, one female may have around six offspring in her lifetime, all going well. *Not enough!*

A suite of measures has been implemented in an attempt to arrest and retrieve this situation, with, as a general rule, the Ministry of Primary Industries managing fishing-related threats and DOC taking care of non-fishing, human-induced threats.

Down south, Hector's dolphins have been protected since 1988 by a marine mammal sanctuary around Banks Peninsula. It doesn't exclude all fishing but targets particularly harmful practices, such as setting nets. Māui's dolphins, however, were not safeguarded in any way until 2003 when set net controls were also introduced on the west coast of the North Island. They were followed in 2008 and in 2013 with further restraints, including the 1200-square-kilometre West Coast North Island Marine Mammal Sanctuary and a raft of other measures to reduce harm from commercial trawling, commercial and recreational set and drift netting, seismic survey, and inshore boat racing. The sanctuary and the fishing restrictions abut and overlap, applying along the coast and in and out of all harbours from Maunganui Bluff north of the Kaipara Harbour to Taranaki's Hāwera in the south and out to varying limits depending on the restriction.

The 2013 amendment was in response to four reliable Māui's dolphin sightings and a fifth that was a 'possible'. The amendment prohibits commercial and recreational set netting between two and seven nautical miles offshore between Taranaki's Pariokariwa Point and the Waiwhakaiho River and increases the prohibition area for set net fishing by 350 square kilometres. It earned anguished howls from New Plymouth-based commercial fishers who feel their livelihoods are being sacrificed to save a creature that many of them have never seen.

In response, marine scientists and conservation groups are sadly certain that the measures are barely sufficient: a larger area and a safe corridor to connect the two dolphin populations might have more chance of success, they say.

It's a gamble and the stakes could not be higher. If it fails, this charismatic creature, friend of the Raglan surfers and loved by many, may join the baiji, the Yangtze River dolphin that was declared extinct in 2006. Or the dodo, extinct from 1662. It doesn't make much difference: once it's gone, there's no coming back.

TARANAKI, A.K.A. 'THE ENERGY PROVINCE', has been a centre of exploration and drilling for oil, gas and condensate, especially since the 1969 discovery of the Māui gas and oil field in the Taranaki Basin. All offshore drilling to date has been confined to the continental shelf at depths of up to 1500 metres but there is now also a longer-term prospect of deep-water drilling beyond the shelf. For many, this evokes the spectre of the April 2010 *Deepwater Horizon* oil spill in the Gulf of Mexico: it's not worth the risk, they say.

Then there are the black sands. Another product of volcanic activity, they contain the mineral titanomagnetite, which makes the region's beaches memorably black and burn-the-soles-of-your-feet hot in summer. The sands stretch from the Kaipara Harbour to Whanganui and are New Zealand's greatest reserve of metal ore. From 1864 people have eyed them thoughtfully but only in recent times have they been successfully extracted and utilised. Today onshore reserves are excavated at Tahora, south of Kāwhia and, as I write, a company called 'Trans Tasman Resources' has an application before New Zealand's Environmental Protection Agency to mine approximately 66 square kilometres of the seabed between 22 and 36 kilometres off the coast of Pātea in South Taranaki. By the time you read this, the outcome will almost certainly be known.

If the application succeeds, up to 50 million tonnes of sand will be dredged annually: ten percent is iron ore and will be extracted and retained but the remainder will be returned to the seabed, creating a giant, long-lasting plume of suspended sediment.

Trans Tasman Resources talks of jobs, a boosted economy and 'confidence in the science' but the scheme's opponents are concerned not only about seabed destruction but also the impact on the wider environment, from the effect of the sand plume on water clarity, phytoplankton and the food web, to the damage to marine mammals, fish and the tourism industry. Only eight of 4840 submissions were in support.

Mine? The ore-rich black sands of the seabed off the Taranaki coast.

ON THE DAY SANDMINING was headlined in the *Taranaki Daily News* (4 February 2014), around 50 migrating Antarctic blue whales (*Balaenoptera musculus intermedia*) were reported south of Cape Taranaki. In the whale-hunting orgy of the 20th century, their population was reduced to one percent of its original size: they are still classed as 'endangered' but for such huge creatures, little is known about them and their ways except that their numbers are believed to be slowly rebuilding.

'It's just mind-blowing,' says DOC ranger Callum Lilley, that 'the largest animal ever to live on Earth has probably been feeding in the waters of the South Taranaki Bight for many years but prior to increased offshore activity (oil and gas), they had seldom been noticed!'

Only four blue whale foraging grounds are known in the Southern Hemisphere outside the Antarctic, none of them in New Zealand waters, but — here are the whales, off the North Island's west coast. It's not as if they're small. And it's not as if they hadn't been hunted, seen and stranded in the South Taranaki Bight before. It was just that, one way or another, no one had connected the dots.

Subsequent analysis by marine ecologist Leigh Torres of all available records, including those from the days of mid-20th-century Soviet whale hunters, further completed the picture. It seems likely that the whales are feeding on the krill that is abundant in the area because of a nutrient-rich upwelling of cold water off Kahurangi Point, south of the bight.

It's an irony that the discovery was triggered because of oil and gas exploration and extraction: along with shipping, which also passes through the bight, it is one activity that has potential to affect whales — although no problems are known so far. The industry goes to considerable lengths to keep it that way, forwarding sightings to DOC, funding research and following seismic survey best practice.

Sandmining, should it go ahead, may be a greater long-term threat because it is likely to cloud the water and impede primary production, which in turn will hamper the growth of phytoplankton at the base of the food web on which the whales rely.

We can only wait, watch and speculate.

Many images of blue whales look like this because it's not easy to photograph (or study) them — their dives last for up to 20 minutes and you can never be sure where they will surface next! They have relatively elongated, tapering bodies, with small dorsal fins (visible as this whale dives).

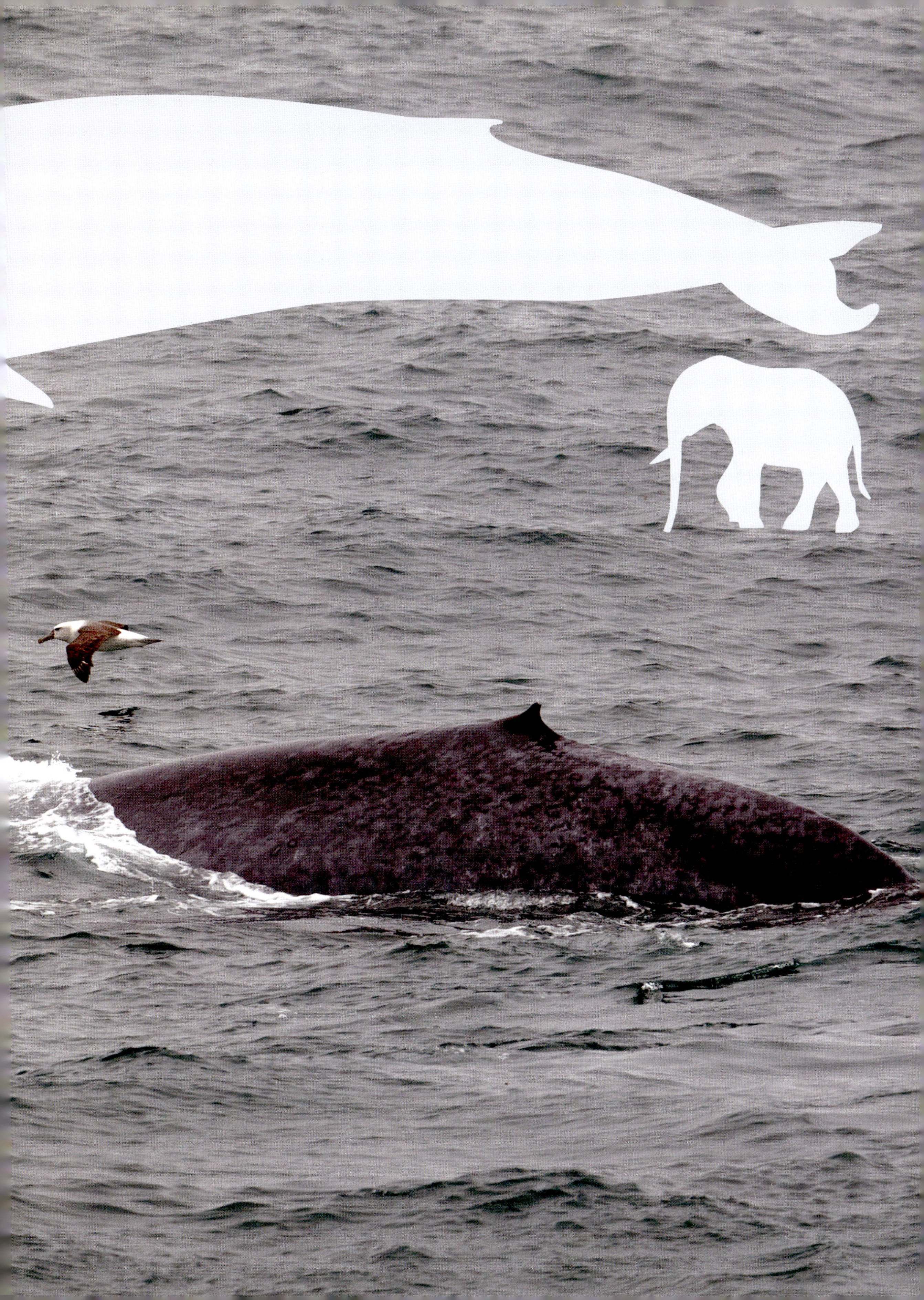

PARININIHI

North of New Plymouth, the coast curves into the North Taranaki Bight. A long series of shingly-rocky-sandy beaches follow the base of increasingly high cliffs to Pariokariwa Point, an impassable headland at the small settlement of Pukearuhe. This marks the southern end of Taranaki's second marine reserve, Parininihi; the other is at Katikatiaka Pā north of the dramatic white cliffs for which the area is renowned. The landscape is in constant flux; twice daily, the tide rises right to the base of the cliffs, nibbling and chewing, collapsing them from below. A little further north again, in the area where Tongapōrutu River empties to a sandy estuary, pinnacles known as the 'three sisters' are sometimes more, sometimes fewer, as the siblings tumble and are ultimately replaced by more carved from the cliffs.

The 1800-hectare Parininihi Reserve was created in 2006. As elsewhere, it was not without controversy and called for compromise: a stretch along the coast at its southern end was excluded as a concession to fishers and to local iwi, Ngāti Tama.

Like Tapuae, Parininihi is regarded as an example of wild Taranaki coastline, with the exception of its main feature, Pariokariwa Reef, in its southwest corner.

The reserve varies in depth between five and 23 metres, with a network of small caves, overhangs, canyons and pinnacles. Aside from a diverse range of fish species and large crayfish population, it has colourful gardens of rare and exotic sponges, bryozoans, anemones and soft corals, which carpet three-quarters of the available rock surface. University of Waikato marine biologist Chris Battershill, an expert on marine sponges, rates the reef as one of the top sponge spots in the world.

The white cliffs of Parininihi. Visitors must be cautious: at high tide the ocean laps against the cliffs and the unwary can easily become trapped.

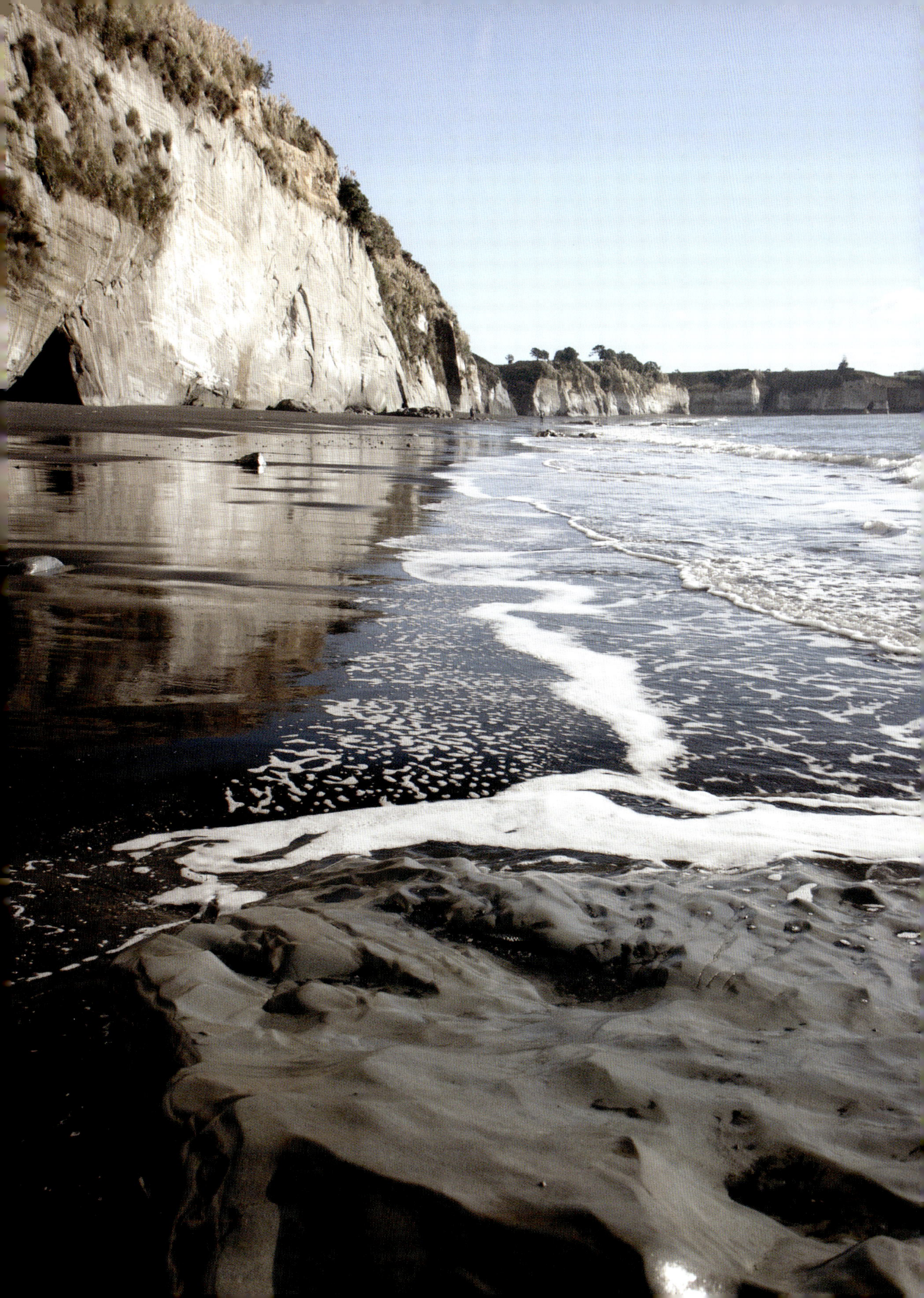

AN OCTOPUS'S GARDEN 'NEATH THE WAVES

Sponges are amazing. Wade Doak writes of swimming into the dark of an underwater cave at the Poor Knights. His torch illuminates 'riotous masses of life forms and colours on the rock walls. All around me are changing surfaces of white, sulphur-yellow, crimson, purple, pink, orange and emerald green . . . Why,' he asks, 'are sponges among the most brilliantly-coloured organisms in the undersea world?'

Why, indeed?

New Zealand has around 700 known sponge species but, as they are not well known or easy to study, it's entirely possible that there are twice this number. Something like 95 percent are found nowhere else in the world. Around 300 species are coastal, living on reefs such as Parininihi's Pariokariwa.

Early naturalists thought sponges were plants: anchored in one spot, brightly coloured and lacking limbs, organs, muscles and nerves — it made sense. It was not until 1765 that it was realised they are, in fact, animals, albeit of a very basic, stay-at-home variety (bright colours notwithstanding).

Sponges are colonies of individual cells that survive through cooperative specialisation — like simple versions of bee colonies, perhaps. They are Porifera, meaning 'pore-bearing' because their framing structures of lime, glass or collagen-like material are riddled with tiny canals or pores. Cells with fine flagella beat seawater into and through the canals, making it available to other cells that remove food before it exits through other pores. It's all very elementary.

The term 'life-span' means little to these creatures: if a piece breaks off, it will develop into a new sponge — and the remaining piece will repair as well. Two sponges may merge into one and some species famously will reassemble themselves if mangled into tiny pieces (pushed through a sieve, for example). Like a more successful Humpty-Dumpty.

Sponges may be vase-shaped, branching, ear- or bud-like, mounded, round, tubular or lobed — and a multitude of variations on these. They live on hard surfaces, such as walls or overhangs, usually in association with other sea creatures such as equally colourful ascidians (sea squirts) and provide shelter and living space for other small creatures such as shrimps, crabs, annelid worms, brittle stars, moray eels, jellyfish-like hydroids, molluscs and tiny fish.

Very few creatures prey on sponges. Some contain poisonous chemicals and who knows, perhaps — as elsewhere in the animal kingdom — the bright colours say it all: keep clear!

OPPOSITE: Encrusting sponges beneath a canopy of kelp, Poor Knights Islands.

Finger sponges and jewel anemones form a colourful display in Whāngārei Harbour Marine Reserve.

6 · BLACK SANDS & VERY SMALL DOLPHINS | TARANAKI

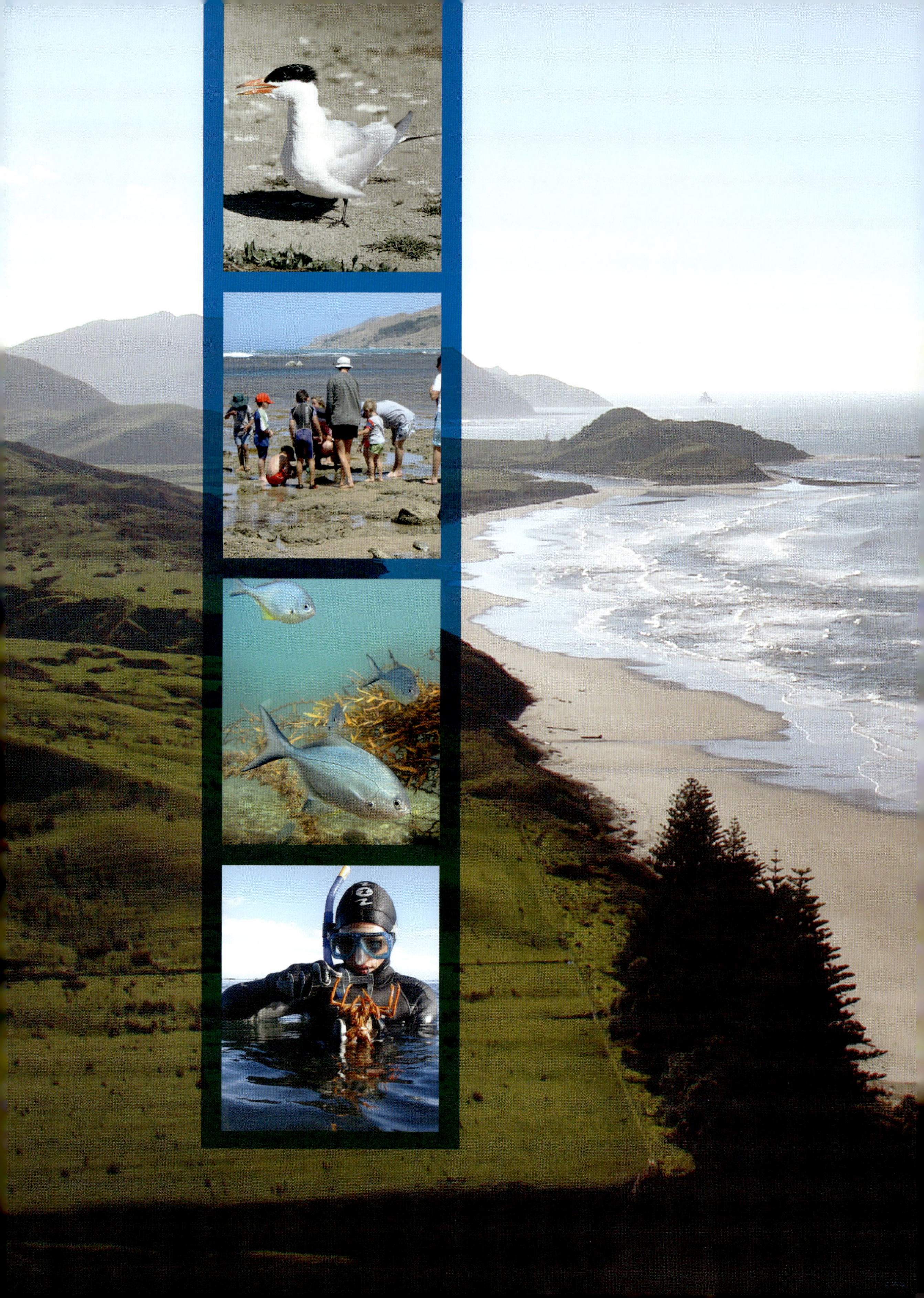

7
WHALE RIDER WORLD

EAST CAPE & SOUTHERN HAWKE'S BAY

There are two marine reserves in the central North Island on the east coast. South of East Cape, around from the Bay of Plenty and Te Paepae-o-Aotea (Volkner Rocks), the coast is picturesque but isolated. The country inland from Hicks Bay to Gisborne is rugged, with ranges of slip-scarred, slumped, creased and folded hills intersected by river valleys opening to the coast. Headlands and cliffs overlook sparkling, blue waters and pearl-grey beaches. Low, pebbly dunes topped with honey-coloured grasses fringe upper shorelines.

PREVIOUS:
Te Tapuwae-o-Rongokako Marine Reserve: a Caspian tern; a visiting school; maomao; a DOC worker takes a crayfish's vital statistics.

The rāhui pou that overlooks the reserve was designed and built by Professor Derek Lardelli, of Ngāti Konohi, renowned Tā Moko artist and also writer of *Kapa O Pango*, the alternative All Black haka.

TE TAPUWAE–O–RONGOKAKO

Te Tapuwae-o-Rongokako Marine Reserve will be familiar even to those who haven't been there as the oceanic setting for the movie *The Whale Rider*. The 2452-hectare reserve was established in 1999, a collaboration between DOC and Ngāti Konohi who wished to honour and protect the realm of Tangaroa, the sea god who has sustained and nurtured their people over many centuries.

The reserve is approximately 16 kilometres north of Gisborne on the Whāngārā Road, close enough to be easily visited and a great resource for schools — it's another of Wade Doak's wet libraries (see p.70). The landward boundary begins in the south at Pouawa River, skirts the headland at Pariokonohi Point and traverses a four-kilometre white-sand beach to terminate at Waiomoko

River in the north. There was once a Ngāti Konohi pā on Pariokonohi Point where old pine trees are the only signs of former dwellings. A large rāhui pole on the headland overlooking the south end of the beach is very much of the present. Public access is at Pouawa, where there's also a freedom camping area.

Down below, there's an inshore reef, intertidal pools, rocky platforms and sandy flats. To the north, but outside the reserve, is the humped form of Te Ana-o-Paikea or Whāngārā Island. The reserve is a typical piece of East Coast, precious because of its marine life — flapjack seaweed, kelp, sponges, kina and the diversity of invertebrate and fish life that accrues when an area is left to itself. Species include spotties, banded wrasse, red moki, hiwihiwi, butterfish, marblefish and parore. Of special note, depending on the time of year, are hundreds of tiny juvenile crayfish that hide in the crannies of the reef.

Kelp forests in deeper waters shelter fish species such as scarlet wrasse, scorpionfish, sweep and leatherjackets, while sponges, hydroids, anemones, soft corals and sea squirts thrive on rock faces and overhangs.

Tapuwae-o-Rongokako, looking south to Pariokonohi Point.

A LONG-STRIDING MAN: RONGOKAKO

There are many stories about the man Rongokako. In one, it is said that when the *Tākitimu* waka came to Aotearoa from Hawaiki, its captain was Tamatea-arikinui. He had a son, the mighty tohunga and athlete Rongokako, who fell into dispute with another mighty warrior, Pāoa. They fought, and Pāoa pursued the fleet-footed Rongokako. As he ran, Rongokako's feet left giant prints — tapuwae — all down the coast, including at Wharekahika (Hicks Bay) and in the rocks of the marine reserve.

Finally Rongokako reached the shores of Raukawa (Cook Strait), took one more enormous stride, and was gone.

MARINE RECOVERY: TE ANGIANGI

Te Angiangi Marine Reserve lies between the small settlements of Blackhead and Aramoana, approximately 30 kilometres east of Waipukurau and Waipawa on the Central Hawke's Bay coast. It was established in 1997 after a number of groups, including representatives from Ngāti Kere, Ngāti Whatuiāpiti and Tamatea Taiwhenua, lobbied the then Ministry of Fisheries for its creation. Following negotiation with fishers and landowners, an area of 446 hectares, approximately one-fifth the size of Te Tapuwae-o-Rongokako, became 'no take'.

As coastlines go, the shores of central and southern Hawke's Bay are not unlike those of East Cape, with tiers of grass-clad craggy hills flowing from inland to fall sharply to sandy, stony, rocky shores. Offshore, the water is a couple of degrees cooler than at East Cape, however, because of the Wairarapa Coastal Current.

The reserve is dominated by a broad, mildly sloping mudstone platform that is dotted with pools at low tide, the largest of which, Stingray Bay, forms a small lagoon popular with divers and snorkellers. The pools contain small fish such as triplefins, juvenile pāua, kina, octopus, crayfish and wandering anemones, while the platforms are strewn with Neptune's necklace, pink coralline seaweed and widespread beds of seagrass. Golden limpets are abundant.

Beyond the platform, in the northern end of the reserve, the seafloor drops steadily to a kelp-covered reef, home to pāua, opal shells, crayfish, and reef fish, such as red and blue moki, butterfish, banded wrasse, marblefish and sweep. On the other side of the reef, there is a boulder bank extending almost as far as the reserve's seaward boundary, with colonies of brightly coloured nudibranchs and sponge gardens. In deeper waters, there are butterfly perch and tarakihi as well as sea perch, scarlet wrasse, large blue cod, common roughy and more crayfish.

The rock pools and platform are a paradise for birds such as kingfishers, eastern bar-tailed godwits, New Zealand and banded dotterels, oystercatchers, herons, pied stilts and the occasional Caspian tern. Once the reserve was established, over 1000 children a year visited to learn about life on the reefs.

In late April 2011 that all changed — albeit temporarily: 650 millimetres of rain over four days saturated the coast and a magnitude 4.5 earthquake ten kilometres offshore triggered a massive slip across the whole reserve. Tonnes of rubble covered the beach and spilled over the platform, devastating the reserve and the life within it. School visits were on hold for a while.

But nature is resilient: DOC ranger Dave Carlton observes that it is remarkable how well the environment has healed itself. 'It's still sorting out what the final coastal shape will look like but it shows that a marine environment that isn't depleted is robust enough to handle a significant event like that and bounce back. It's been fascinating to see.' Research shows there are still more marine creatures living in the reserve than on the coast either side of it and school visits have resumed, with students helping replant some of the slips. The birds are back hunting at low tide — as Dave says: 'the biggest long-term casualty has been the toilet block!'

It's a crumbly old coast: the cliffs, rock platform and pools show evidence of past slips and slumps.

POP GOES THE SEA-BEAD

Unfortunately, just because it contains the word 'weed', 'seaweed' suggests a land-based plant that grows where it's not wanted — a transference of a terrestrial concept to a marine environment! It's not so. 'Seaweed' simply refers to a large and diverse group of simple marine organisms that are more properly called 'algae' (the Latin word for 'seaweed'). Although some make their way to places where they are not welcome, on the whole, they are an entirely natural and essential component of the ocean ecosystem, providing food and shelter for a multitude of sea creatures.

Seaweeds — algae — range in size from microscopic, single-celled organisms to multicellular monsters, such as 60-metre giant kelp. They don't have the complex structures of land plants — no true roots, stems or leaves; instead, they have a holdfast, which is not a root but which does exactly as it says — holds fast, to a rock or other firm surface, a blade (which may be divided into fronds) and sometimes a stalk (called a 'stipe') connecting the two. Where plants on land must take nutrients from the soil and transport them to the leaves, seaweeds absorb them directly into their blades from the water.

There are three major groups, based on colour: green, brown and red,

A crayfish in the flapjack, a medium-sized brown seaweed found in the low-tide zone on the offshore platform up the coast at Te Tapuwae-o-Rongokako.

although, as scientist Malcolm Francis says, 'it may be hard to decide whether greens are browns or reds are really brown or green. Brown seaweeds can be golden yellow-brown to dark olive. Red seaweeds have the greatest range of tone — pink to purple, red, and brown to nearly black.'

Green seaweeds, such as sea lettuce, are found where there is plenty of sunlight, in the intertidal zone. (The seagrass at Te Angiangi is not a seaweed but a flowering plant.) Brown seaweeds such as kelps are found in deeper water, where there is less light, and red seaweeds are deeper again, in water up to 25 metres.

New Zealand has about 1000 native seaweeds, a third of them found nowhere else. Like the wandering anemone, the brown seaweed known as Neptune's necklace (*Hormosira banksii*) is found in Australia and New Zealand. It often grows in association with the pink encrusting red alga *Corallina officinalis* and familiar to most of us. Its strings of hollow, olive-green bobbles resemble children's pop-beads, keeping it afloat on the current and in the sunlight. It is covered in a slimy layer that retards drying when it is exposed at low tides.

AND OFF IT GOES

Sea anemones somewhat confusingly share their name with a genus of flowering plants — but are actually animals, members of the same group as corals and jellyfish, of the phylum Cnidaria. Cnidarians have a central gut cavity surrounded by venomous tentacles that, in the case of anemones, often appear like soft, colourful petals. At last count, 1112 cnidarian species were recorded in New Zealand waters.

Sea anemones are usually attached to a surface but the largest New Zealand species, the wandering anemone or hūmenga, moves about. During the day, it looks rather like a substantial tea cosy made of baked beans (around 150 by 350 millimetres) but by night it becomes both more flower-like and more deadly: it ties up to a seaweed in a favourable current and extends the fringe of stinging tentacles around its mouth, and nabs passing plankton and small invertebrates as they float by.

Wandering anemones are found only in New Zealand and Australia.

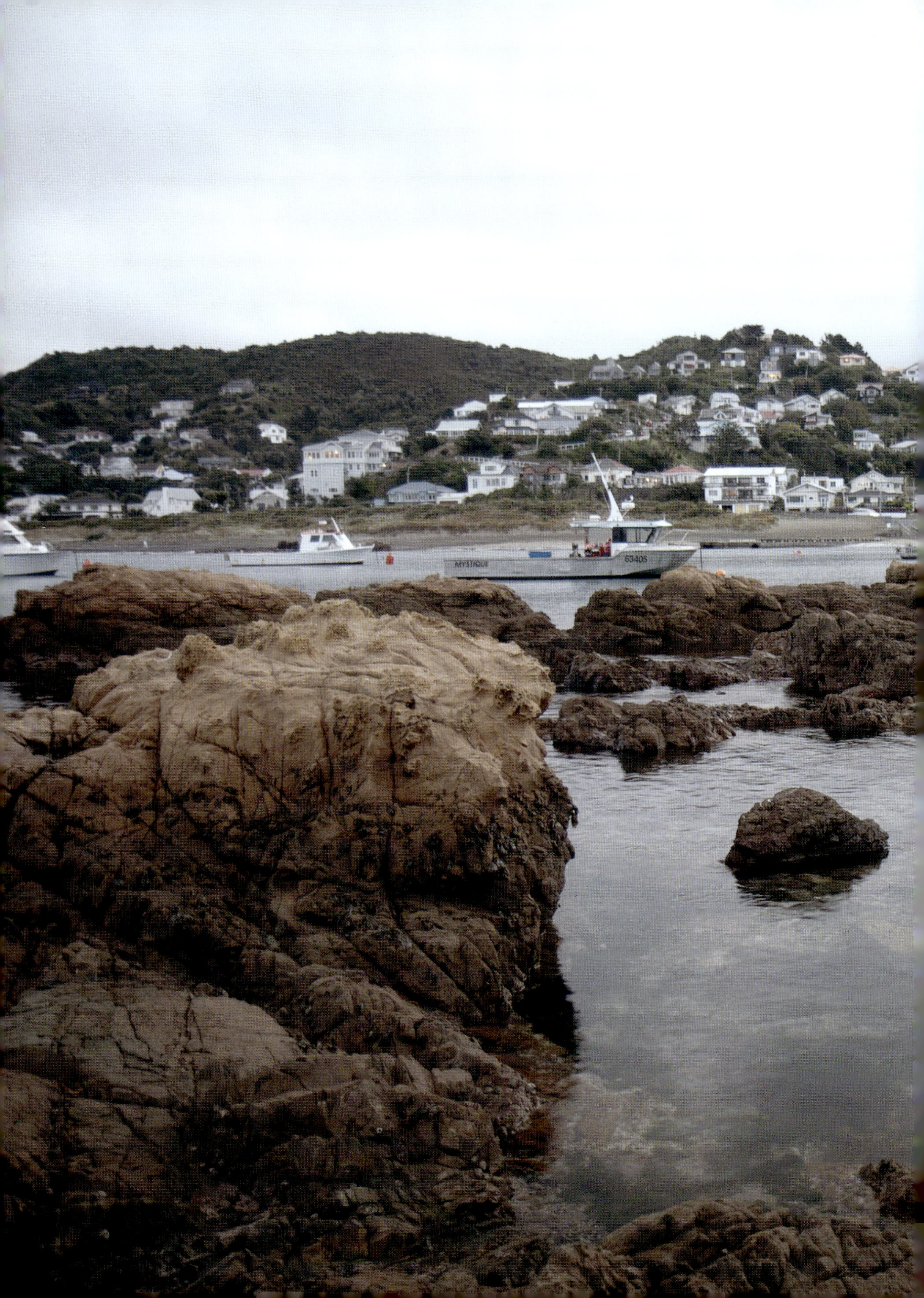
MYSTIQUE
63405

8

CITYSIDE

KAPITI & TAPUTERANGA

There are two marine reserves in the lower North Island; one of the oldest, Kapiti, is off the populated Paraparaumu–Waikanae coast and was established in 1992, while one of the more recent, Taputeranga in Wellington's Island Bay, was established in 2008.

KAPITI: MORE THAN A MARINE RESERVE

PREVIOUS:
Early morning in Ōwhiro Bay above Taputeranga Marine Reserve.

—

Kapiti Island from Raumati Beach.

—

Kapiti Marine Reserve connects Kapiti Island Nature Reserve to the mainland's Waikanae Estuary Scientific Reserve, creating an unbroken sequence of protected areas that includes open ocean, island forest, comparatively sheltered channel and freshwater estuary.

Unimpeded flow between such a range of environments is relatively rare and therefore all the more precious. It is particularly important for birds that feed in coastal waters but return to land to roost and, in some species, to breed. Birds of many different feathers live on and around the island, including shags (black, spotted, little and pied), variable oystercatchers, reef herons, sooty shearwaters, little blue penguins, red-billed and black-billed gulls, white-fronted terns, Australasian gannets, Caspian terns and diving petrels. Some also visit the estuary where they mingle with its contingent of largely wetland birds, including the royal spoonbill.

The sea-to-shore-to-river sequence also benefits native freshwater galaxiid fish like inanga, kōaro and shortjaw kōkopu (juveniles of several galaxiid species are commonly known as 'whitebait') because they have both marine and freshwater stages in their life cycle. In autumn at the height of spring tides, the adult fish lay eggs among plants around the high-water mark on the edge of the estuary. In the following month or so, diminutive larval fish develop inside the eggs and at the next high tide these tiny creatures — less than one millimetre long — hatch and are washed out to sea where they remain over winter, feeding on even tinier crustaceans. In spring, they return to the freshwater, and in the usual way of things on most New Zealand rivers, run the gauntlet of whitebaiters' nets. The fish at Kapiti have only natural predators to avoid, however, and although the wetland birds don't know about the fishing ban in the estuary, there's a good chance the inanga will safely make it to a stream or creek in the southern Tararua Ranges, where they will remain for between one and ten years before returning to the river mouth to spawn and again set the cycle in motion.

THE ISLAND OF KAPITI has a long and complex history. It is the upper portion of a submerged mountain range, with a major fault line along its western edge, where sheer cliffs have been uplifted to a crest over 500 metres high. It had great strategic value for early Māori because of its commanding position north of the entrance to Cook Strait, and is especially famed as the stronghold of Ngāti Toa chief Te Rauparaha, who lived there from the 1820s with as many as 3000 of his people.

In the late 1820s, they were joined by whalers who, by the 1830s were operating as many as seven stations on the island and three on offshore islets dedicated to the pursuit and slaughter of humpback whales as they swam between the island and the mainland. By the early 1840s, the whale boom was over and the people of Ngāti Toa had largely departed. Much of the island was subsequently cleared for farming, which meant the introduction of a throng of domestic and feral animals such as goats, pigs, dogs, possums, rats and cats. Although the island was designated a 'bird sanctuary' in 1897, the last of these animals was not finally removed or eradicated until 1996, almost a century later. Today it is a premier refuge for some of New Zealand's rarest creatures, among them kiwi, kākā, takahē and tīeke (North Island saddleback).

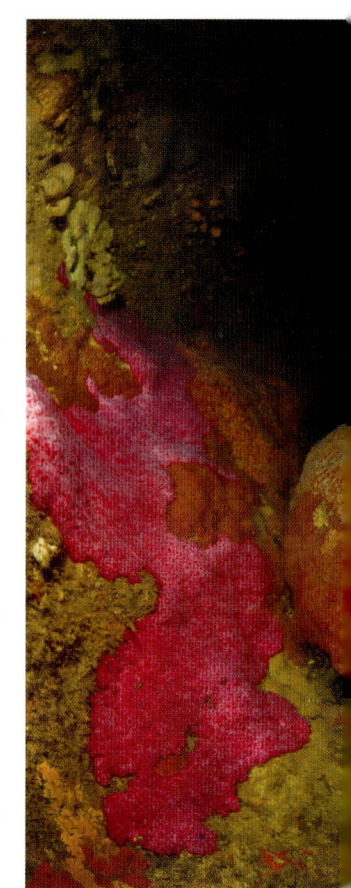

KAPITI MARINE RESERVE is in two sections. The roughly oblong, ten-by-two-kilometre island is approximately five and a half kilometres offshore, sitting more or less parallel to the coast, with high cliffs backing to the open sea and the Rau-o-te-rangi Channel (the 'moat') separating it from the mainland. The bulk of the 1825-hectare reserve is in this area, an approximate triangle from the island's northeast side across to the mouth of the Waikanae River and back; the 342-hectare remainder is off the northern corner of the island, extending not quite halfway down the western coast.

Three currents converge in the Kapiti–Wellington region, the Westland Current from the south, the warmer D'Urville Current from the east and north and the Southland Current, flowing up the east side of the South Island and then through Cook Strait. Each brings a different blend of salinity, clarity and temperature along with its own consignment of marine life, from seals and penguins to subtropical fish, including sharks.

Strong winds, tidal currents and swells dominate the island's waters, especially on the exposed, western side where kelp forests grow on boulder reefs; there are carpets of jewel anemones and fish such as snapper and red moki are abundant. The water in this area is relatively clear and the underwater scenery is spectacular, especially an underwater tunnel known as the Hole-in-the-Wall, where divers swim among clouds of fish including blue cod, banded wrasse, silver drummers and red moki, and are often accompanied by seals from a haul-out base on the western shore. Crayfish, pāua and octopus, as well as kina and more sponges, starfish and anemones are found in deeper zones.

The landward side of the island is more sheltered although there are still strong currents. Narrow, shallow boulder reefs are interspersed with sandy areas, silt and gravel to depths of 80 metres. Notably, there are beds of rhodoliths and of horse mussels.

A diver is inspected by red moki and dwarfed by boulders in the slot known as the Hole-in-the-Wall.

Local man Ed Skelton scores a 9.4-kilogram snapper. Ed has observed a huge difference not only in the fishing outside the reserve but, as one who dived around the island in the days before the reserve was established, has also noticed huge changes for the better in the undersea life and landscape.

WHEN THE MARINE RESERVE was established, a survey was undertaken by NIWA's predecessor, the New Zealand Oceanographic Institute. Although not as comprehensive as later assessments, it established an important baseline against which to measure change within and outside the reserve. There have since been a number of surveys by DOC, NIWA and by university departments. Comparisons are not straightforward and it's even less easy to draw absolute conclusions, but the trend is clearly in the direction of an overall improvement in the density, diversity and size of marine life.

As well, while there is no way to quantify the community's experience, its members also acknowledge and appreciate the reserve's benefits. Recreational fisher and former Kapiti member of the Wellington Regional Council Chris Turver recalls that it was the first reserve to be proposed in a heavily populated area, and attracted strong opinions, with people either fiercely for or against. The initial proposal encompassed about two-thirds of the waters around the island, and was not supported on safety grounds by boating clubs at Waikanae, Kapiti and Ōtaihanga.

However, a compromise was reached after DOC reduced the reserve's proposed area. 'We could live with that,' says Chris who organised much of the recreational fishing opposition. And, 'irony of ironies', he found himself the recreational fishers' representative on the marine reserve committee, a position he held for 13 years before DOC 'regrettably disestablished it'.

It took up to five years after the reserve was designated before there were observable changes within it, but then fishers also began to notice increased sizes and volumes of shellfish species, specifically pāua and crayfish, *outside*, while reef fish such as blue cod and butterfish became 'bountiful'. The reserve is now wholeheartedly supported by the community, Chris says. 'It's done exactly what it's supposed to and is an international showcase for regenerating a marine environment.'

RHODOLITHS: FREE-LIVING PINK STONES

They don't look like plants — or seaweed, for that matter. If anything, they resemble pinkish-red, multi-branched, knobbly, limestoney knucklebones: they are formed when coralline red algae deposit calcium carbonate inside their cell walls, making coral-like structures called 'rhodoliths'. Like corals, rhodoliths come in a range of shapes from leafy to lumpy but, whereas corals are animals and filter their food from the water, rhodolith-making algae photosynthesise their own.

Unlike most seaweeds, however, rhodoliths don't have holdfasts and are not attached to any fixed surface; they roll with the motion of the water like tumbleweeds in the breeze, especially when they are small. Once they have grown and are heavy enough, they settle into beds and form firm surfaces in otherwise sandy and gravelly areas that in turn become significant habitats for communities of other algae and marine animals such as invertebrates and juvenile fish. Like the mussel beds that once filtered the Hauraki Gulf, they are biogenic and build an environment all of their own.

Rhodoliths are widespread in the world's oceans and are thought to date back 55 million years. They will, however, be one of the organisms affected by acidification of the seas.

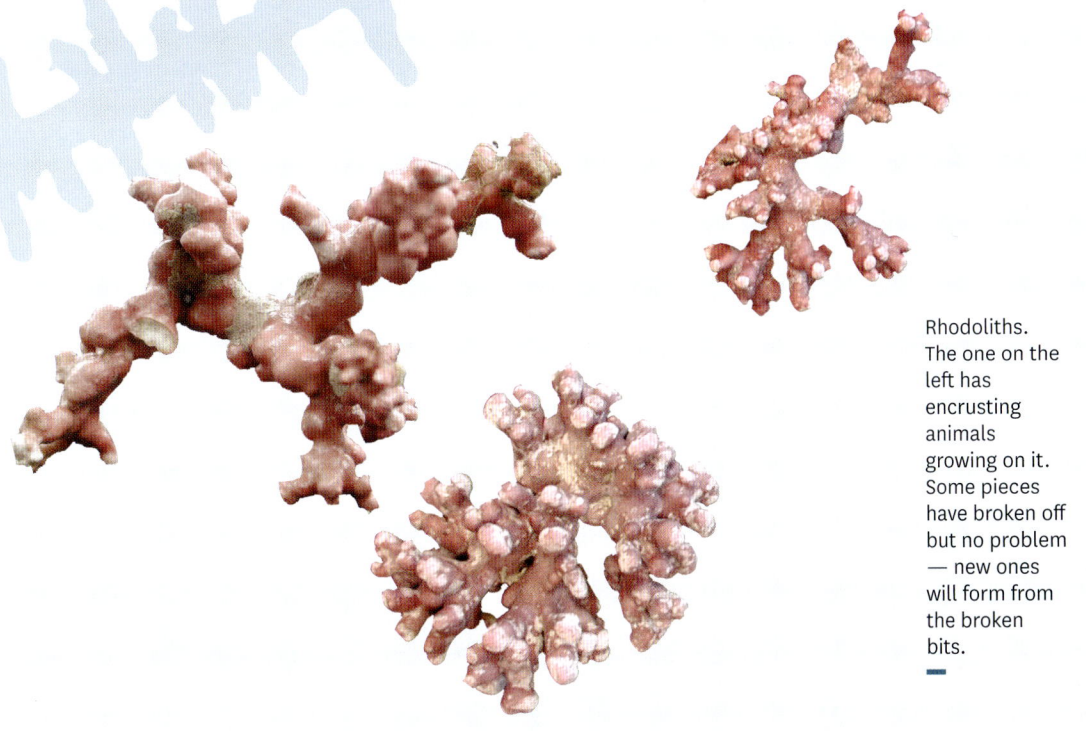

Rhodoliths. The one on the left has encrusting animals growing on it. Some pieces have broken off but no problem — new ones will form from the broken bits.

TAPUTERANGA: A CAPITAL PLACE

Taputeranga is the only fully accessible marine reserve in the heart of a large population centre. Unlike Motu Manawa/Pollen Island, which is similarly central in Auckland but not easy to visit, Taputeranga, which is on the shores of Cook Strait, is just six kilometres from the city of Wellington's central business district, immediately below the streets and houses of the hillside suburbs of Ōwhiro Bay, Island Bay and Houghton Bay. It is very much part of the city's life: it is supported by an active Friends of Taputeranga Marine Reserve group, the Experiencing Marine Reserves programme runs here, there's an aquarium on the shore in Island Bay, there's Te Kopahau open-air visitor shelter and a marine education display at the western end, a state-of-the-art Victoria University Coastal Ecology Lab and, for those who want to explore on their own, a snorkel trail similar to that at Te Whanganui-a-Hei.

Two yellow triangles on the benches of a disused quarry announce the western boundary of the 854-hectare reserve. The pit is carved into the massive hills of the southern North Island, its exposed and tilted seams dramatically illustrating the tectonic forces at work in this most unstable of regions. Below the hills and the quarry, there's a small bay with a shingle beach, where driftwood and seaweed tangle and pile at the high-tide line. A walkway beyond the reserve boundary to the west leads to two further scientific reserves, a 200-million-year-old outcrop of pillow lava known as Red Rocks, and Sinclair Head/Te Rimurapa, where in winter months there is a colony of non-breeding New Zealand fur seals. Dolphins, orca and southern right whales pass through the strait.

Around the headland in the other direction, the walkway becomes a road with a string of houses nestled at the foot of the bluffs on the other side,

A calm day in the rocks and pools of Taputeranga, looking east towards the island (at left), with the entrance to Wellington Harbour and Pencarrow Head beyond.

the houses' relative smallness serving only to emphasise the magnitude of their stark backdrop.

But it's the rocks that are significant. The reserve stretches along approximately five kilometres of coast and 2.3 kilometres out to sea, with the island after which it — and Island Bay — is named, at its heart. The complex underwater landscape is like a piupiu of scraped and striated, bare-bones, toothy strands of rock interspersed with gravel-filled channels that stretch from shore to surf. Their small pinnacles break the waves and at low tide their pools, some of them as deep as 2.4 metres, are full of life.

A calm day is rare in these waters. Currents and tidal flows in Cook Strait are especially complex, often storm-tossed and wind-blasted, slapping and hurling at the land. The waters vary, depending on shape and depth of the underlying seafloor, shape and slope of the coast, the season, the time and height of the tide, the wind, and the salinity, density and temperature of the water. Three currents converge on the reserve at different times: the Southland Current, which travels up the east of the South Island, largely turns east towards the Chathams around Kaikōura but a small portion flows north and west into the strait; the Westland Current flows up the west coast of the South Island and similarly divides, with some flowing towards Kapiti and some funnelled through the strait; while the D'Urville Current crosses the Tasman and again sometimes passes through the strait. Some currents, such as the Westland, occasionally even reverse, depending on the tide and prevailing wind.

Consequently, this constantly colliding and churning sea is the northern limit of some fish and the southern limit of others — over 180 species in all. Among them are blue cod, blue moki, crayfish, butterfish, marblefish, spotties, banded and scarlet wrasse, crabs, starfish and octopus. Seaweeds also hold tight and flourish, with around 400 species in the reserve. Large brown species do particularly well, with kelps growing to 20 metres. Beneath them there are sponges, hydroids, anemones, nudibranchs and big-bellied seahorses.

Murray Hosking, chair of the Friends group and one-time forester, describes swimming in the reserve:

Even in small pools at the reserve's edge there is a huge diversity of life, shape and colour including a tiny, almost-transparent fish (centre).

Snorkel 'floating' over a south coast reef is akin to flying slowly over a New Zealand terrestrial high forest. The ecological elements are strikingly similar, with major kelp forests harbouring epiphytes and a host of small invertebrates and bacteria. Secondary forests and shrubs abound. Burrowing animals attack holdfasts and fish fly-swim amongst the forest fronds. On a micro scale there are coralline algae turfs, which also carry epiphytes and critters as mini-ecosystems vital to marine food chains. The seaweed provide the forest structure and the shelter and habitats for so many marine creatures.

GRUMPY OLD COD

Sometimes it's almost impossible to avoid imposing human traits upon an animal. Blue cod have thick-lipped, down-turned mouths that make them look as if they are not only in a bad mood but seriously, most terribly disapproving; they rest their pectoral fins and tails on the seafloor, scowling cheerlessly. In fact, they are on the bottom because they don't have swim bladders and they have a pompous *looking-at-you* expression because they are on the prowl for passing supper or, because they are strongly territorial, for intruders.

This makes them appear inquisitive, approaching divers, nibbling and tugging at dive gear, peering into masks and having a go at their own reflections. Others interpret this behaviour more kindly, describing blue cod as endearing, curious and comical. It's even possible to stroke their heads.

Blue cod (*Parapercis colias*) are endemic to New Zealand. They are beautiful: slightly mottled, silvery-blue-green on the back and sides, with white bellies. They are seafloor dwellers that tend to remain in a preferred and defended home range. They are voracious feeders and eat small fish, molluscs, crustaceans and marine worms — anything they can swallow, in fact. They have only small teeth in their jaws but also have grinding structures further back in their very large mouths.

Blue cod (rāwaru or pākirikiri) are not 'cod' at all but belong to the weever or sand perch family. Although found in New Zealand's northern waters, they are larger and more prevalent south of Cook Strait. They grow up to 600 millimetres in length and live at depths of up to 70 metres.

Blue cod are important not only as an indicator species for marine reserves but also a prized commercial and recreational catch. This has placed them under so much pressure that some fisheries have been closed while others have limits on size and number. Blue cod form an important commercial fishery in places such as Stewart Island/Rakiura, where they are caught in baited pots. Good reason to be grumpy!

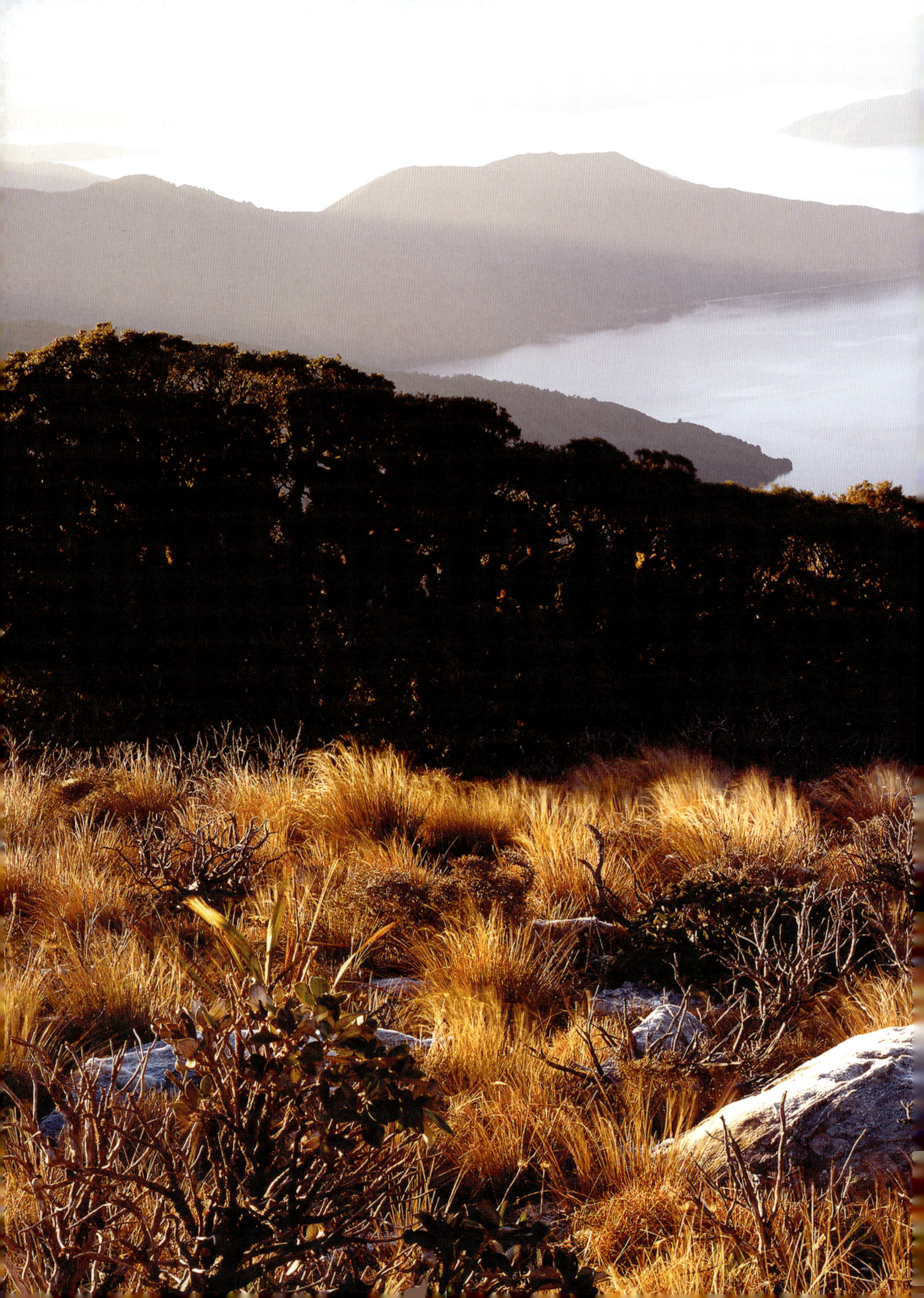

9
SOUNDS & BOULDERS

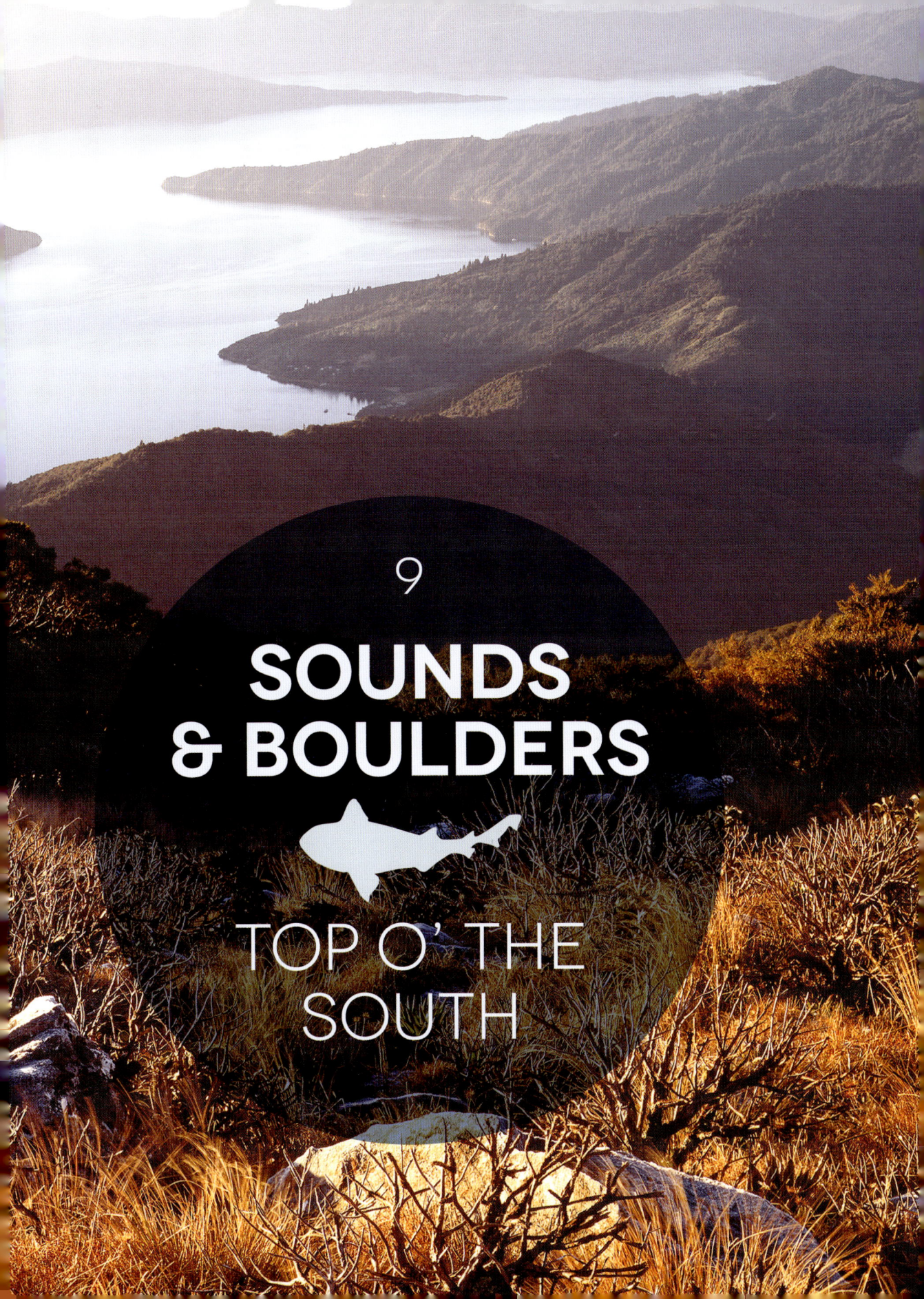

TOP O' THE SOUTH

Four marine reserves are spread evenly across the top of the South Island. The first is Long Island–Kokomohua, northwest of Wellington's Taputeranga and across Cook Strait on the outer limits of the Marlborough Sounds; next is Horoirangi, 12 kilometres north of Nelson city; then comes Tonga Island, in the Abel Tasman National Park; and finally, just around the hook of Farewell Spit, tucked inside Whanganui Inlet on the northwest tip of the island, is Westhaven (Te Tai Tapu).

LONG ISLAND– KOKOMOHUA

The Marlborough Sounds are another outstanding New Zealand land-and-seascape. They are a maze of fragmented, irregularly shaped, narrow inlets whose blue-green waters wash against jagged-edged, largely bush-clad peninsulas, eroded craggy islands and bare rock stacks.

The chain of islands and rocks that are the nucleus of Long Island–Kokomohua Marine Reserve are at the outer end of Queen Charlotte Sound, 35 kilometres from Picton. Long Island is four kilometres long but only one kilometre at its widest, like a taniwha with a long bony spine, stretched out with its chin in the sea to the north. The marine reserve extends 463 metres from high-water mark around Long Island, Kokomohua Island and a number of rocky pinnacles to their north.

The reserve can be reached only by water: there are no jetties but landing is possible on the east of Long Island, and there is a flat area to the southwest that may be where Captain James Cook landed in 1770. He was so enchanted that when he returned in 1773, he planted a hearty range of

PREVIOUS:
Looking into Queen Charlotte Sound from Mount Stokes.

vegetables including potatoes, carrots, parsnips, turnips, onions, cabbages, beans, peas, broad beans and wheat — none of which remained when he called back four years later.

Following a similar pattern to Kapiti, the island was heavily fortified during Māori occupation through the mid-1800s, then later cleared for farming through the late 1800s to the 1920s. It became a scenic reserve in 1926, with the last stock removed in the 1930s. The bush has since regenerated and is an important wildlife refuge and home to little spotted kiwi, fluttering shearwaters, yellow-crowned kākāriki or parakeets, toutouwai (South Island robins), tīeke (South Island saddlebacks), Maud Island frogs and tuatara. The island was again fortified in World War II, with construction of barracks and an anti-submarine defence station.

The spine of a taniwha: Long Island.

In the late 1980s, Marlborough dive clubs noticed declining fish numbers around the island. They voluntarily called a halt to fishing themselves and began to promote the idea of a marine reserve: it became the South Island's first when it was officially signed onto the books in 1993.

THE RESERVE IS TYPICAL INNER Marlborough Sounds, with boulder reefs around the south, east and west sides of Long Island, an underwater reef connecting the islands, and a sand and gravel seafloor in the deeps beyond. It is known for abundant, friendly blue cod as well as marblefish, spotties, blue and red moki, sea and butterfly perch, banded and scarlet wrasse, leatherjackets, tarakihi, and small fish such as triplefins, gobies and clingfish. Crayfish are large and plentiful and there are kina, brightly coloured nudibranchs, brittle stars, anemones and pāua. The latter are slowly recovering after being seriously depleted. Seals and dolphins — common, bottlenose, dusky and Hector's — are sometimes seen around the islands as are little blue penguins and on occasion, orca.

Encrusting seaweed, a sea star and an anemone in the Marlborough Sounds. Some local residents are concerned that salmon farms proposed for the area will threaten these clear waters and its marine life.

A SMALL SWIM WITH A SLIGHT SHARK

During the day, the young carpet shark rests beneath an overhang near the base of a narrow slot between two rocky outcrops. In the blue-green light at around five metres depth, her light tan body appears almost white, mottled with dark patches, bars and streaks, a brilliant camouflage that renders her almost invisible — and is the reason for her name, being carpet-like. (She is also sometimes called a 'swell shark' because she can inflate her body when alarmed.)

As evening falls, she swims, undulating her body side-to-side, much as a dog wags its tail. She is not at all conventionally shark-like and, at a little over 600 millimetres long, is not fully grown, with two smallish dorsal fins well down her body, and stumpy, round-ended, triangular pectoral fins. She has a broad head with a flattened nose that is rodent-like in profile. Her standout feature is her large oval eyes, as clear as a marble.

She cruises along an encrusted wall at the northern end of the reserve, past a company of crayfish, also waking for the evening, their whip-like antennae a defensive thicket of waving, slender feelers. They are so many in number that their bodies touch, armoured flank to armoured flank, and they are large, with knobbly-prickly thoraxes, full, rounded tails and staring eyes. Below them, above the sandy floor, small fish dart and disappear.

She passes anemones, chitons, kina, a seven-armed starfish, before entering a forest of larger seaweed, swimming through the stipes below the blades. Beyond the rocks the floor is open, pebbled and flat, with only an occasional rounded shape — a horse mussel standing in the soft substrate, like a dolmen on a plain. Some of the mussels are encrusted with algae: red and brown, fine, branched.

There are boulders, a reef, another slot. She enters the gloom, flicks her tail, and is gone.

HOROIRANGI

West of the jumbled islands and channels of the Marlborough Sounds, the coastline opens into the triangle of Tasman Bay, with the city of Nelson close to its southern tip. Horoirangi Marine Reserve is approximately in the middle of the triangle's eastern side, a 904-hectare rectangular area extending 1852 metres offshore from Ataata Point in the north along a narrow shoreline below the steep, scantily vegetated face of Mackay Bluff to the small seaside settlement of Glenduan in the south.

The bluff is an integral part of the reserve's story because it is the source of the dark, granite-like, volcanic rock granodiorite that not only makes up its distinctive boulder reefs, but also a rare neighbouring landform, the 13-kilometre-long Nelson boulder bank. The bank stretches southwest from the southern tip of the reserve, arching away from the coast to form a roughly parallel barrier that encloses Nelson Haven, a protected tidal estuary. The spit is made of graded, interlocking boulders and is thought to have developed over 6000 years.

In the reserve, especially towards its north, the boulders form a wide intertidal zone that stretches offshore for up to 400 metres, to depths of 20 metres. The endless motion of boulders and rocks on the upper shore scrubs them relatively clear of anything living but deeper reaches attract a rich array of marine life — shellfish, anemones, nudibranchs, snails, starfish, crustaceans and fish. Sponge gardens between ten and 15 metres, with a wide range of sponges — finger, golfball, red, yellow, orange and grey — provide important habitat for juvenile fish including triplefins, tarakihi, blue cod, leatherjackets, red moki, banded wrasse and spotties.

Beyond the sponge gardens, the seafloor is silty and muddy with a different complement of inhabitants including worms, shrimps, crabs, cockles, scallops, horse mussels and the echinoderms: sand dollars, heart urchins, brittle stars and sea cucumbers.

When the reserve was established in 2006, edible reef fish were uncommon both within it and outside: over time, however, one of the monitored species, blue cod, clearly increased in abundance of legal-sized fish compared to the control area (although sub-legal blue cod had the same increase in both places). There were no appreciable improvements for either blue moki or tarakihi but there were more and larger crayfish inside the reserve, while pāua inexplicably declined in size in the reserve — but increased outside.

MĀORI HAVE COLLECTED HAMMER STONES from the boulder bank and have lived in and visited the area for hundreds of years. The reserve's name, Horoirangi, comes from a 657-metre peak behind Mackay Bluff and is also the name of an ancestor of Ngāti Tama Manawhenua Ki Te Tau Ihu. The reserve came into being in 2006 after it was realised that the bay's marine life was suffering from decades of fishing and harvesting. Ngāti Tama suggested the site and also initiated the establishment of the Whakapuaka Taiāpure, a customary fishing area in Delaware Bay, to the north of the reserve.

The graded rocks and boulders that characterise this reserve extend along the Nelson boulder bank.

TONGA ISLAND

Tonga Island Marine Reserve is a stretch of typical coastline also inside Tasman Bay, but on the bay's northwestern side, not far from Separation Point, where the coast doubles back into Golden Bay. The 1835-hectare reserve extends one nautical mile (1852 metres) from mean high water, from the headland immediately north of Bark Bay in the south, to Awaroa Head in the north. It includes a number of descriptively named smaller bays and headlands — Mosquito Bay, Foul Point, Arch Point, Tonga Quarry, Onetahuti, Shag Harbour and Abel Head — as well as the small, bush-clad island opposite Onetahuti beach after which the reserve is named.

The reserve borders the beautiful Abel Tasman National Park and contributes to its popularity. Its waters are jewel-like, often brilliantly turquoise and offset by broad, curving golden beaches; its dramatic, creamy-white granite reefs and headlands are framed by a backdrop of intense forest-green and summertime-rātā crimson. There is no road access but visitors either walk the coast track to Onetahuti or arrive by kayak, boat or water taxi.

As with Long Island–Kokomohua and Horoirangi, Tonga Island Marine Reserve's establishment in 1993 was a response to falling fish numbers. Despite its name — 'Tonga' refers to the south wind — it is largely sheltered from the southerlies that howl through the not-far-distant Cook Strait and batter the lower North Island.

As well as the natural beauty of the landscape, the area is rich in wildlife: little blue penguins, godwits, herons, oystercatchers, dotterels and shags frequent the shores and estuaries; there's the occasional pod of dolphins and one of the main attractions, New Zealand fur seals and their pups on and around Tonga island.

Beneath the water's surface, the reserve is dominated initially by rocky, bouldery reefs with sandy-silty seafloor beyond. Unlike many other marine reserves, with their flourishing kelp forests, the seaweed cover here is relatively scant, amounting to pink encrusting coralline algae over much of the rock surface and a fringe of brown flapjack seaweed. There are, however, mussels, barnacles, cat's eyes, starfishes, kina, limpets, Cook's turbans and green topshells as well as sea anemones and nudibranchs, and triplefins, banded wrasse and leatherjackets swimming above them.

Both blue cod and crayfish have benefited from the reserve's 'no-take' status and are plentiful and of good size, but many other species — spotties, red moki and tarakihi among them — have been slow to improve. Scientists speculate that this may be due to a number of factors including heavy fishing pressure and low stocks prior to the reserve's establishment, continued fishing in adjacent areas, the comparative isolation of the area in terms of other populations and the low productivity and fertility of the catchment. Snapper have likewise been slow to show improvement, although local recreational fishers reported a good season — outside the reserve, of course — in 2013.

Curious juvenile fur seals inspect a kayaker near Tonga Island.

WESTHAVEN (TE TAI TAPU)

If *boulders* are at the heart of the Horoirangi and Tonga Island stories, then *mud* is the key to Westhaven (Te Tai Tapu) Marine Reserve, the largest wetland of its kind on the South Island's west coast. Estuaries are a true union of land and sea: freshwater flows from hills and mountains towards the coast where it slows, deepens and begins to meander and spread. Twice daily, it meets an influx of salt carried on tide and wave, and, depending on the lie of the land and the flow of the current, the two mix, although not always evenly. Nevertheless, they form a zone of transition between the fresh and the salt, the sheltered and the wave-tossed — and are important environments in their own right, filtering and cleaning the waters that arrive at the sea, and hosting a huge diversity of plants and animals. They are among the most productive ecosystems on Earth.

WESTHAVEN (TE TAI TAPU) MARINE RESERVE is unique among marine reserves in being completely within a tidal estuary, the Whanganui Inlet. Situated just around from Golden Bay, opening to the sea 19 kilometres southwest of Cape Farewell, it is 13 kilometres long and two to three kilometres across. Around 6500 years ago, it was a low-lying river system that was drowned by rising sea levels towards the end of the last ice age. It has a substantial bar across its ocean mouth and two major arms, one to the north, one to the south. The incoming tide fills channels down the middle of the arms before spilling onto the extensive tidal flats.

The surrounding landscape is hilly and steep, some in pasture but much clad in coastal forest, with many creeks and rivers that feed the inlet. Like all estuaries, it receives a certain amount of sediment and sand from its two water sources, its tributaries and the ocean. However, because of the surrounding bush and relatively unmodified countryside, Whanganui Inlet is one of the most pristine estuaries in the country.

The Māori occupants of the inlet (in turn, Ngāi Tara, Ngāi Tūmatakōkiri, Te Ātiawa, Ngāti Tama and Ngāti Rārua) fished its waters, harvested the wetland and left several pā sites and middens around its margin. Europeans in their time took to the area with enthusiasm, constructing wharves, mills, roads, tramlines and bridges in order to fell and extract the original rimu, kahikatea and beech forests and later to gather and mill the abundant flax. Coal and gold were both mined in the early 20th century, when there were also a number of unsuccessful attempts to drain the wetland. Most signs of this enterprise have long since disappeared as the inlet returns to its natural state.

THE MARINE RESERVE WAS ESTABLISHED IN 1994. It occupies 536 hectares in the southern arm and includes all the tidal sand flats with their extensive seagrass beds and all channels in the south of a straight line between Melbourne Point and the nearest headland on the opposite side, as well as three small additional areas upstream of causeways along Dry Road, southeast of and including the Wairoa River. It does not include a

Bluffs, forest, a wetland and a skein of mist are reflected in the waters of Mangarākau Swamp, part of the interconnected sequence of water bodies at Westhaven.

small area around the Mangarākau wharf. The reserve is surrounded by hills covered in coastal forest, with thick rātā, kahikatea, pukatea, beech, rimu and nīkau rising above the reeds and rushes of the saltmarsh.

As elsewhere, one initial suggestion was a 'no-take' reserve over the entire inlet but the desire among locals to be able to occasionally throw a line off the wharf or shoot a duck or two (in season) eventuated in a two-part compromise, with the Westhaven (Te Tai Tapu) Marine Reserve at one end and the 2112-hectare Westhaven (Whanganui Inlet) Wildlife Management Reserve at the other. The wildlife management reserve is partially protected but allows a limited amount of recreational gamebird hunting, traditional fishing and whitebaiting as well as accommodating kaimoana collection for cultural purposes.

Both zones teem with life. Approximately 30 species of marine fish have been identified in the inlet and, as at Kapiti, freshwater fish such as inanga, banded kōkopu, red-finned bullies and long-fin eels are able to migrate seamlessly from freshwater to salt and back at different stages of their life cycles. The seagrass beds and channels are also important spawning and nursery areas for shellfish and fish such as snapper, flounder and kahawai. Over 163 species of invertebrate have been recorded, among them many varieties of crabs, worms, starfishes and snails as well as whelks, cockles, pipi, nut shells, wedge shells, snapping and mantis shrimps.

Wading birds that feast on this bounty include banded dotterels, eastern bar-tailed godwits, knots, oystercatchers, kingfishers and white-faced herons. Little shags and southern black-backed gulls nest around the inlet.

BUT THAT'S NOT ALL! The south end of the marine reserve is fed by water from the 360-hectare Mangarākau Swamp. The largest remaining freshwater wetland in the upper South Island, it is also an outstanding natural landscape, with diverse habitats including fern and mānuka scrublands and rush and reed communities. Nelson botanist Edith Shaw has a plant list of over 800 from this wetland and it is home to at least 54 bird species including banded rail, fernbird, spotless crake and Australasian bittern. There are frogs, eels, kōkopu, inanga, kōura, freshwater shrimps and a species of brown mudfish that is wholly the region's own.

Some of the wetland is public land managed by DOC but a block of

160 hectares is owned by the New Zealand Native Forest Restoration Trust. It is covenanted, and is cared for by volunteers from the Friends of Mangarākau Swamp Incorporated Society, who also run an accommodation lodge and an information centre. Over time, they have removed mountains of weeds and exterminated pest animals such as stoats, rats and weasels. Despite setbacks of major fires in 2002 and 2004, they continue to build tracks, plant and tend seedlings including hundreds of majestic swamp-loving kahikatea and to plan for the wetland's total restoration — 500 years hence, they say, taking the long view.

THE ULTIMATE: RAMSAR LISTING

The whole complex of Mangarākau Swamp, Lake Otuhie to its south and Whanganui Inlet area with the marine reserve and wildlife management area (including the wharf) is in line to become one of New Zealand's next Ramsar sites, a move that will accord it worldwide recognition. As of March 2014, the long and detailed application process only awaits formal acceptance by the New Zealand Ramsar representative before being presented to the international Ramsar committee.

In her assessment in support of the application, botanist Bev Clarkson ranked the wetland 21.25 out of 25, putting it up there with the top 15 percent of New Zealand swamps. It is, she says, 'a good example of an intact, relatively large swamp system containing a variety of indigenous vegetation types and, unlike most swamps elsewhere in New Zealand, has not been modified by weed invasion.'

The Convention on Wetlands of International Importance is commonly called the 'Ramsar Convention' after the small Iranian resort town where its first meeting was held in 1971. The convention came into force in 1975 and New Zealand signed on in 13 December 1976. There are currently 168 signatories.

The convention's flagship initiative is the Ramsar List, a register of 2178 sites representing 2,085,232.2 square kilometres of wetland. New Zealand has six sites on that list, including Farewell Spit in Golden Bay. The others are Whangamarino in north Waikato, the Firth of Thames in the Hauraki Gulf, the Kōpuatai Peat Dome on the Hauraki Plains, the Manawatū Estuary near Foxton and the Awarua-Waituna wetland complex in Southland. Look for Mangarākau Swamp any time soon.

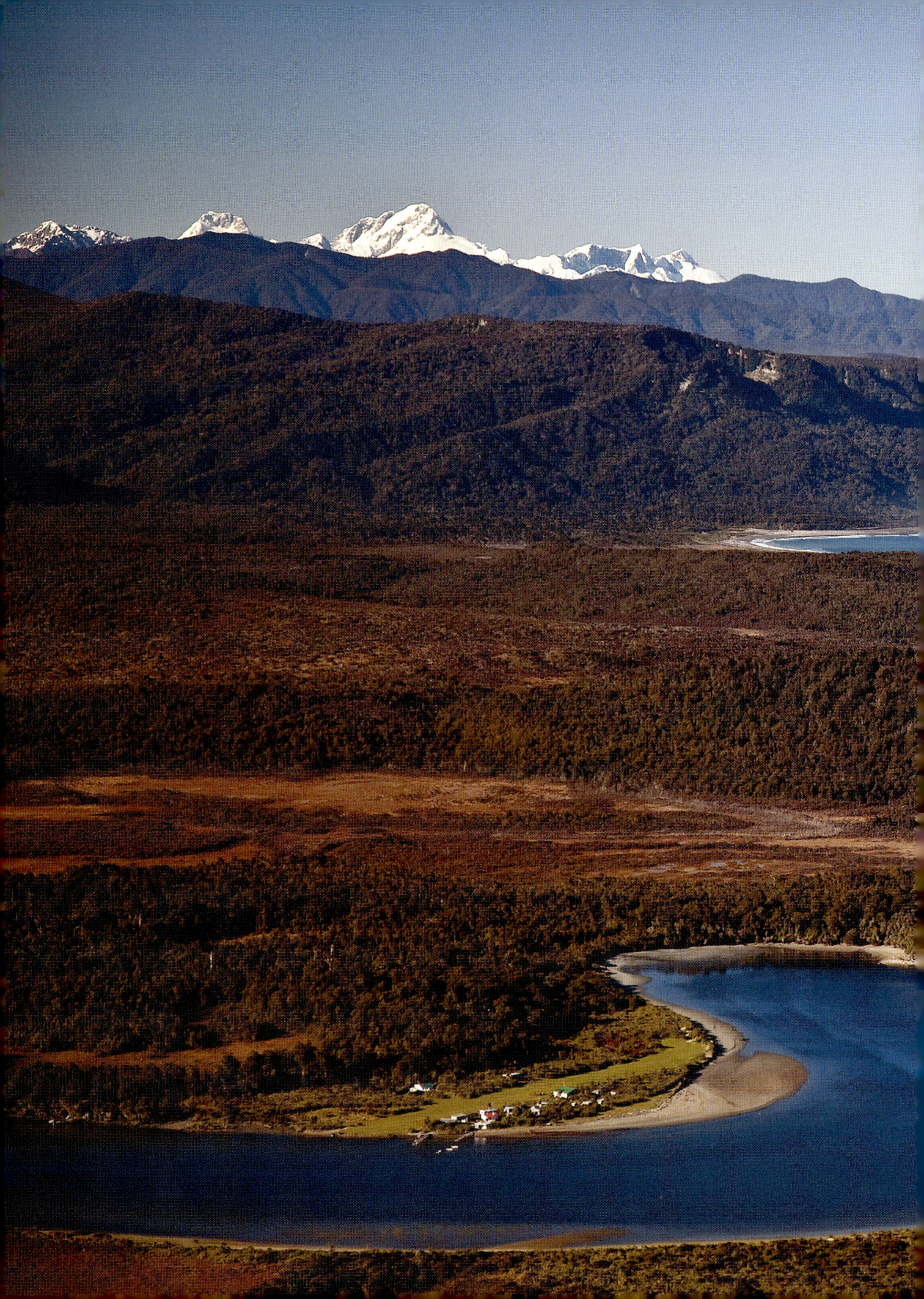

10
TE WAIPOUNAMU

UPCOMING WEST COAST

For many years there has been only one marine reserve in the central South Island — Pōhatu Marine Reserve at Flea Bay on Banks Peninsula. However, this is all about to change, with seven new reserves on the horizon, five on the west coast and two on the east.

THE WEST COAST REGION stretches 600 kilometres from Kahurangi Point in the north to Awarua Point in the south. Its shores are the wildest in New Zealand: exposed, dynamic, dramatic, stark and beautiful. Its waters are classified as 'high energy', with average wave heights of two to three metres and a mere six to eight seconds from one to the next. Their white tips often fleck the cobalt-blue sea from shore to horizon.

Wave action is often compounded by prevailing west winds and by the north-flowing but generally weak Westland Current, which brings relatively warm water from its parent, the Tasman Current. Inland, the Southern Alps rise sharply for much of the region's length, with several large rivers and around 80 estuaries discharging a constant burden of forest debris, gravels and sediments as well as a significant volume of freshwater.

It's a demanding environment. Nevertheless, the region is home to nearly 200 species of fish over the inshore shelf, hundreds of invertebrate species, as many as 175 species of seaweed, over 23 species of marine mammal including 11 classed as 'threatened', and around 100 species of birds, 18 of which are also classed as 'threatened'.

The West Coast Marine Protection Forum was established in 2005. It included people with a specific interest in the management of the coast including Ngāi Tahu, commercial and recreational fishing groups, conservationists, and people from local government and tourism, and was endorsed by the Ministries of Fisheries and Conservation. Its brief was to develop a policy to halt the decline in marine biodiversity across the region

PREVIOUS: An aerial view of a small whitebaiting settlement on the Cascade River on the West Coast.

at the same time — importantly — as it minimised the impact on existing users and accommodated Treaty settlement obligations.

In 2010, after five years of planning and consultation, the forum presented the ministers with a package proposing a range of options across a spread of habitats and ecosystems. The options included five marine reserves, 11 mātaitai reserves and a number of Type 2 Marine Protected Areas such as marine mammal sanctuaries and areas that, for whatever reason, would be open to only limited fishing practices.

A year later, the Minister of Conservation Kate Wilkinson and Fisheries Minister Phil Heatley, with heartiest congratulations to the forum, announced the government's intention to go ahead with the marine reserves, which will be known as Kahurangi, Punakaiki, Waiau Glacier Coast, Hautai and Tauparikākā. The reserves' combined total of 17,528 hectares is a mere drop compared with the 26,000 square kilometres in the South Island's national parks but does at least begin to add a degree of marine equivalence. The ministers also notified the intention to use the Fisheries Act 1996 to protect an additional 9557 hectares adjoining the Punakaiki and Hautai marine reserves from bottom trawling, dredging and Danish seining.

Each of the five proposed marine reserves contains as few as three and as many as eight of 17 different habitat types identified in the region based on depth and substrate characteristics. They encompass a broad range of habitats and ecosystems, both north-to-south up and down the coast as well as out to sea, across the continental shelf. Although smaller than initially proposed, three — Kahurangi, Punakaiki and Waiau Glacier — are generously sized; Kahurangi and Waiau Glacier will become the largest around New Zealand's mainland.

Larger, of course, protects a broader range of habitats, each of which is also able to be a good size, which in turn means greater interconnection between habitats, to the benefit of those species that move from one to the other at different stages of their lives. The reserves' larger sizes may also provide opportunities to research the 'edge effects' of fishing and other disturbance around marine protected areas.

Further, despite being relatively isolated, in order to minimise impacts on existing users the proposed reserves will be accessible to the public. Each belongs to a spectacular coastal landscape and is also adjacent to either a national park or a World Heritage area: trampers of the Heaphy

Track will walk part of the way alongside the waters of the Kahurangi Marine Reserve; the Dolomite Point walkway and Truman Track adjoin the massive cliffs, blowholes, caverns and waterfalls of the Punakaiki site; walkers can take the coastal leg of the Three Mile Lagoon walk at Ōkārito (Waiau Glacier Coast) at low tide; and one of the walks at Tauparikākā leads to a lookout with magnificent views overlooking the reserve and coastline south to Jackson Head.

KAHURANGI AND PUNAKAIKI

The first two proposed reserves are typical of the *northern* West Coast, with alternating rocky coasts and beaches bordering the broad, gently shelving seabed of the continental shelf.

The Kahurangi Marine Reserve (8466 hectares) will adjoin the national park of the same name, extending approximately 15.8 kilometres south from Wekakura Point to near Crayfish Point, and approximately 5000 metres offshore. The steep, rugged shoreline is some of the least-modified coastal land in the Buller–northwest Nelson region, and the proposed reserve echoes that ruggedness, with rocky and sandy habitats reaching out to the inner continental shelf areas to depths of about 50 metres.

An envoy from the terrestrial to the marine: a fur seal pup takes a first look at its future world.

Punakaiki Marine Reserve (3558 hectares) will extend approximately 10.8 kilometres south from Perpendicular Point to Maher Swamp, and 3704 metres offshore. It adjoins Paparoa National Park and includes the internationally renowned Dolomite Point pancake rocks and blowholes, a site of national scientific significance and a major tourist attraction in itself. There are rocky, gravel and cobble shore habitats reaching out to sandy seabed areas to depths of about 20 metres.

WAIAU GLACIER COAST

The proposed Waiau Glacier Coast Marine Reserve (4641 hectares) is typical of the *central* West Coast, with open gravel beaches and moraine bluffs of glacial origin. It adjoins the coastlines and catchments of Westland Tai Poutini National Park and Te Wāhipounamu–South West New Zealand World Heritage Area. It is close to the internationally renowned Ōkārito Lagoon and other estuaries that are important spawning and nursery spots for indigenous fish, such as giant kōkopu and inanga, and also adjoins the Ōkārito Mātaitai Reserve. Its coastal boundary will run approximately 10.7 kilometres south from the vicinity of Kohuamarua Bluff to the northern side of Ōmoeroa Bluff, with its outer boundaries approximately 3704 to 4200 metres offshore. Beneath the waves, there are moraine boulder and gravel shore habitats reaching out to sandy and muddy seabed areas to depths of about 25 metres.

TAUPARIKĀKĀ AND HAUTAI

The proposed sites for Tauparikākā Marine Reserve (16 hectares) and Hautai Marine Reserve (847 hectares) are typical of the *southern* West Coast, with sandy beaches and boulder shores bordering a narrow inner-shelf zone with deeply incised submarine canyons beyond. Both run off the coast of Te Wāhipounamu–South West New Zealand World Heritage Area.

The small Tauparikākā Marine Reserve is an educational site and will extend approximately 630 metres from Tauparikākā Point southwards to near the southern lookout on the Ship Creek Beach walk, and approximately 200 metres offshore. The proposed site includes the coastal marine area of Ship Creek/Tauparikākā, with pristine beaches, tidal lagoons and coastal dunes, and adjoins the Tauparikākā Mātaitai Reserve. Its sandy shore and river-mouth habitats reach out to depths of about five metres. An unusually high number of Hector's dolphins are seen in this area.

The Hautai Marine Reserve, with the working title of 'Gorge', will extend approximately 5.8 kilometres south from near Longridge Point to Hacket River, and approximately 1000 to 1300 metres offshore. It includes boulder and sand habitats reaching out to seabed areas to depths of about 30 metres, with canyons and rocky reefs beyond. This section of coast has habitats of high wildlife value, including marine mammals and seabirds.

LIFE ON THE ROCKS: OPEN BAY ISLANDS

Open Bay Islands are little more than two rocky islets five kilometres west of Haast, directly opposite the mouth of the Ōkuru River. They are not part of any marine reserve but are almost the only islands on this turbulent coast. They are low — to 30 metres — and small: Motu Taumaka to the north is a mere 660 by 260 metres and its tiny companion, Popotai, is 400 by 200 metres. The only reason they exist at all is their gritty foundation of limestone and granite, with all softness and almost any hint of topsoil long since thrashed into oblivion by wave, wind and rain. Their crags support only scrubby vegetation, tangled flaxes, ferns and shrubs. They are surrounded by low platforms and boulder reefs, their tops white with foam and tossed with spray. Despite their savagery, the waters are rich with nutrients from the Southern Ocean and provide for a diverse company of creatures, from the most minute zooplankton to the 4000 New Zealand fur seals (*Arctocephalus forsteri*) that claim this spot as their own blue backyard.

THE OPEN BAY ISLANDS were the setting for a dramatic episode in New Zealand's early colonial history. For a brief, heady time from the 1770s to the 1850s, fur seal and sea lion populations in New Zealand, Australia and around the world were ravaged by hunters keen to make their fortunes from a market hungry for pelts. Unlike most marine mammals, fur seals have a relatively thin layer of blubber, relying instead for warmth and insulation on an outer layer of stiffer hair and a soft, waterproof underfur that made their skins highly desirable for both fur and leather.

In February 1810 the brig *Active* dropped ten men on Open Bay Islands under the leadership of a young man named David Lawrieston, intending to return for them in a couple of weeks. The men set up camp at the northern end of Taumaka and duly set about clubbing, skinning and salting the helpless resident seal population.

By November, they had cured 11,200 skins and virtually snuffed out all the animals. It was by then abundantly clear that the *Active* was not returning any time soon — they were the last to have seen it — and that the team was in serious trouble: the rush for skins, like the fever for gold, entailed great secrecy, so, alas for them, no one knew the sealers were there.

They were not rescued until the end of 1813, almost four years later. Having slaughtered their one major food source, the seals, they were near starvation much of the time. A difficult and hazardous trip to the mainland failed to improve their lot. Ultimately, their survival on that little outpost was, we surmise, due to teamwork and Lawrieston's leadership.

Unfortunately, by the time they returned to civilisation, the market for skins had collapsed and they were denied even the compensation of a large payout on their harvest: it had all been for nothing.

On the bright side, the falling returns almost certainly saved the

Motu Taumaka with the hut just visible to the right and the mainland in the distance.

remaining seals. The last season closed in 1875 and sealing was finally banned completely in 1894. That prohibition was further strengthened almost 60 years later by the passing of the Wildlife Act of 1953 and again by the Marine Mammals Protection Act of 1978. Although they were pushed within a whisker of extinction, the fur seals are now in full recovery mode.

BOTH FUR SEALS AND NEW ZEALAND sea lions belong to the family Otariidae, meaning that they have external ears — albeit small — and hump along on all four flippers when on land, unlike their cousins the true seals, which have no external ears and drag their hind flippers. They clamber into astonishing places and can put on quite a burst of speed when it's needed but still appear ungainly and ponderous out of the water.

It's a different story in the ocean, however, where they are agile and graceful, and speed around in explosions of bubbles at up to 50 kilometres per hour. They roll and twist, turn over, around, upside down and back as they scan surface-to-seafloor and 360 degrees in one fluid movement. Little escapes their large, round eyes, whether prey (squid, small mid-water fish and sometimes larger species such as octopus, conger eels, barracuda, mackerel and hoki) or predator (sharks — seven-gill and great whites). The large eyes and long, vibration-detecting, Lorax-like moustaches are

OPEN BAY OPPORTUNISTS

Marooned! Weka were placed on the Open Bay Islands by sealers, ostensibly as a food source — though you have to speculate that this must have been after the time of Lawrieston and his men, for they would surely have eaten them all. These hen-sized, brown birds have wings but have long given up flight, and they're not seabirds. They have powerful homing instincts and are known to swim long distances when sufficiently motivated. Five kilometres back to the distant blue mainland must have been beyond them, however, and now memories of their former home are well gone.

They survive on the islands by picking a living wherever they find it: sand-hoppers in seaweed, shellfish dropped by gulls, scraps of fish, lizards, snails, eggs and young of other birds, dead seals and seal afterbirth. They're below gulls in the pecking order but they're not fussy; they wait their turn.

especially useful at night, their usual feeding time. Their dives average three to five minutes but can be as long as eleven. They have been recorded at depths over 270 metres.

THE NHNZ TELEVISION CREW who filmed the series *Our Big Blue Backyard* spent weeks both on the islands and in the water with the animals, shooting the first weeks and months of the life of a female fur seal.

The Open Bay Islands pong — seals urinate and defecate whenever and wherever. But human sensibilities aside, the islands' hidey-holes, crags and ledges are an ideal maternity ward for the 600-or-so pups that survive their first year: approximately one-third die, casualties of drownings, squashings, separations and desertions. There's a shallow pool on the southwest corner of Taumaka that opens to the sea via a narrow, rocky-sided surge channel, a convenient if turbulent front passage to the island. The pool is where the pups spend most of their days, romping like wet dogs, wriggling, manoeuvring, mouthing, playing, honing swimming skills. Like all youngsters, they are practising and preparing for being adults.

Hungry neighbours. A moulting crested penguin cannot enter the water until its feathers are replaced, while the juvenile seal must wait for its mother's return to feed.

Kina Scollay, underwater cameraman, spent hours with them in the pool, in the channel and in the waters beyond, patiently filming. It was a challenge. Visibility in the churned, sediment-laden southern waters is rarely good and the weather around the islands is fickle. Nevertheless, he and Max Quinn, topside, captured many intimate and special moments.

'I quietly made my way into the colony,' Kina says, 'and lay there for hours and hours. After a while the adult seals forgot I was there. The pups weren't scared and came up to check me out. One even thought I was its mum and tried to suckle under my armpit. It was the coolest!'

One memorable shot shows the young pup's first foray into the water — as a small fish might see it (see p.222). It begins with the skin of the water's underside: gleaming, green-golden, stippled and alive with light and motion. Suddenly, the eight-day pup's whiskery head bursts in, eyes huge and wide, looking from its birth world into its future, the element it will soon consider its own. In the filtered light, it sees bare rock, gravel and small boulders, some encrusted with white-pink algae. There are kina sporting stones on their spikes, green-black mussels, yellow-white anemones, kelp, gold-white starfish, small fish, a spiky-knobbly nudibranch and snails.

It's rich and colourful, full of wonders to explore: *welcome to Open Bay Islands, little seal.*

Low tide: juvenile seals play in the surge pool or snooze on the rocks while diver Kina Scollay films (that's him on the right).

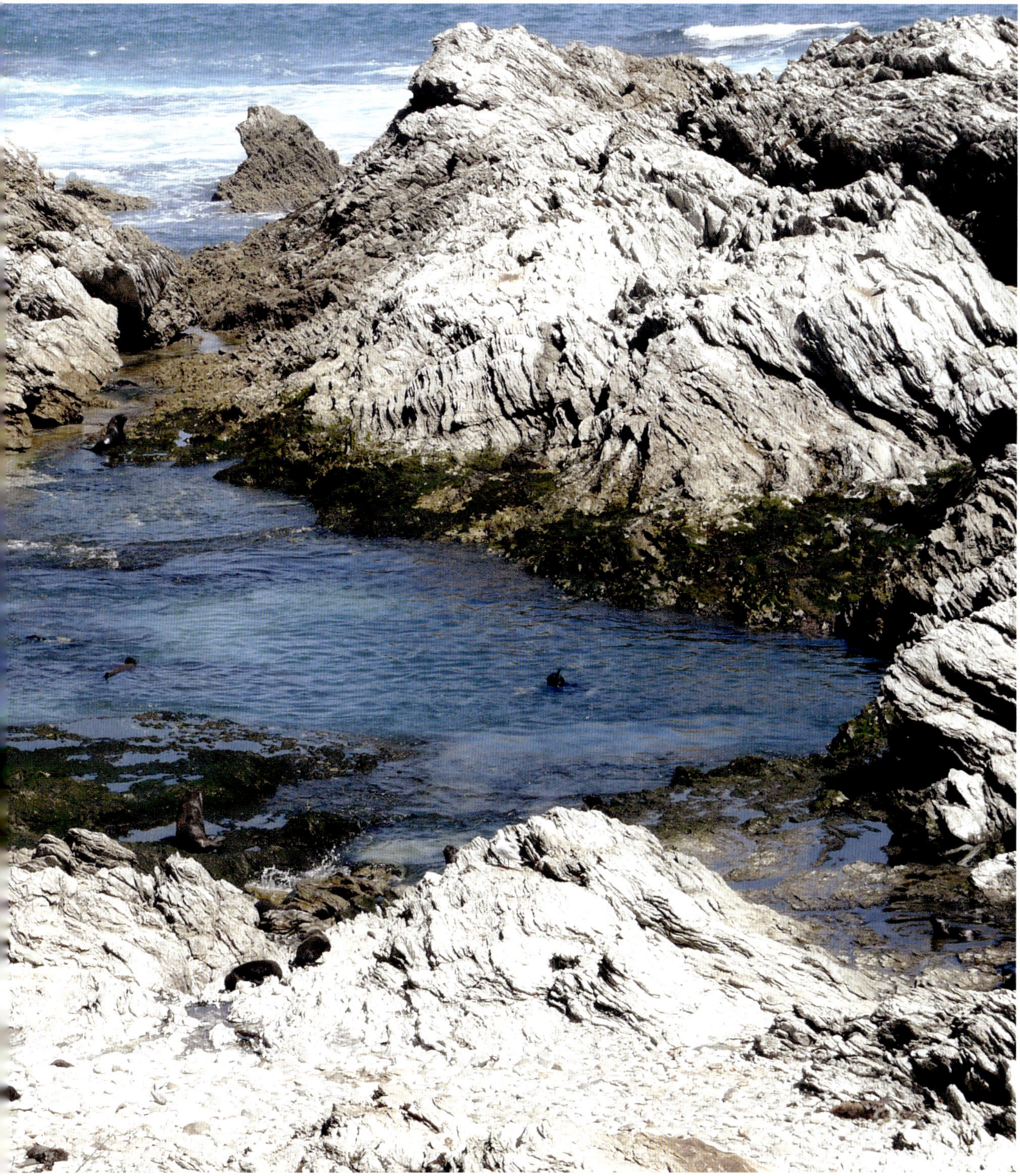

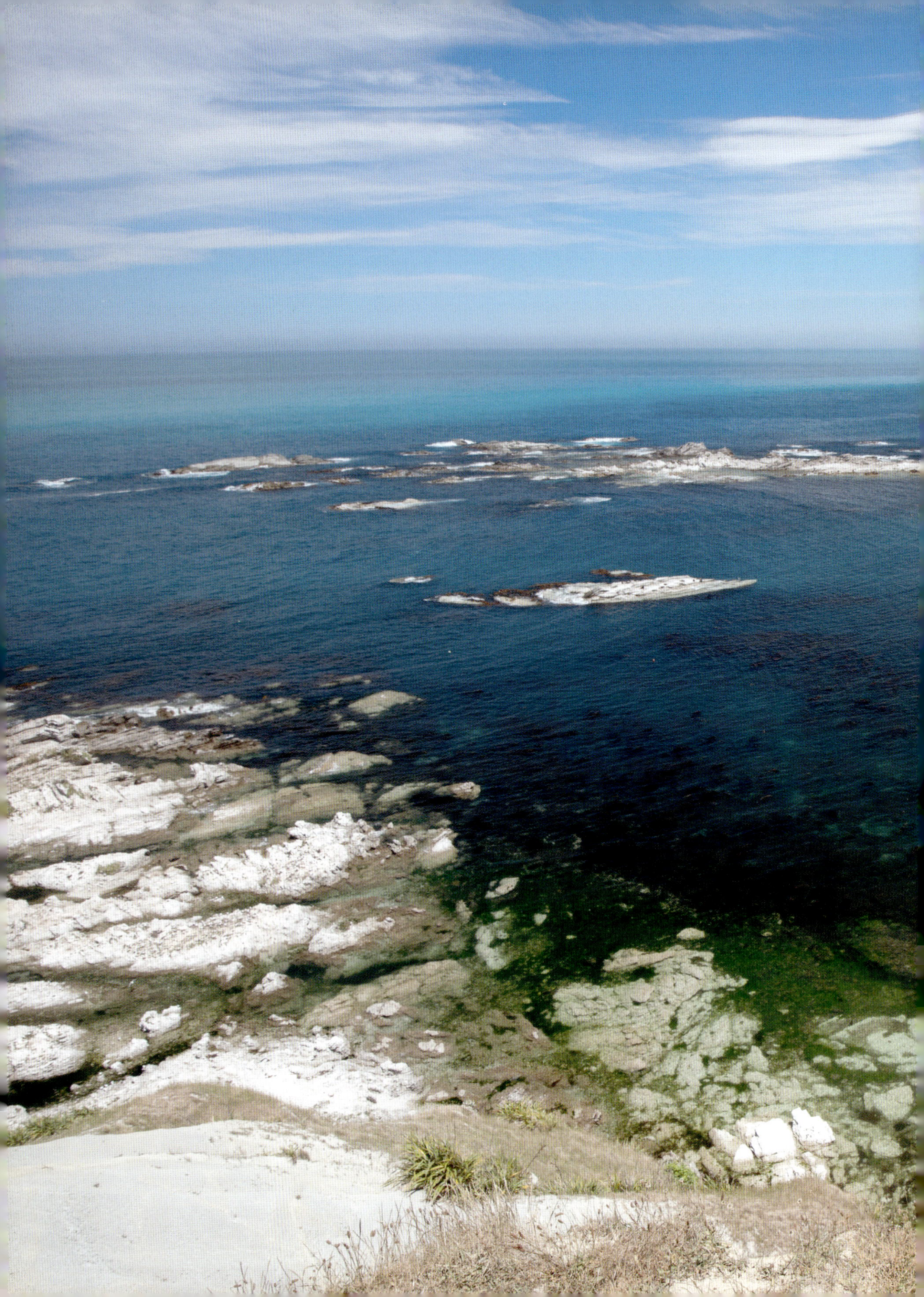

11
CANYONS & PENINSULAS

SOUTH ISLAND EASTSIDE

Ka ora te mauri me te wairua o 'Te Tai-o-Marokura' i a tātou ngā kaitiaki nō te hapori tonu, ka ora hoki ko ngā wai, ko ngā uri, ko ngā taonga a Tangaroa, hei painga mō tātou, ā, mō ngā uri ā muri ake nei. • *From the heights of Te Tapuae-o-Uenuku above, to the depths of Hikurangi below, it is Te Tai-o-Marokura in between that sustains the wellbeing of the people.*

KAIKŌURA: TE KOROWAI MARINE PROTECTION

The Kaikōura Peninsula is 195 kilometres from Punakaiki, on the east side of the South Island. The region's marine setting is unmatched in New Zealand because of its proximity to the deep ocean. The massive Kermadec Trench from north of New Zealand narrows into the Hikurangi Trench off the Wairarapa region, curves in a long arc towards Marlborough and terminates in the Kaikōura Canyon, a deeply incised channel that reaches depths of 1200 metres and slices 60 kilometres across the continental shelf to within a few hundred metres of the shore. Immediately to its south, the broad plateau of the Chatham Rise reaches east.

The waters in the region are influenced by this complex undersea topography as well as by an intricate convergence of currents: north-flowing subantarctic waters meet and combine with south-flowing subtropical waters and are topped up by cold upwellings from the deep ocean. The subantarctic waters are particularly rich in nutrients and plankton and attract a multitude of greedy mouths, from the seabirds that live on and visit Kaikōura's cliffs to the crabs and other invertebrates in the

PREVIOUS:
The white rocks and clear waters of the Kaikōura Peninsula.

rocks and reefs of the nearshore zone and the seals, dolphins and whales that gorge on the surfeit of food further out. It's astonishing to think that, up till now, the only marine protection was a rāhui around Waiopuka Reef on the north side of the peninsula and a closed set net area along the coast.

PROTECTION WAS A LONG TIME COMING. In 1992, the Royal Forest & Bird Protection Society unsuccessfully proposed that part of the Kaikōura Peninsula be set aside as marine reserve; ten years later, alarmed by dwindling fish and shellfish stocks, Te Rūnanga o Kaikōura and the Kaikōura Marine and Coastal Protection Society placed the rāhui on Waiopuka Reef. In 2005, as momentum was building for a more comprehensive solution, a group called 'Te Korowai ō te Tai Marokura/ the Kaikōura Coastal Marine Guardians', or 'Te Korowai', came together under the leadership of Ngāti Kurī of Ngāi Tahu.

As with the West Coast Marine Protection Forum, Te Korowai includes not only Ngāti Kurī but also representatives of commercial and recreational fishers, the Kaikōura Boating Club, local businesses, tourism operators and Forest & Bird. The group was supported by wider agencies including DOC, the Ministries of Primary Industries and the Environment, Environment Canterbury, the Kaikōura District Council and Te Rūnanga o Ngāi Tahu.

Te Korowai spent seven years preparing a *Kaikōura Marine Strategy* central to which is a 'gifts and gains' approach to negotiation and consensus building. One interesting — and unconventional — outcome of this process is an irregular shape to parts of the marine reserve.

In 2012 an integrated package was taken to government and in early March 2014 Prime Minister John Key announced its acceptance and adoption in full. The Kaikōura (Te Tai-o-Marokura) Marine Management Bill was introduced to the House on the 20th of the same month by Hon Dr Nick Smith, who hopes to have it passed and implemented in 2015.

The package is a tapestry of overlapping zones, some contained entirely within others. It includes a marine reserve, a marine mammal sanctuary, three mātaitai reserves and two taiāpure. There will also be changes to recreational fishing regulations and a ministerial advisory committee will be established. In total, this will be the largest marine protected area off the New Zealand mainland.

THE HIKURANGI MARINE RESERVE is at the heart of the proposal. It will cover approximately 10,416 hectares, with a landward boundary at Goose Bay south of Kaikōura township of a mere 1.95 kilometres but a seaward extent of 23.4 kilometres. That takes it into and over the Kaikōura Canyon, a biodiversity hot spot containing far more marine life than ever seen before at such depths. The canyon includes much of the area thought to be critical for sperm whales at Kaikōura while at the landward end there are rocky reefs, boulder outcrops and a sandy-muddy seafloor. All mining, fishing and harvesting is banned but, as with other marine reserves, tourism activities will continue. Management of the reserve will be reviewed after 25 years with a view to assessing its performance and effects on the community.

TE ROHE O TE WHĀNAU PUHA/ Kaikōura Whale Sanctuary has two overlapping portions. The outer sanctuary will include 91 kilometres of shoreline from the Clarence River north of Kaikōura, to just north of Gore Bay down the coast; it will cover an area of 4686 square kilometres; the inner portion will comprise perhaps half that but have more stringent protections. The total sanctuary will extend to around 56 kilometres from shore. As marine mammals are protected anyway, the sanctuary is largely aimed at reducing or eliminating potential impacts of seismic survey activities. The sanctuary is designed primarily for the welfare of the mammals but also, with tourism in mind, is intended to keep the whales coming.

Watching whales has become synonymous with bringing visitors to the town. The great upwelling of nutrients and life in the canyon attracts a year-round population of sperm whales: the biggest toothed whales and the largest predators in the world, they weigh in at 57 tonnes and live for over 60 years. They can stay underwater for over two hours while they hunt giant squid in the deeps of the canyon.

Whale species on migration from Antarctica to the tropics also pass through: 40-tonne humpbacks are often seen over winter, swimming with the characteristic action that gives them their common name, breaching and flipper-slapping, feeding on krill and small fish in the upper layers. Minke whales, pilot whales, blue whales, beaked whales and southern right whales are all occasional visitors.

Whale Watch, an award-winning nature tourism company, was formed in 1987. It revolutionised the fortunes of Kati Kurī Māori, a hapū of Ngāi Tahu, who mortgaged their houses to start the business and began with small, inflatable vessels. The business caught on. Whale Watch had to expand first to a larger boat, *Uruao*, and then another and another. Today their fleet includes custom-designed catamarans departing from a specially constructed marina in South Bay.

They honour the ancestor Paikea, who came to New Zealand on the back of the whale Tohorā and represents the 'spiritual bond between the human world and the natural world . . . and the possibilities that reveal themselves when the world of nature is revered rather than exploited'.

The largest toothed cetacean, a diving sperm whale, in the waters off the Kaikōura coast. Males grow up to 18 metres long. These giants routinely dive to depths over 1000 metres as they hunt giant squid.

ŌHAU POINT NEW ZEALAND FUR SEAL SANCTUARY will be north of Kaikōura, centred on the most significant New Zealand fur seal breeding colony on the South Island's east coast. Access to the shoreline and intertidal seal habitat will be restricted, although visitors will be able to continue to observe the animals from existing viewing platforms.

The proposal also draws on traditional knowledge and customs to ban commercial activity and protect the fisheries of Te Tai-o-Marokura: there will be three mātaitai reserves and two Te Korowai taiāpure local fisheries which will jointly protect Ngāti Kurī food-gathering areas at Mangamaunu, Mussel Rock and Oaro and around the Kaikōura Peninsula and Oaro Blocks/Haumuri. Neither mātaitai reserves nor taiāpure local fisheries will affect public access to the beach or marine environment.

Changes to fishing regulations will reduce recreational fishers' daily bag limits for a range of finfish and shellfish. There will also be a daily limit on the harvest of seaweeds such as karengo and bladder kelp, a complete prohibition on the take of red moki and an increase in minimum legal sizes for blue cod.

Elements of Te Korowai's Kaikōura Marine Strategy that may be implemented in the future include seeking World Heritage status, further integrating land and water management, improving biosecurity, gaining an 'Important Bird Area' classification to lift awareness of seabird life and environments, as well as voluntary codes of practice for commercial fishing and other education and compliance initiatives.

ALWAYS GOING BACKWARDS

It's crowded at the base of the food web where the tiny, bug-eyed squat lobsters (*Munida gregaria* or kōura rangi) live in unnumbered abundance. They resemble lobsters but are, in fact, small crustaceans known as 'false crabs'. The adults live on the seafloor and are rarely seen but their bright red, 30-millimetre offspring are free-swimming and congregate over summer in vast pink-red clouds in the water column, where they are eaten by everything larger than they are.

The juveniles have short bodies and tucked-under tails that they use to propel themselves backwards, like oarsmen always looking aft and never seeing where they are going. They are common as far south as Otago where they sometimes wash ashore in vast quantities.

RED-BILLED GULLS

There are red-billed gulls (*Larus scopulinus*) throughout the Southern Hemisphere. They are an inescapable part of the New Zealand beach experience; unashamed scroungers that can be seen wheeling above seaside cities, in carparks, at restaurants. Perhaps because of the abundant krill and those pink squat lobsters, there's a breeding colony at Kaikōura, the largest in the South Island and third-largest in New Zealand.

Unfortunately for some female gulls in the colony, because they tend to live longer than males, there's a sex-ratio imbalance — 55 percent female to 45 percent male.

The *Our Big Blue Backyard* crew filmed the plight of one of these females: she waited for seven barren years for a mate and finally solved her problem by seducing an already-paired male — he obligingly performed the deed and promptly returned to his mate.

This left her with the prospect of an egg but no means of brooding it or raising a chick, a task that requires equal contribution from two parents. Problem solved: she teamed up with another mateless female and together they successfully raised two offspring.

PLAYING THE SEAWEED GAME: THE DUSKY DOLPHINS OF KAIKŌURA

The *Our Big Blue Backyard* film crew spent some time in the waters off Kaikōura filming dusky dolphins (*Lagenorhynchus obscurus*). These medium-size cetaceans are sleek and immaculate, with white-grey undercolour and blue-black stripes spray-painted nose-to-tail along the back. They are about two metres long and, like their small cousins, the Hector's, their heads slope continuously from blowhole to the tip of the snout. They live up to 25 years and are common in waters south of East Cape.

By day they loaf, rest and play in shallower inshore waters but at sunset they head into the deep Kaikōura Canyon where they capitalise on the massive nightly migration to the surface of zooplankton such as krill and squat lobsters. The dolphins eat the fish that eat the zooplankton, using echolocation to zero in on their prey. Despite their size, they are themselves occasionally preyed on by orca or sharks. Their response is a safety-in-numbers approach, living in pods of up to 100 individuals or using their high-speed swimming and superb agility to evade pursuit.

As the crew filmed, the dolphins swam around them in a graceful, ever-moving tableau of streamlined silver and blue-black bodies. Sometimes, however, they touched, shouldered or bumped into one another and while this was possibly just friendly social contact, it was also likely it was a consequence of them sleep-swimming. When, as all creatures must, dolphins doze off, they can't switch off the absolute requirement of surfacing to breathe, so they rest half the body at a time. One eye droops and one hemisphere of the brain powers down to match. This also, as it were, enables them to keep one eye out for danger.

Duskies are gregarious, constantly whistling, squealing and squeaking to each other and engaging in virtuoso displays of acrobatic ability, with extraordinary leaps and somersaults that are thought to reinforce social order. Sometimes they play with objects, including one of the most readily available resources — seaweed.

It goes like this. If you are a dolphin, you first locate a suitable strand of weed, about a metre long, maybe with a couple of bobbles, and hold it tantalisingly in your mouth. Then, without pause, you let it go and almost imperceptibly catch it, draping it disarmingly several times round your pectoral flipper. You attract immediate attention.

Then you swim a few metres, and nonchalantly drop it. Another of the pod will just as casually scoop it up and dangle it, using momentum to hold it against her flipper, looking for all the world like a woman toting a handbag until she, too, calmly lets go. Hello, the next to take the weed slings it around his dorsal fin until he shrugs it off and . . . picks it up with his tail.

It's endless fun, apparently.

For the fun of it: dusky dolphins in the wake of a vessel leaving Bluff.

BANKS PENINSULA: THE STOREHOUSE OF RĀKAIHAUTŪ

From the skies above, it's instantly clear that Banks Peninsula, a rounded bulge protruding from the flatness of the Canterbury Plains, is a place apart. It was once an island formed from the near-circular remains of two, possibly more, overlapping, extinct volcanoes that were active between eleven and six million years ago. The peaks have long since eroded to a fraction of their original heights, their flooded craters forming today's Lyttelton Harbour to the north and Akaroa Harbour to the south. Each is the epicentre of a starburst of ridges and valleys radiating to the coast and terminating in a multitude of smaller harbours and bays, every one with its unique combination of gravel-sandy beaches, estuaries, reefs, stacks, arches and starkly eroded cliffs and headlands. Like the craters, the bays are drowned valleys, formed when the seas rose 6000 years ago.

The warm Southland Current flows around the peninsula, with giant kelp and bull kelp flourishing in the shallow reefs beyond the harbour entrances. The seabed is shallow, sloping to the north and south of the peninsula, but is relatively steep to the southeast where it drops rapidly to 40 metres.

The peninsula was sometimes known by Māori as Te Pātaka-o-Rākaihautū — 'the storehouse of Rākaihautū'. Ecologically, it is still a storehouse and an island, an enormously diverse physical environment for a matching variety of wildlife, fish, mammals and birds — another marine hot spot, in fact!

PŌHATU

Pōhatu Marine Reserve is on the south coast, east of the entrance to Akaroa Harbour. As marine reserves go, it's small — a mere 215 hectares, the smallest outside Fiordland. Since its opening in 1999, it's the only one on the South Island's east coast. It was a compromise, a temporary solution to an impasse over a proposed reserve within Akaroa Harbour itself. It is named after Pōhatu pā, the traditional home to Kāi Tahu chief Tūtakahikura and his people in pre-European times; it is a taonga for his descendants, Te Rūnaka o Koukourarata of Kāi Tahu.

The reserve includes the bay and a rectangle extending into the open sea around 500 metres beyond its entrance. The bay is approximately two kilometres long by half a kilometre wide, with two sand-shingle beaches. It is a sample of characteristic peninsula coast, with boulders, rock stacks, reefs, kelp forests and cold-temperate reef fish. But there is another good reason for this reserve — it is a breeding site for over 4000 white-flippered penguins. These 30-centimetre-high birds are little blue penguins or kororā (*Eudyptula minor*) but as their name suggests, they have a distinct white edge around each flipper.

White-flippered penguins are found only in Canterbury, mainly at Flea Bay and at Motunau Island at the northern tip of Pegasus Bay. Because they interbreed with little blue penguins, they are not considered to

THE MAN WITH A PASSION FOR LAKES — RĀKAIHAUTŪ

In stories of the early Māori settlement of Aotearoa, Rākaihautū was the captain of *Uruao*, a great waka from Hawaiki, that carried both giants and humans, the ancestors of the Waitaha people. As the party journeyed south, Rākaihautū, who was a bit of a superhuman himself, accomplished a number of extraordinary feats. He lit the first fires in Te Waipounamu and then, because he found the land lacking in inland watering places, moved across the country using his digging stick, Tūwhakarōria, to excavate most of the great lakes. Among the last of his creations were Waihora (Lake Ellesmere) and Wairewa (Lake Forsyth).

At this point, he ceased his roaming, making his home at Akaroa, and planted Tūwhakarōria into the ground: it became Tuhiraki or Mount Bossu, one of the peaks on Banks Peninsula. Rākaihautū's son, Te Rokohouia, was the first to discover the rich seafood resources of the region, including the abundant seagull eggs at Kaikōura.

A little blue penguin (not white-flippered) emerges from its overnight refuge.

be a separate species or subspecies, although genetic analysis in 2006 suggested the possibility, and many locals believe that to be the case. There were once tens of thousands of these seriously cute birds but dogs, cats and mustelids, as well as all the things that people do to modify and destroy penguin living space, have so reduced their numbers that they are considered 'nationally vulnerable' by DOC.

Flea Bay, however, is one of their strongholds. Its steep hills are several hundred metres high and have been replanted in native bush. Predators are being kept at bay through trapping by locals, making it safe for the penguins to spend their nights sheltering and snoozing under tree roots, in crevices and burrows, often some distance from shore.

The reserve is also a safe refuge for many other seabird species including the occasional, equally vulnerable yellow-eyed penguin or hoiho, spotted shags, fairy prions, terns and gulls. Dolphins visit and fur seals are often seen dozing on the rocky platforms.

There's bull kelp at the entrance to the bay; divers and explorers will see colourful mixed algae, mussels, limpets, chitons, sea squirts, sponges, whelks, crabs, cat's eyes, barnacles, periwinkles and tubeworms in shallower waters while the depths are alive with a range of fish such as triplefins, lumpfish, moki, wrasses, butterfish, leatherjackets, lobsters, pāua, blue cod and rockfish. Large octopuses also inhabit the deeper waters.

BANKS PENINSULA MARINE MAMMAL SANCTUARY

The Banks Peninsula Marine Mammal Sanctuary, established in 1988, was New Zealand's first legally protected area for either cetaceans (whales, dolphins and porpoises) or pinnipeds (seals, sea lions and walruses). Curving south from Sumner Head on the north side of Lyttelton Harbour around the peninsula as far as the Rakaia River on the other side of Lake Ellesmere, it first extended four nautical miles from the coast, but in 2008 was increased to 12 nautical miles. It protects 4130 square kilometres.

The sanctuary's focus and reason for being is to protect the endangered Hector's dolphin or upokohue (*Cephalorhynchus hectori*). Hector's grow to one and a half metres long and are the smallest marine dolphin in the world, much loved for their friendly and inquisitive natures and antics such as bow-riding and playing in the wake of boats. Like the Māui's dolphin, Hector's favour inshore waters where they are in danger of accidental death caused by human activities — boat propellers, for example, kill Hector's calves while they are still learning to swim and spending most of their time near the surface. The sanctuary is protected by an array of restrictions including limits to commercial set netting and trawling.

The sanctuary also benefits seals and whales, particularly the southern right whale. These massive creatures, up to 15 metres long and black, with no dorsal fin, often come close to shore.

Southern right whales are readily identified, not only by species but also as individuals, by the patterns of the rough patches of skin or callosities on their heads.

AKAROA

The Minister of Conservation, Hon Dr Nick Smith, opened Akaroa Marine Reserve on World Oceans Day, 8 June 2014. The reserve had been a long time in the making, undergoing an on-again, off-again, sometimes acrimonious, process that has consumed 17 years and passed under the noses of no fewer than six different ministers (Dr Smith twice).

The new reserve is alongside an area known as Dan Rogers Bluff on the eastern side of the Akaroa Harbour entrance, a spot with volcanic cliffs, sea caves — including the largest, Cathedral Cave — and stacks that fall through the water to the seabed. There are encrusting marine communities, huge

Akaroa Harbour on Banks Peninsula, with Pōhatu Marine Reserve just out of shot to the right.

boulders, overhangs, spectacular scenery and fish life to match. The peninsula's many cruise boats frequently bring tourists to this area to watch and, in some cases, swim with the dolphins and penguins.

As elsewhere, the initial proposal was trimmed from 530 hectares to 475 to accommodate customary and recreational fishers. However, the removed section will still be under some degree of protection, albeit lesser, because it will be part of the Akaroa Harbour Taiāpure, which will occupy the remaining 90 percent of the harbour and extend around the outer coast as far as Flea Bay. Fishing will be permitted within the taiāpure but will be subject to restrictions determined by a committee whose membership is drawn from local rūnanga and recreational fishers.

The reserve will be adjacent to, and benefit by its proximity to, three small terrestrial reserves: Nīkau Palm Gully, Dan Rogers Creek Nature Reserve and the historic Akaroa Head Lighthouse Reserve. It is an important feeding, breeding and roosting habitat for seabirds such as terns, gulls, white-flippered penguins and spotted shags.

And now the reserve is open, it will only get better.

The Minister of Conservation, Dr Nick Smith, chats with the locals in Akaroa Harbour, 2013.

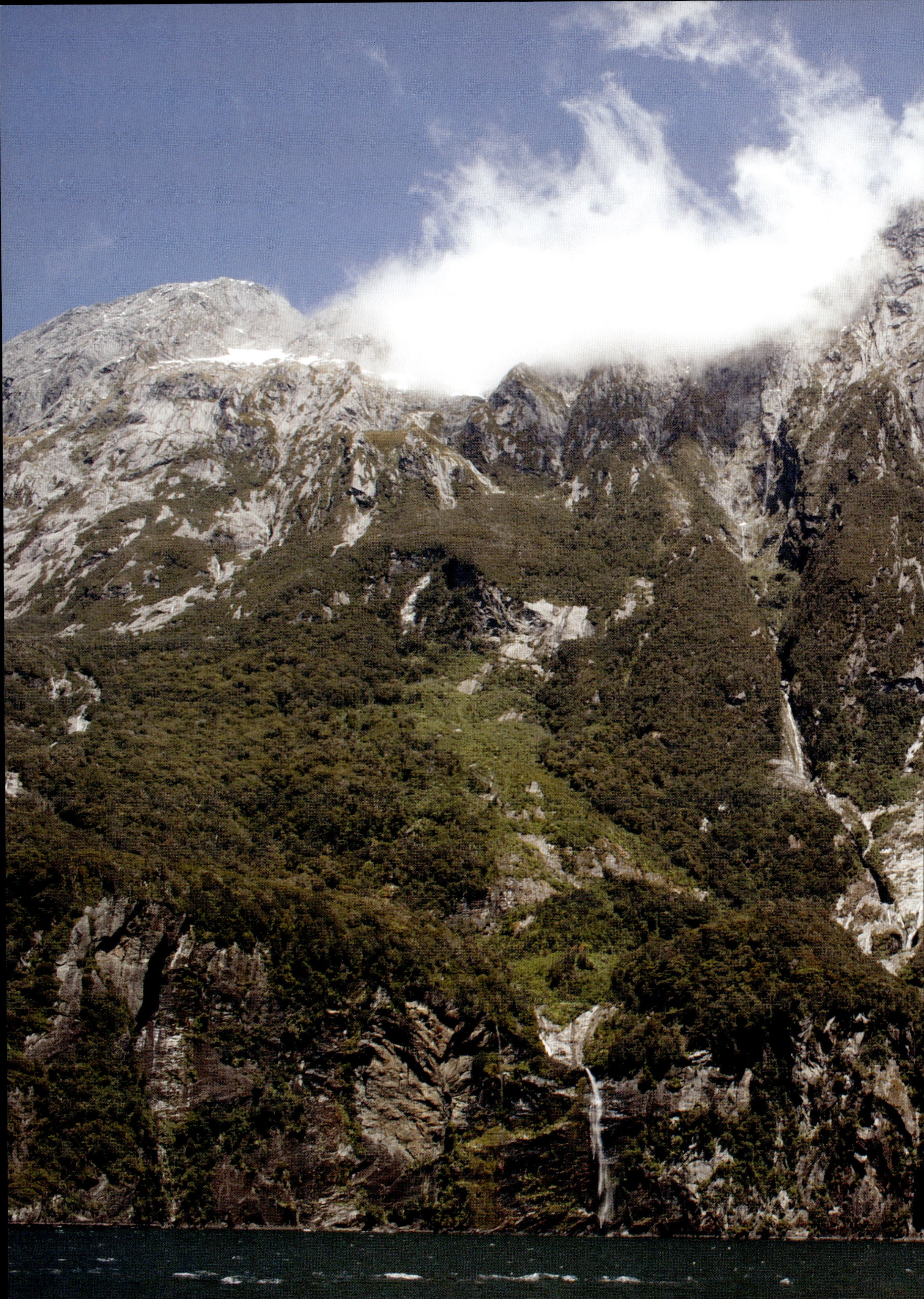

12
FIORDS & MUTTONBIRDS

SOUTH OF THE SOUTH

PREVIOUS:
Large volumes of water continually tumbling from Fiordland's peaks are strained through leaf litter and fall into the fiords.

—

The blue-green backyard that conceals the secret of the fiords.

—

Tucked away in the remote, uninhabited, southwest corner of the South Island, there is a nest of not one or two but *ten* marine reserves. Two, Piopiotahi (Milford) and Te Awaatu Channel (the Gut, in Doubtful Sound), were established in 1993, with the other eight added in 2005. They are a marine complement to this country's largest national park, Fiordland. They range in size from 93 to 3672 hectares, and in total include over 10,000 hectares of inner-fiord marine habitat.

From north to south, they are: Piopiotahi in Milford Sound, Te Hāpua in Sutherland Sound, Hāwea (Clio Rocks) in Bligh Sound, Kahukura (Gold Arm) in Charles Sound, Kutu Parera (Gaer Arm) in Bradshaw Sound, Te Awaatu Channel (The Gut) in Doubtful Sound, Taipari Roa (Elizabeth Island) in Doubtful Sound, Moana Uta in Wet Jacket Arm between Breaksea Sound and Dusky Sound, Taumoana (Five Fingers Peninsula) in Dusky Sound and Te Tapuwae-o-Hua (Long Sound) in Preservation Inlet.

Until the 1970s, when divers first began to descend into the depths of the fiords as part of the work on the Manapōuri Power Station and tailrace tunnel, people were largely unaware of the world hidden beneath the surface of the region's 14 fiords. From above, the waters appeared pristine and beautiful but not otherwise remarkable. Little did they know.

FIORDLAND: SECRET WORLD

Every detail in the Fiordland story knits into everything else in a chain of cause and effect.

First, the physical setting. The mountains are a massif of diorite, granite and gneiss, and contain some of New Zealand's oldest known rocks, at 400–500 million years old. Forged deep underground, they are crystalline, hard and resistant to erosion. As a result, Fiordland's valleys and peaks are often sharp and steep-walled and, although they are densely forested with mature stands of southern beech and podocarps, there is scant topsoil.

The only thing that could move the mountains was the greater power of slowly grinding rivers of ice: over 200,000 years, successive ice ages ripped sheer-sided, U-shaped basins through the massif as they bulldozed ridges of rock debris before them to the coast. In time, when the ice melted and sea levels rose, the basins flooded and became the extensive system of fiords we know today. Their average length is 24 kilometres and they are deep — some to 400 metres. Their sea mouths are partially blocked by debris sills from 30 to 145 metres deep, that impede the in–out flow of ocean waters.

Then there's the climate. Fiordland is the wettest corner of New Zealand, receiving an annual *average* of seven metres of rainfall. It cascades down those steep sides, into rivers and streams and ultimately, the fiords. The water is relatively clear, carrying little sediment because of the forest cover and lack of topsoil but is stained a strong-ale golden-brown by tannins from decaying vegetation.

Combine these elements, and interesting things happen. The vast quantity of freshwater from the mountains is less dense than seawater and because there's little mixing in the relative shelter of the fiords, it lies on top of the salt water in a richly coloured layer that can be as much as ten metres

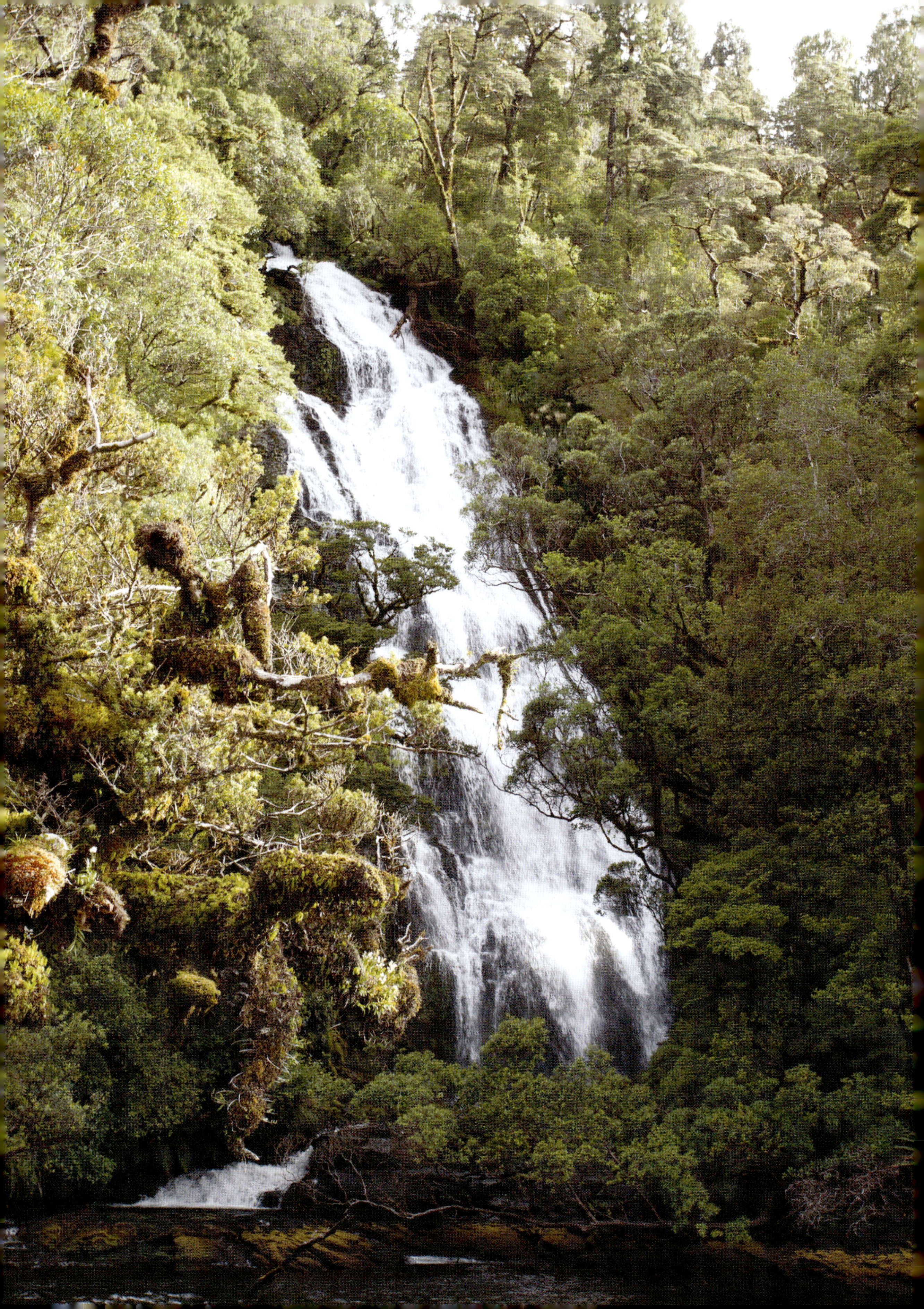

thick, depending on the weather. This layer is so discoloured that very little light penetrates, meaning almost no sun-loving seaweed at depths where it would otherwise grow. In its place, marvellously, in a phenomenon termed 'deep water emergence', the waters *below* the buoyant fresh-to-low-salinity layer harbour an assortment of species that would usually be found only in the deepest of the deeps.

This zone only slowly becomes more saline as it deepens. First, there are organisms tolerant of low salinity, such as black lichens, tufted red algae, barnacles, deep-green algae and an ensemble of freshwater snails, tiny shrimp-like crustaceans, Neptune's necklace seaweed and blue mussels.

Then there's a relatively empty zone where the water is more evenly blended but is uncomfortable for low-salinity lovers and high-salinity specialists alike: only creatures with broad tolerances, such as blue mussels, barnacles, some sponges, bryozoans, tubeworms and some algae survive.

It's below that, however, in the truly saline environment, that the excitement begins. For around 40 metres, it's magic. The fiord walls are adorned with bryozoans, nudibranchs, lamp shells, sponges, starfishes, urchins, corals, tubeworms, sea pens, gorgonian fans, feather stars, anemones, crayfish. There are over 150 species of fish as well as passing and resident bottlenose dolphins.

Sometimes a landslide tips trees and rocks into the water from the cliffs above, stripping the walls below in one stroke. There are, however, places that are immune to this periodic destruction — small submarine islands that were impervious even to the might of the glaciers. Divers and scientists call them 'China Shops' (there are 23) places where everything is so fragile that you wouldn't want to drop a craypot or an anchor, and even diving calls for extreme caution to ensure against inadvertent damage.

OPPOSITE: Myriad waterfalls deliver tannin-stained freshwater to the fiords.

Brittle stars come in a multitude of colours and patterns.

THE STARS OF THE CHINA SHOPS and of the fiords in general are corals, especially, but not exclusively, the light-shy black coral *Antipathes fiordensis*. When the coral is alive, the dark-coloured skeleton that gives it its name is obscured by tiny, interconnected but individual, anemone-like creatures called 'polyps', each of which has six stumpy, non-retractable tentacles that comb the water for microscopic plankton.

The corals are as elegant and as delicate as spun glass: some take the forms of winter skeletons of terrestrial deciduous trees while others resemble whips, fans or feathers. Some are adorned by colourful, rubbery-looking bands twined tightly around limbs and branches — yellow, red-brown, black-and-white, often-striped brittle or snake stars, long-armed relatives of starfish and kina. They have a mutually beneficial relationship with the coral, using its structure in return — it's thought — for keeping it clear of sediment. They unwind at night to feed on plankton.

Black corals grow very slowly; some larger individuals, up to five metres tall, are estimated to be hundreds of years old. There may be over seven million colonies of these extraordinary animals in the fiords, most of them in that magic 40-metre zone; if you want to see any of New Zealand's other black coral species — there are over 50 — you need to find a way to get down to between 200 and 1000 metres! Black coral colonies overseas have been destroyed by illegal harvest for the manufacture of expensive jewellery. Fiordland's species are protected by national and international law.

Black coral, brittle stars, anemones and passing locals — an underwater wonderland.

LAMPS, PENS & FEATHER-DUSTERS

As well as black corals, the fiords are internationally important for brachiopods or lamp shells, with one of the largest concentrations in the world — up to 500 individuals per square metre in some places. Brachiopods were abundant 570 million years ago when there were something like 30,000 species — they are actually more common today as fossils than living animals: around 300 species survive, 32 of them in New Zealand waters. They look like clams but are otherwise very different. Their name comes from their resemblance to an ancient Roman lamp.

Sea pens are named for their resemblance to quills — although not all of their order are feathery. They are octocorals — their polyps have eight tentacles. One single polyp makes up the central rib or shaft, with rows of feather-tipped feeding polyps to either side. When the body is pumped full of seawater, a sea pen stands about 300 millimetres high. Sea pens put on a spectacular nocturnal light show, with pulses of electric-green bioluminescence rippling across their surface.

As diver Dave Abbott discovered when he observed a fanworm bed (see p.72), tubeworms rapidly withdraw into their calcareous tubes when disturbed. This one is a feather-duster (*Protula bispiralis*).

FIORDLAND'S FIRST TWO MARINE RESERVES were proposed by the New Zealand Federation of Commercial Fishermen. However, no two fiords are the same and it was evident that all were under a range of pressures calling not only for more reserves but other protective measures. Local people also wanted to be involved.

In 1995 a forum representing commercial and recreational fishers, charter boat and tourism operators, environmentalists, marine scientists, community and tangata whenua (Ngāi Tahu) formed the group that ultimately became the Fiordland Marine Guardians.

The guardians developed the *Fiordland Marine Conservation Strategy* which identified sites for an additional eight reserves and also, using the same 'gifts and gains' approach as was later employed at Kaikōura, negotiated a suite of other measures with stakeholder groups, including reducing fish and shellfish quotas for some species and stopping fishing for others altogether. It was published in draft form in 2002.

Three years later, the Fiordland (Te Moana-o-Atawhenua) Marine Management Act 2005 was passed. As well as the eight new marine reserves, it amended fisheries regulations for non-commercial harvesting, excluded commercial fishing from large areas of the internal waters of Fiordland and implemented a range of other measures including formally recognising the guardians group as an advisory body. It also gave special protection to the 10 China Shops that fall outside the marine reserves, including restrictions on anchoring or mooring in their vicinity.

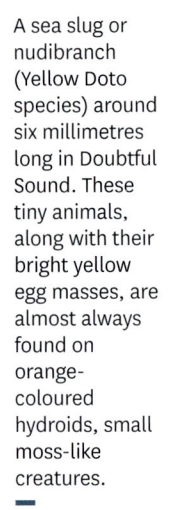

A sea slug or nudibranch (Yellow Doto species) around six millimetres long in Doubtful Sound. These tiny animals, along with their bright yellow egg masses, are almost always found on orange-coloured hydroids, small moss-like creatures.

MARKING THE DIFFERENCE

The usual signs for marine reserves are yellow triangles but the markers for the Fiordland reserves are poupou designed by Cliff Whiting, carved by Bubba Thompson and erected by the Fiordland Marine Guardians and the iwi Ngāi Tahu, Kāti Māmoe and Waitaha. They are more in keeping with the wilderness values of the region and are kaitiaki, evoking 'ancestral connections with Fiordland, the deities, the explorers, the Whānau, Whānui who have travelled these pathways before us.'

Each of the poupou is unique, with small and subtle differences from the others.

The poupou for Wet Jacket Arm (right) and Charles Sound (below).

ULVA ISLAND/TE WHARAWHARA

The Stewart Island/Rakiura instalment of the television series *Our Big Blue Backyard* begins with two brief, scene-setting sequences. The first, which weaves through the episode like a refrain, is the blunt snout, toothy gape and vacant eyes of a great white shark; the other is an aerial shot of Paterson Inlet at dusk.

IT'S ESTIMATED THAT A POPULATION of between 100 and 200 great white sharks (a.k.a. white sharks or *Carcharodon carcharias*) cruise the waters around Stewart Island over summer months. They have been protected in New Zealand waters since 2007 but are slow breeders, producing around 10 pups per litter and breed every two to three years. It takes them up to 20 years to mature and they may live as long as 50 years. It was thought until recently that these magnificent fish, which may weigh as much as one tonne and have a top speed of around 40 kilometres per hour, spend their winters in cooler regions but no one really knew, and there was a pressing need to find out: even an apex predator can't compete against accidental entanglement in set nets or lines and, unless you know where a creature goes and how it behaves, you can't safeguard it.

Beginning in 2005, NIWA scientists began to address that situation. Over a number of years, they attached various kinds of electronic tags to the animals' fins — a delicate exercise in itself, because as anyone who has seen *Jaws* knows, these beasts are extremely dangerous. The data gathered provided insight not only into the complex lives of individual sharks —

many of which received names, such as Ella, Shack, Slash, Geoff and Dave — but of the population as a whole. Of particular interest was the discovery that the sharks travel up to 3300 kilometres in winter, as far afield as the Great Barrier Reef, New Caledonia, Fiji and Tonga. Some dive to great depths — Dave, a 4.8-metre male, has the great white shark world record for a dive of 1245 metres. It's not known exactly what he was doing down there but it is likely that he was hunting squid and fish.

While in the Stewart Island area, the great whites snack on the occasional seabird that is feeding on the surface but for their main course they are mostly interested in New Zealand fur seals from the large colonies in the area.

Ella, Shack, Geoff or Dave? One of Stewart Island's great white sharks.

STEWART ISLAND'S MĀORI NAME is Rakiura, or 'glowing sky', a reference to vivid dawns and sunsets, their effect doubled by reflection on the still waters of the island's largest harbour, Paterson Inlet or Whaka-a-Te Wera — named after Te Wera, a Ngāi Tahu leader who lived on its shores prior to the arrival of the first whalers and sealers. It is the site of our final inshore reserve, Ulva Island (Te Wharawhara) Marine Reserve.

Like the fiords, but a fraction of their depth at an average 20 metres, the inlet is an ancient, submerged, rock-walled river valley on the eastern side of the island. Its upper reaches extend 16 kilometres into Rakiura's heart, to the tidal estuaries of Freshwater and Rakeāhua rivers. It is surrounded by low mountains and bush-clad hills with tree cover from ridge to shoreline, ensuring exceptionally clear waters below — there's little sediment and no pollutants. The inlet is almost enclosed and is sheltered from the often stormy waters of Foveaux Strait by a long peninsula called The Neck, as well as by Ulva Island and two smaller islands.

The 10,000-hectare inlet as a whole is semi-protected: since December 2004, aside from the marine reserve and a marine farming area, it has been Te Whaka-a-Te Wera (Paterson Inlet) Mātaitai Reserve, established in recognition of the inlet's centuries-old value to Rakiura Māori for mahinga kai. Significant traditional fishing and food-gathering areas are maintained by the prohibition of commercial fishing and restrictions or bans on bag limits, fish and shellfish sizes, hook sizes, craypots, drag nets, set nets and dredges.

By contrast, the marine reserve is, of course, 100 percent 'no take'. It is in three parts, centred on and complementing Ulva Island, itself a 266-hectare, predator-free open sanctuary known for its prolific bird life including Stewart Island weka, South Island saddlebacks, Stewart Island robin, brown creeper and Stewart Island brown kiwi or tokoeka.

The reserve includes representative samples of the inlet's habitats including different combinations of direction, substrate, slope, depth and exposure to waves. As in the fiords, it is one of the few places in the world where normally depth-loving brachiopods or lamp shells are found in large numbers in relatively shallow water. The inlet is also relatively easy to get to and is of long-standing interest and value to the scientific community.

Stewart Island/Rakiura has more varieties of seaweed than anywhere in New Zealand, with 270 species inside the inlet, including bull and bladder kelp closer to its mouth and meadows of small red seaweeds on the sand seafloor. All provide food, shelter and a nursery area for many communities of invertebrates and at least 56 marine fish species including blue cod, blue and red moki, butterfish, banded and scarlet wrasses, ling, leatherjacket, thornfish, southern pigfish, butterfly and sea perch, dogfish, carpet sharks, electric rays and skates as well as pāua, scallops, crayfish and kina.

The islands, hills and forested shores of Paterson Inlet.

NEW ZEALAND'S SEAHORSE

They are found all around the New Zealand coast but are so cryptic — so well camouflaged — that they are not easily or often seen. They are New Zealand's only species of seahorse or manaia, one of approximately 32 worldwide (ours is *Hippocampus abdominalis*). They are also, at around 300 millimetres, one of the largest. And although they are fish, their equine-shaped heads earn them a special place in our hearts and folklore.

The seahorse filmed by the *Our Big Blue Backyard* crew around Stewart Island is a daffodil-yellow, all the better to blend with the seaweed beds where it hangs out, curling its prehensile tail around a convenient strand and waiting for a small piece of prey to drift by. It has no teeth — just a mouth at the end of its long snout, that sucks small crustaceans directly into its continuous sort of in-one-end-out-the-other digestive tract (it has no proper stomach either). Its eyes swivel independently: in this fish-eat-fish world, it's good to be alert.

Seahorses have an unconventional, unfish-like reproductive arrangement: after an elaborate courtship that includes increasing posturing and repeated changes of colour brightness — *heightened natural glow* — the pair swim to the surface, heads pointing up and tails pointing down, spiralling, belly to belly. The female then transfers her eggs to the prominent, whitish pouch on the male's midriff and that's her part complete. He fertilises them and broods them for around 30 days, after which he ejects a cloud of, on average, 270 miniature seahorses from 13 to 22 millimetres long, their tiny horsey faces just visible. They are on their own.

Unusually for kiwi, which are otherwise strictly forest-dwellers, Stewart Island's tokoeka have extended their range to the coast and may be seen on a starlit night fossicking among kelp and driftwood for sand-hoppers, going so far as to plunge bills — and sometimes heads — deep into the sand. *What's so remarkable about that?* It's a great example, you might think, of adaptive behaviour. The only potential problem is that kiwi nostrils are uniquely sited in the *tip* of their bills — perfect for scavenging in leaf litter, but likely to clog in sand.

THE STORY OF THE WATERS of Stewart Island/Rakiura is not complete without mention of seabirds, especially sooty shearwaters (*Puffinus griseus*), also known as tītī or muttonbird, the latter for their flavour when fresh. These medium-sized birds (40–46 centimetres long) breed in summer on islands all around New Zealand but are most numerous in the south where they sometimes flock in tens of thousands. They are long-distance migrants and in the southern winter fly north to the Arctic.

Tītī roost and breed in vast numbers on three chains of islands around Rakiura. Young birds, on the verge of taking to the air, are considered a delicacy by descendants of Rakiura Māori who harvest around 400,000 from 1 April to 31 May each year for eating fresh or salting for longer keeping. Hone Tuwhare, whose poem opens this book, looked forward every year to receiving a few buckets of tītī. They were one thing this normally generous man did *not* offer to share.

Tītī, or sooty shearwaters, flock around the muttonbird islands in their tens of thousands.

CAMERAMAN DAVE ABBOTT and his dive buddy, NHNZ intern Andrew Scott, share memorable experiences from filming around the island.

Stewart Island has some amazing marine creatures in its cool green waters, from alien red sea cucumbers to great white sharks. While filming for this episode we had a couple of interesting underwater encounters with some of its larger marine inhabitants. Fortunately the only white sharks we saw over the course of this shoot were from inside a cage!

On one dive near the Heron River we were quietly filming trumpeter and moki amongst the weed beds, when I sensed a dark shadow right on the edge of my mask. I knew Andy was behind me but when I turned my head, I was looking straight into the face of a large grinning seven-gill shark! She brushed past me as though I was a commuter that had got in her way on the sidewalk and swam slowly off, giving me just enough time to get an 'away shot' as she disappeared into the green gloom — a very cool encounter!

A New Zealand (Hooker's) sea lion filmed in the waters around Auckland Islands in the Subantarctic Islands.

On another dive we were filming on the sand edge just outside a beautiful tall kelp bed, when a big dark shape came rocketing past in a stream of bubbles at close range, circled unbelievably fast and came back with toothy mouth agape! It was a big Hooker's sea lion who obviously didn't want us around in 'his' bay. He proceeded to charge us repeatedly, getting more and more aggressive and trying to nip at our arms and fins.

Finally, after enduring this for ten minutes, unable to concentrate on filming anything else and tired of being driven into the kelp and entangled, we bailed back to the shallows and surfaced, hopefully with some useable sequences out of the dive!

Strong currents along Stewart Island's southwest coast.

13
WAY, WAY OFFSHORE

THE KERMADEC & SUBANTARCTIC ISLANDS

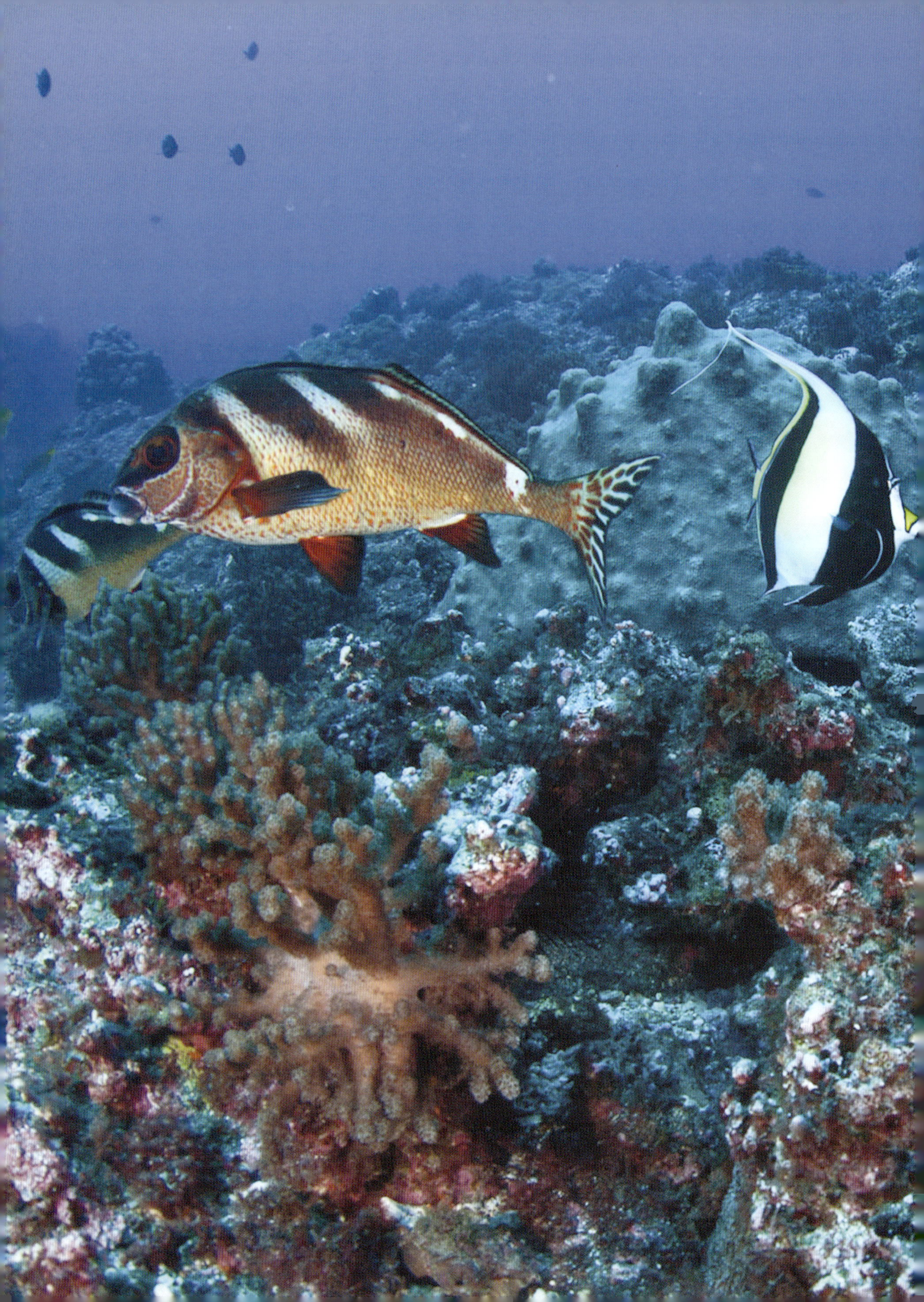

Our final marine reserves are places most of us will never see. The first, the 745,000-hectare Kermadec Islands Marine Reserve, is almost 1500 kilometres northeast of Wellington while the 484,000-hectare Auckland Islands (Motu Maha) Marine Reserve is at the opposite extreme, 1200 kilometres from Wellington, in the far south. Three new offshore reserves were added in early 2014, covering an additional 435,000 hectares: the Antipodes (Moutere Mahue), Bounty (Moutere Hauriri) and Campbell (Moutere Ihupuku) Islands marine reserves.

KERMADEC ISLANDS

In 1954, when the British government was seeking an out-of-the-way spot to test a hydrogen bomb, their eyes fell on the Kermadec Islands. Had they gone ahead, things may have been a little more explosive than they anticipated, however, because although there had been an eruption in the area as late as 1870, they didn't realise they were contemplating bombing an active volcano . . . fortunately, they were refused permission.

WHAT WE KNOW as the Kermadec Islands are the upper peaks of a number of substantial underwater volcanoes. They are towards the middle of an extensive chain of around 80 mostly submarine seamounts and volcanoes dotted in an arc to the west of the Kermadec Ridge, which runs like a massive welt in the seafloor for 2600 kilometres from New Zealand's White Island to Tonga. The cause, again, is that titanic duo, the pushy Pacific Plate and the resistant Australian Plate: as the Pacific dives beneath

PREVIOUS:
An Antipodean albatross in its element in the vicinity of the Auckland Islands.
—
Exotic and colourful: a painted moki (left) and a Moorish idol in the waters around the Kermadecs.
—

the Australian, it furrows out the 10,000-metre-deep Kermadec Trench, rolling the seafloor up to form the ridge on its western side. It is a region of great instability, its young, steep-sided volcanoes prone to submarine rumblings and burpings, eruptions and earthquakes.

The Kermadec portion of the ridge is a series of small islands and rocks spread over 240 kilometres. The largest, Raoul, is the most active volcano and is inhabited some of the time, with freshwater, a field station and living quarters on its northern shore used and maintained by DOC. A few kilometres off its northeast coast, there are three groups of islets, Meyer Islands, Herald Islets and Napier and Nugent islands. Macauley Island and Haszard Island are about 110 kilometres to its southwest, with Curtis and Cheeseman islands a further 35 kilometres south and L'Esperance Rock 80 kilometres further south again.

The Kermadec Islands were declared a nature reserve in 1937 and the marine reserve was added in 1990. It is New Zealand's largest, single 'no-take' zone; it encircles each island group to a distance of 12 nautical miles (just over 22 kilometres) and includes abyssal depths to 3000 metres. Moves are currently afoot to extend protection to 200 nautical miles and create the Kermadec Ocean Sanctuary. If successful, it will be the largest no-take reserve in the world (620,000 square kilometres).

THE KERMADECS ARE TRUE OCEANIC ISLANDS, having never been joined to any other landmass; as a consequence, a unique assemblage of plants and animals has evolved, both above and below the waterline, a 'marine oasis in an ocean desert,' according to Dr Tom Trnski from Auckland Museum. The islands are up to five degrees closer to the equator than Cape Rēinga, and occasionally experience cyclones, but the climate is otherwise placid and mild and the waters warm. Marine life is diverse, with many species at the limits of their range from either direction — temperate or subtropical. Because the area was too isolated to have been heavily fished before it became 'no take', it required little recovery and consequently is an ecosystem in balance, with all animals present in natural numbers, from the numerous sharks to the tiniest crustaceans.

However, compared with New Zealand's other reserves, there are a number of habitats and species that are not present. There are no sheltered bays; no fringing reefs, lagoons or estuaries; no large kelp forests and no kina; and although there are 17 species of reef corals, seven soft corals and coral colonies up to 2.4 metres in diameter, the waters are too cool for full reef building.

After visiting the Kermadecs for the first time, diver and underwater film-maker Steve Hathaway observed:

A Japanese fishing vessel wrecked on the steeply-shelving shore at Denham Bay, Raoul Island.

> *How different the underwater landscape looked and felt compared with the rest of New Zealand . . . It was especially strange not to see large seaweeds covering the rocks. It seemed to be a barren moonscape until we looked closely and saw rocks covered with hard and soft coral and smaller tufting seaweeds — a myriad of life. What a difference just a couple of degrees' water temperature can make. It was remarkable too to see large schools of fish such as blue maomao, which are common around northern New Zealand, alongside tropical species.*

He was particularly impressed by the sharks. 'It's a real privilege to see one in New Zealand waters but here, at times, there are over 20 below our fins! It's a great sign of a pristine marine environment,' he said.

Despite the absence of kelp, there are more than 165 other species of algae. Also of note are a giant limpet and a crown of thorns starfish, as well as herbivorous fish including caramel drummer, Kermadec scalyfin and Kermadec triplefin. Large predators such as Galapagos sharks and kingfish are abundant but the undisputed stars of the reserve are the world's only major population of spotted black grouper (*Ephinephelus daemelii*), a territorial reef fish that grows close to two metres and is thought to live over 50 years.

They are magnificent creatures with a great, unhurried presence and a strong sense of curiosity. Like the little seahorse, they have the trick of rapid colour change, from almost white to almost black (or the reverse) and many shades of grey in between. Wade Doak comments that he has watched one move from sand to rock, and transform itself to match from one to the other. In fact, little is known about the biology of these fishes other than that they are slow growing and change gender as they go through life, becoming male in their later years. They are protected in all New Zealand waters.

The Kermadecs are also a transit zone for migratory species such as humpback whales, which are among seven whale species present, including sperm whales. The humpbacks journey from Antarctica to the tropics in winter to breed, and between late August and early November swim south again with their calves, passing Raoul Island along the way. Five of the world's seven sea turtle species also pass through the islands' waters.

And of course, there are seabirds — 35 species, adding up to between ten and 15 million individuals, breeding on the islands and feeding from their seas, making the reserve an internationally important refuge. Most

Majestic and unhurried: a spotted black grouper.

are tropical or subtropical including the red-tailed tropicbird, the masked booby, two species of noddy, terns and the grey ternlet. A number of New Zealand's endemic seabirds breed here, including the white-naped petrel, Kermadec little shearwater, Kermadec storm petrel, New Zealand sooty tern and the world's largest population of black-winged petrels.

Two-spot demoiselles pass above an encrusted rock and a crown of thorns sea star.

FOLLOWING SIR PETER

No cellphone! No phone! No internet! No television! *No problem!* From 8 to 19 August 2012, a group of 30 young people joined a team of 25 scientists, business leaders and adventurers from across New Zealand to travel to the Kermadecs on the inaugural Young Blake Expeditions voyage. Sir Peter didn't ever visit the islands himself, but the expedition was made in his spirit, to inspire and mobilise a new generation of Kiwi leaders and environmental ambassadors.

It was, the young voyagers agreed, life changing. Among other things, they overcame seasickness; shared the sea with sharks; snorkelled with turtles, giant kingfish, wrasses, needlefish, black spotted grouper and various other tropical fish; buddied with scientists to assist with shark tagging, dolphin DNA sampling and plankton monitoring; rescued a Kermadec storm petrel; learned about the navy; saw dolphins and humpbacks; stayed on and trekked across Raoul Island; were awestruck by the region's intensely blue waters; appreciated what it means to be somewhere truly remote; and in the end, exhausted all superlatives. There were not even any obvious signs of *nomophobia* (no-mobile).

Rose Mickleson of Havelock North described Raoul as 'archaic, untamed and dangerous', while Felix Bornholdt of Wellington was astounded by the colour of the water: 'a deep, rich blue, both inviting and also somewhat unnerving.' For him, 'the sense of space and isolation is a huge presence; it is both humbling and somewhat surreal to be in a place like this, and you often find that you need to remind yourself that you're moored off an island 1000 kilometres away from civilisation and sitting on top of a ten-kilometre deep trench.'

Time to make a splash. Samara Nicholas is at centre.

HE SAID IT

Sir Peter Blake (1948–2001) was literally and figuratively a giant of our times. A commanding figure at 1.93 metres tall, he dedicated his life to the sea — in the first instance, as a supreme yachtsman, and in his later years, as a conservationist.

In 2000 he established 'Blakexpeditions' with the aim of educating and inspiring people to care about the oceans and its creatures. In 2001 he became a Special Envoy for the United Nations Environment Programme. People around the world were horrified when he was killed in early December of that same year while defending his vessel *Seamaster* and its crew against pirates near the mouth of the Amazon in Brazil.

In my first couple of Round the World races, our yachts, when in the Southern Ocean, would be surrounded by large albatross, day after day, in all weathers. As the years went by (I raced every four years or so through the same waters), I noticed there were fewer and fewer of these great birds. The last time through the Indian Ocean, in 1994, we were lucky to see one large albatross a week. Their numbers have been decimated, mainly by indiscriminate fishing techniques. And they are being killed at a faster and faster rate. It has to stop or very soon we will have killed off one of the most beautiful and awe-inspiring creatures on the planet.

I have also been fortunate enough to have had encounters with whales that have left me with no doubt as to their intelligence and understanding.

I have watched a large female fin whale come up behind our race yacht, on a light-airs day in the cold of the southern Atlantic Ocean. The whale closed in until its 'snout' was only one metre behind our transom. We could clearly see it examining us with its enormous eyes. Its cream underbelly sported a patch that extended up and over its right eye.

After a while, it turned belly-up and swam under our yacht from stern to bow, the great flukes of the tail wider than our boat. It then surfaced just in front of us and blew — 'whoosh'. Then it turned on the surface and took up station astern of us again, just a metre away. It did this several times.

Our yacht was 24.5 metres long. The whale, we estimated, was approximately 23 metres long. A magnificent giant of the oceans — yet they are still being hunted. Again, the needless and senseless slaughter has to stop, or the world is going to be a much poorer place for losses of species that can never be replaced.

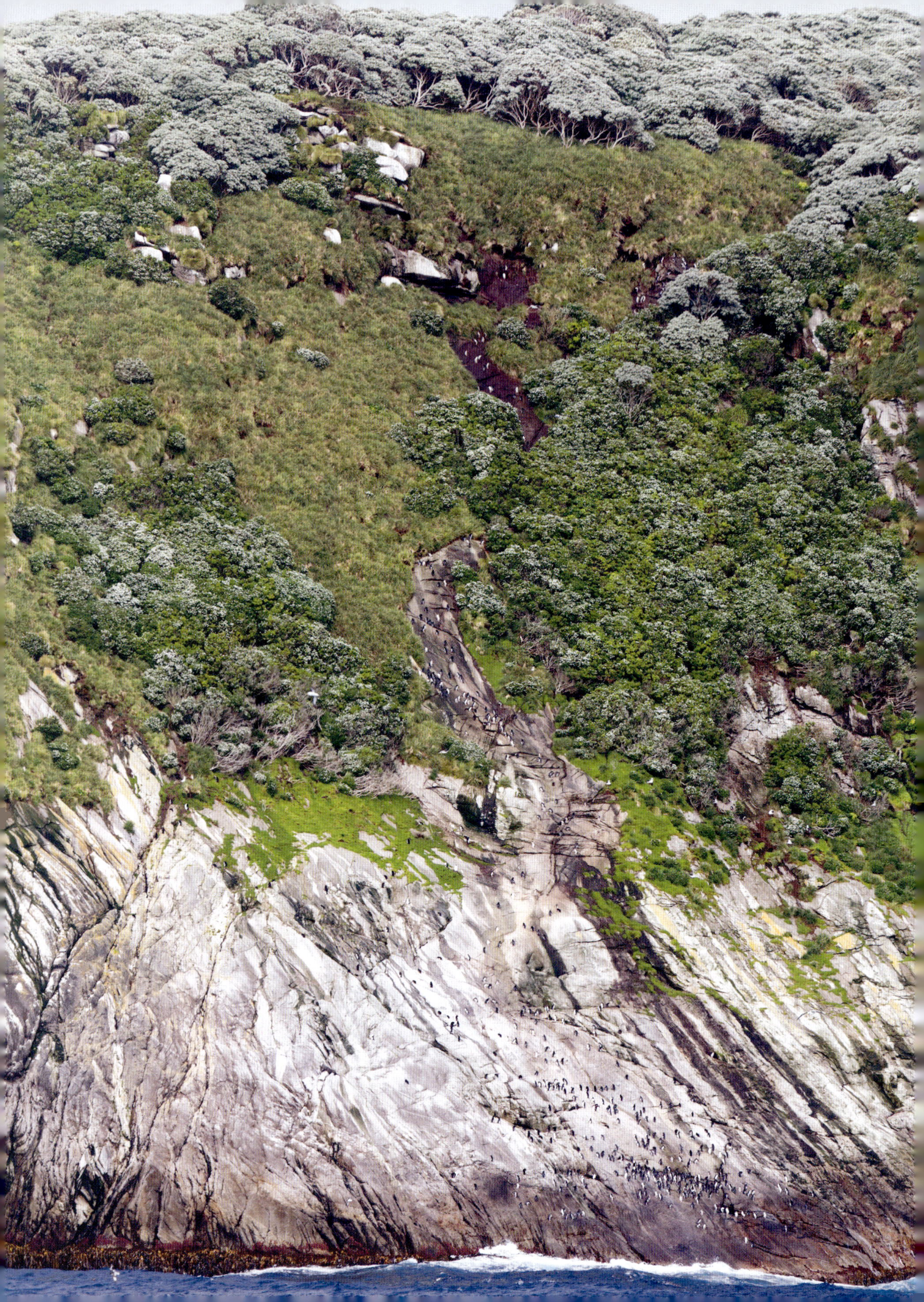

THE SUBANTARCTIC ISLANDS

It is 2792 kilometres from the Kermadecs to Campbell Island, the most southerly of New Zealand's Subantarctic Islands. The islands — the Snares, Auckland Islands, Antipodes Islands, Bounty Islands and, of course, Campbell Island — have little in common with the Kermadecs except extreme remoteness, but, as with the Kermadecs, it's the remoteness that makes them exceptional: aside from the devastating years of sealing and whaling and doomed attempts at farming in the 19th century, they are simply too difficult to exploit.

Although the islands all come under the 'subantarctic' umbrella, some are pristine while others are in various degrees of recovery following the removal of introduced animals and plants. All lie on the vast but, at 600–1000 metres, relatively shallow, underwater Campbell Plateau, but they are widely separated, each with a different geology and distinctive combination of plant, terrestrial and marine life.

FROM 47 DEGREES SOUTH and on through the 50s and 60s, it's open slather for the world's westerly-driven winds and currents, which are impeded only by the southern tip of South America as they romp around the globe whipping up gales and mountainous seas. For air-breathing creatures, such as birds and the marine mammals that require land to breed, the Subantarctic Islands are vital havens, life rafts in a hostile ocean.

All are national reserves under New Zealand's Reserves Act 1977 and are protected by an assortment of statutes. None are inhabited and landing is strictly controlled. In 1998 their outstanding conservation values were

Snares crested penguins make daily treks up and down this steep rocky slope on their stumpy legs. You can see them right near the top before they enter the bush.

recognised internationally when they and their surrounding seas to 12 nautical miles were made UNESCO World Heritage sites.

The two northernmost groups, the Snares and the Bounty Islands, are uplifted granite and metamorphic rock over 100 million years old, while the southern trio are eroded volcanoes dating from 10 to 15 million years old. The Auckland Islands and Campbell Island have steep, eroded cliffs to the west and sheltered inlets and fiords on the east. The Antipodes are least eroded, with many sheer coastal cliffs and pinnacles that plunge to the seabed.

THE ISLANDS WERE THE SCENE of great hardship, heroism, suffering and endurance in the 19th century. First, in the early 1800s, sealers moved from one Subantarctic Island to the next, clubbing, shooting and harpooning southern elephant seals, leopard seals, New Zealand sea lions and New Zealand fur seals in turn to the point of extinction, departing only when there was little left to economically exploit.

They were followed in some cases by farmers who brought with them domestic and feral animals and alien plants. Most memorably, in the mid-1800s, with the marine mammals and their hunters gone, a contingent of British settlers was enticed south to the Auckland Islands by promises of a utopia where crops would grow tall and animals would thrive: they were rained on 320 days of the year and even when it wasn't raining, it was about to — the skies were constantly overcast; the peat soil was acidic, potatoes were the size of marbles and the sheep got lost in the tangled undergrowth. It was utterly depressing. They persisted for almost three years before decamping to Sydney.

Small as they are in their wide expanse of ocean, the islands were especially dangerous to ships en route from Australia to Great Britain around Cape Horn; numerous wrecks inspired the establishment of castaway depots and further liberation of sheep, pigs and other animals. The introduced creatures remained long after their owners had departed and the risk of wrecks was reduced, with long-lasting, detrimental consequences for the islands' flora and fauna. All are now removed.

THE SNARES/TINI HEKE

Each day they go to sea to feed and each night they surf ashore on a wave, leaping out of the kelp that fringes the island to painstakingly clamber on stumpy legs up steep rocky faces and into the shelter of the scrubby, tree daisy forest. There, they waddle single-file beneath tangled and wind-shorn limbs, following pathways beaten smooth by countless feet over hundreds, perhaps thousands of years. Finally they reach a flat open space where hundreds of their kind are already gathered. It's a safe colony where, depending on season, mates with eggs or chicks may wait. They are Snares crested penguins and these, the tiny (341-hectare) islands after which they are named, are their only breeding site in the world.

The Snares, about 100 kilometres due south of Rakiura and perched on the western rim of the Campbell Plateau, are not a marine reserve although the islands themselves are protected. They are home not only to the endemic Snares crested penguin but are also famed for sky-filling flocks of sooty shearwaters, the islands' surfaces honeycombed by the birds' burrows. The Snares have never had alien animals on their shores and are a near-pristine environment.

Snares crested penguins line the rocks above the kelp in this fish-eye view of the shore.

AUCKLAND ISLANDS/ MOTU MAHA

The Auckland Islands are 250 kilometres beyond the Snares, also on the edge of the Campbell Plateau. They have a long but intermittent history of human contact, with indications that Polynesian people were present as long ago as the 13th century.

The oceans around the islands are a mix of warm subtropical currents and cool Antarctic waters. They are surprisingly productive and feed countless mouths: four species of penguin breed on the islands and another seven penguin species visit; vast populations of seabirds include petrels and the majestic albatrosses, the southern royal, Campbell and wandering albatrosses and white-capped, Salvin's and shy mollymawks. The Auckland Islands are breeding grounds for New Zealand sea lions and southern right whales; baleen whales such as minke, sei, fin, blue and humpback whales as well as their toothed cousins, sperm whales, orca and dusky dolphins are all seen in these waters.

In 1993 a 498,000-hectare marine mammal sanctuary was established around the Auckland Islands, principally to protect the breeding population of New Zealand sea lions (*Phocarctos hookerii*). Its establishment prohibited commercial fishing to within 12 nautical miles of the shore; the marine reserve, created ten years later, covers the same area, namely eight islands with their associated reefs, boulders, inlets and bays. Its inshore seas drop to 100 metres but, because it is on the edge of the Campbell Plateau, it also includes depths of 3000 metres. The marine reserve, covering the same area as the marine mammal sanctuary, was created in 2003.

The Subantarctic Islands are a seabird haven: a pair of southern royal albatrosses.

101 THINGS TO DO WITH A NEW ZEALAND SEA LION

On the night of 3 January 1864, the schooner *Grafton*, having run deep into Carnley Harbour on the south coast of Auckland Island, broke her starboard anchor chain in a heavy squall and began to drag towards the shore. 'From 10 pm till midnight the gale blew with the most terrific violence, and at precisely midnight the ship struck . . .' Captain Musgrave recorded later. The vessel was broadside to the beach with waves breaking over her with 'the most unimaginable violence,' he wrote.

The five crew were in the hire of François Raynal, 33, Frenchman, sailor and a miner who was about to return to France when he was persuaded to investigate a rumour of minable tin on Campbell Island. Raynal was acting second mate to the American Captain Thomas Musgrave, 30; there were also two seamen: a Norwegian, Alick Maclaren, 28, and an Englishman, George Harris, 20; and a Portuguese cook, Harry Forgès, 23. Over the following months, the five salvaged all they could from the wreck and in time built a relatively comfortable hut and established a routine that included a roster for cooking duties and evening 'classes' to keep themselves entertained.

Their survival over the following 19 months was due to three things: teamwork and a happy combination of personalities, the thoughtfulness and creativity of Raynal and ... sea lions: the *Grafton* had foundered in the vicinity of a breeding colony shortly after the pupping season in December. The males, which scrap over territory and assemble harems from November on, were still in the neighbourhood while the females and their pups were living on the beaches and in the island's rātā forests. The men soon found that they could club the animals without too much difficulty.

They ate sea lion flesh boiled, roasted, stewed and in soup, and they used the skins to make clothes and footwear: green skins quickly wore out but the inventive Raynal worked out how to tan them, build lasts and make enduring shoes. The oil, which is copious off an adult sea lion, was used at every turn: for healing wounds, making soap, as fuel for lamps, to make black and white paint (for a chess board), for deep-frying — an attempt to make island vegetation more palatable ('it bore a tolerable resemblance to sawdust,' said Raynal, and would not touch it although it was his idea), to make pitch by combining it with tar scraped from the wreck and to produce caulking for an escape boat by mixing it with lime.

Both Raynal and Musgrave used sea lion blood mixed with tannin and salt to write their journals once they had exhausted the ink supplies from the *Grafton*.

Few people have probably ever experienced such prolonged and intimate observation of the animals: by the end of their stay, there was little the men didn't know about them. And they were not unsympathetic. They felt remorse at killing young pups — they were much better eating — and when the main sea lion clan disappeared to sea over winter, they were sad to kill an old male they had affectionately named 'Royal Tom'. Both Raynal and Musgrave published detailed accounts of the animals in the years after their return.

New Zealand sea lions (known as Hooker's sea lions until 1995, after Joseph Hooker, the 19th-century botanist) were once found right around the New Zealand mainland but although they haul out over a wider area, they currently breed only on Auckland Islands beaches and at smaller rookeries on the Snares, Campbell Island and the Otago coast. They are the rarest of this species in the world in large part because, despite measures to limit deaths, thousands have been accidentally drowned in the trawl nets of the squid fishery that has operated around the islands since the 1980s. Unfortunately, although the marine reserve offers protection, sea lions forage well beyond its limits and continue to be imperilled.

HE WOULD BE KING

Raynal described a titanic evening clash shortly after their arrival. His companions had nodded off but he was lying awake, dimly aware of the calls of females and their pups on the beach. Suddenly 'a confused noise of crackling plants, and panting breath, and hoarse coughs rose all around us'. It was followed by 'extraordinary turmoil', branches splintering and the sound of blows. Two male sea lions were battling it out within paces of their tent.

Each was about eight feet long, and nearly six and a half feet in girth at the shoulders. From thence the body narrowed, until it terminated in a couple of little fins. It was covered with a short, thick, smooth hair, of a chocolate colour. The fore-paws, from four to five inches in length, wore, on their upper surface, a fine and delicate fur, tawny, or rather bronze, and underneath, a thick, black, corrugated skin. These large fins, or paws, were attached, by means of a short, thick arm, to their enormous shoulders. The latter, as well as the neck, and a part of the head, were covered with a shaggy, iron-gray mane, which, during their combat, the two champions bristled up, and shook every now and then in fury.

Pressing one against the other, their eyes glowing, their nostrils expanded and snuffing the air with a loud noise, their lips, trembling with rage, turned upwards, these monsters opened wide their enormous jaws, surmounted by long, stiff moustaches, and displaying the most formidable tusks. Every moment they flung themselves upon one another, and bit and gnawed, tearing away great shreds of flesh, or inflicting gashes whence the blood flowed in abundant streams. They exhibited an audacity, a vigour, and a fury truly worthy of their terrestrial homonym — the monarch of the African deserts.

CAMPBELL ISLAND/ MOUTERE IHUPUKU

Campbell Island is the location of the first of New Zealand's newest marine reserves. It is New Zealand's southernmost limit at 53º latitude south, in the middle of the Campbell Plateau east-to-west, 550 kilometres southeast of Steward Island/Rakiura. The reserve covers 39 percent of the island's waters, with Type 2 Marine Protected Area restrictions over the remainder to prohibit bottom trawling, Danish seining and dredging.

The island is the eroded remains of a shield volcano, with large cliffs, boulder beaches and a few sandy bays. Its marine environment ranges from about 100 to 200 metres deep and it includes sheltered inlets, exposed rocky reef and deep soft sediment. There are towering basalt pinnacles, extensive sponge beds, reefs encrusted with bright pink coralline seaweeds and boulder fields dominated by giant spider crabs. Six of the 22 species

Southern royal albatross on the Col Lyall track, Campbell Island. The head of Northeast Harbour is in the background.

of albatross and mollymawk, including the world's largest population of the southern royal albatross, breed here, as well as eastern rockhopper penguins, New Zealand sea lions, southern elephant seals and New Zealand fur seals.

When Sir Joseph Hooker visited the island in the 1840s, he was impressed by fields of unexpectedly large flowering plants, commonly now known as 'megaherbs'. Where some plants respond to harsh weather and impoverished soil by becoming stunted, these plants have gone the other way, with enormous leaves that are thought to be an adaptation to low levels of sunlight.

The island was farmed as late as 1931, when the farmers departed leaving around 4000 sheep, up to 30 cattle, some cats and rats. It was not until 2001 that the last of these animals was removed. The megaherbs had taken a thrashing but began to recover once the sheep were gone.

Megaherbs on Campbell Island: *Pleurophyllum criniferum* to the left with the Campbell Island daisy, *Pleurophyllum speciosum*, to centre and, right, among *Bulbinella rossii* (the burnt orange flowers).

BOUNTY ISLANDS/ MOUTERE HAURIRI

Despite the lack of cover on land, the skies and waters around the Bounty Islands are full of birds including these Salvin's albatrosses.

Across the other side of the Campbell Plateau, 700 kilometres east of Rakiura are the Bounty Islands, the second of the new reserves. As with Campbell Island, the marine reserve is partial, covering 56 percent, with Type 2 controls over the rest.

At first glance, the Bounty Islands barely qualify either for the word 'island' — because they are essentially a group of around 20 granite islets and rocks — or for the word 'Bounty', for the same reason. They are continually washed by rain and waves and have no topsoil, scant plant life and no safe anchorage or easy landing sites — although sealers somehow managed to obtain enough footing to kill 50,000 fur seals in the 1820s. The largest, Depot Island, is only 800 metres long and 88 metres at its highest point. They suit their Māori name, Hauriri or 'angry wind'.

But names and appearances aside, they are bountiful — the rocks are shared by around 20,000 New Zealand fur seals and by thousands of Salvin's mollymawks, Antarctic terns, erect-crested penguins, fulmar prions, Snares cape pigeons, southern black-backed gulls and a small population of Bounty Island shags, the world's rarest cormorant. All of them generate copious amounts of excrement and make such a racket that they can be smelled and heard some distance away.

Some of the bird droppings have baked into a shiny topping on the rocks, but they also provide a habitat for an endemic beetle, a wētā, a pair of spiders and a couple of flightless moths.

A large quantity washes directly to the sea where it nourishes communities of encrusting animals, barnacles, sponges and large mussels. There are giant masking crabs and, once again, giant spider crabs.

Salvin's albatrosses on their rocky home.

ANTIPODES ISLAND/ MOUTERE MAHUE

Toroa pango or the light-mantled sooty albatross, breeds on the Auckland, Campbell and Antipodes islands.

OPPOSITE: In 2011 DOC volunteer Melanie Heather counts erect-crested penguins on Antipodes Island, their only breeding site in the world. 'The noise, the smell — a sensory overload!' she said. The islands were 'magic, so pure and untouched'.

A little further south of the Bounty Islands, 860 kilometres from Stewart Island/Rakiura, on the eastern rim of the Campbell Plateau, is the volcanic Antipodes Island and four smaller islets. The last of the new reserves, this group has 100 percent protection to 12 nautical miles and includes waters 3000 metres deep.

The islands were discovered in 1800 by Captain Waterhouse of HMS *Reliance* and originally named 'Penantipodes' because they are nearly opposite London, the implied centre of the world. Their Māori name 'Moutere Mahue' refers to their isolation and means 'abandoned'.

There has been very little fishing around the Antipodes, making this one of the least disturbed and therefore most precious marine environments in New Zealand. Sheer cliffs rise from the sea to a tussocky plateau where the endemic Antipodean albatross breeds. There are also large colonies of erect-crested and eastern rockhopper penguins, southern elephant seals and New Zealand fur seals.

Marine life in the clear waters below is diverse, with rock walls encrusted in layers of bright pink seaweeds, habitat for a range of creatures such as sponges, anemones and bryozoans. There are more than 100 described seaweeds including massive beds of an endemic kelp that grows to four metres tall. There are few nearshore fish species here, but one of the most common is the Antarctic cod. Ling and Patagonian toothfish have been recorded offshore.

13 · WAY, WAY OFFSHORE | THE KERMADEC & SUBANTARCTIC ISLANDS 287

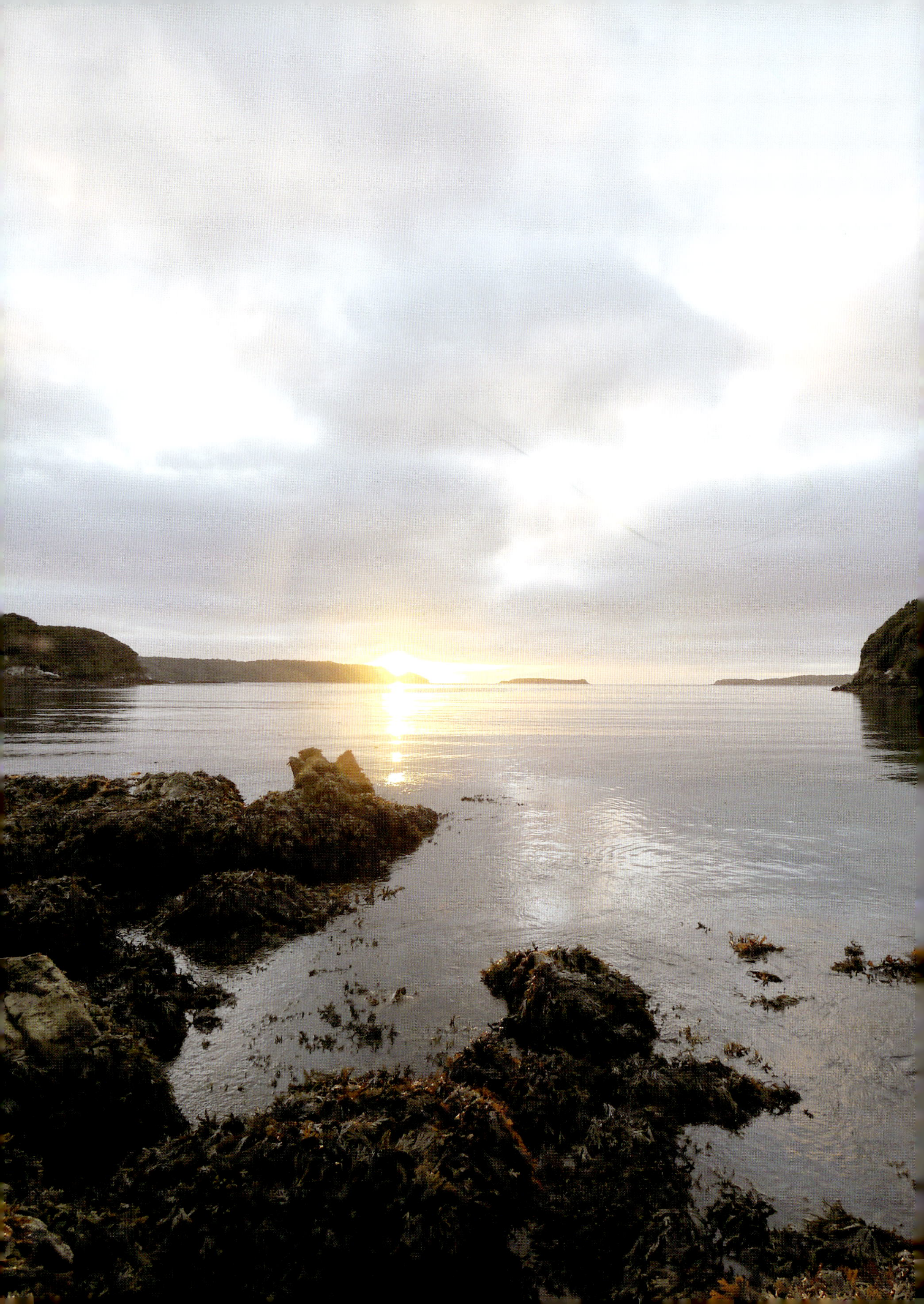

CONCLUSION

At the end of day, as the last rays brighten the waters and the terrestrial world tucks in for the night, out at sea, the guard is changing. Microscopic creatures, beyond number, begin their daily vertical migration to the ocean's surface at the same time as others, such as New Zealand fur seals and dolphins, head into the deeps for a night's foraging. At the base of the rock wall, kina and crayfish emerge to feed just as the Sandager's wrasse tucks his family into the sand for the night.

It's an alien, fascinating world below the waves, with different rules and animals and plants to match. It is both robust and fragile, an uncompromising world where the only certainty is that everything will be eaten, sooner or later, by something else. It is intricate, complex and beautiful. Much of it is yet unknown but increasingly we have another small window through which to view it — marine reserves.

Their numbers are increasing — which is great — but there are not enough by any means. And progress is slow. This book is not about the reserves that have been planned and failed, but there are many, including Tiritiri Matangi, Great Barrier, French Pass and, at the time of writing, possibly Waiheke. Time and again, communities engage in often-divisive, always time-consuming, lengthy, frustrating debate and at the end, it comes to nothing.

But change is incremental and momentum is building: more and more people (including you, dear reader) now appreciate their wonder, understand their value and talk to and show others what treasures you have found. Those we have will grow — possibly not in the directions we anticipate, or even necessarily the directions we would like, but we will visit and watch and learn, scientists will measure and evaluate, and Samara and her cohort will take the children down to the sea. They run up the shore shouting: 'I saw a fish! I saw a fish!'

Rakiura or glowing sky: sunset over the entrance to Paterson Inlet.

HOW TO VISIT A MARINE RESERVE

Marine reserves are ideal for scientific study, education, snorkelling, diving, eco-tourism, kayaking, swimming, taking photographs and exploring rock pools. Each reserve has its own particular characteristics, which are described in DOC brochures and available online.

They all share one thing, however: they are NO TAKE. All marine life, whether plant or animal, living or non-living, within reserve boundaries is protected. No fishing, collecting of marine life or unnecessary disturbance is allowed. The seabed, foreshore and all natural materials such as sand, rocks and shells are also protected. Leave everything as you find it, including stones and rocks in rock pools: if you turn them to peek underneath, turn them back when you are finished.

It could be said that marine reserves are NO ADD as well! You must not feed fish, discharge anything, build unauthorised structures or drop litter. If you boat within a reserve, take care not to drag your anchor because this may damage the very life you have come to see. Take care to ensure you do not accidentally take pests, such as mice, rats, non-native ants and weeds with you to reserves where you are allowed to land.

You are a visitor to a magic realm. Respect its difference, its other-worldliness.

Enjoy . . . but on its terms.

Two female gulls at Kaikōura (p.237) settle their chicks for the night.

GLOSSARY

Abyssal plain. Largely flat, featureless ocean floor from depths of 4000 to 6000 metres. It's very cold, dark and pressure is extreme.

Algae. Another term for seaweed. Algae range from microscopic, single-celled organisms to multicellular monsters, such as 60-metre giant kelp.

Antarctic Circumpolar Current or 'West Wind Drift'. An important body of water that flows eastwards around Antarctica.

Aristotle's lantern. Mouthparts of sea urchins.

Benthopelagic or benthic. On the sea floor.

Biogenic. Building its own environment.

Bioluminescence. Light emitted by a living organism.

Black coral. Slow-growing with dark-coloured skeletons that are obscured by tiny, anemone-like creatures called 'polyps'. There are over seven million black coral colonies in the fiords.

Brachiopods or lamp shells. Resemble clams but are otherwise very different. From 30,000 species 570 million years ago they are down to around 300 species today, 32 of them in New Zealand waters.

Cetacean. The order of whales, dolphins and porpoises.

Colonial animals. Collective life forms such as corals and salps.

Continental shelf. The portion of the continent that lies below the ocean.

Continental slope. The division between the inshore shelf and the continental shelf proper.

Deep Towed Imaging System. The high-definition video camera, still camera and lighting apparatus deployed by NIWA to explore the deep ocean.

Deep water emergence. When unusually low light levels in the upper layers causes plants and animals to migrate from the deep waters where they are most commonly found.

Diatoms. The most common plankton.

Diorite, granite, gneiss. Some of New Zealand's oldest known rocks, at 400–500 million years old. Forged deep underground, they are crystalline, hard and resistant to erosion.

East Australia Current. The current that forms the West Auckland and East Auckland currents and has a major influence on New Zealand seas.

Echinoderms. The phylum that includes kina, starfish, brittle stars and sea cucumbers.

Exclusive Economic Zone (EEZ). 200 nautical miles from land; three-quarters of New Zealand's EEZ is between 1000 and 6000 metres deep.

Extended continental shelf. A legal term that describes the alignment of the jurisdiction of a maritime nation with the physical form of the seafloor or continental shelf.

Galaxiid fish. Native freshwater fish such as inanga, kōaro and shortjaw kōkopu (juveniles are commonly known as 'whitebait'). They have both marine and freshwater stages in their life cycle.

Gondwana. The single landmass or supercontinent that lay west and south of our present location 540 million years ago. A portion of eastern Gondwana ultimately became Zealandia.

Granodiorite. A dark, granite-like, volcanic rock.

Ice age. In the past 120,000 years there have been at least five glacial periods. The last was approximately 20,000 years ago when the average surface temperature was about 5° lower than today and sea levels were 125 to 130 metres lower than at present.

Inshore shelf. A relatively shallow platform of varying widths adjacent to the coast; approximately 130 metres at its deepest.

Kaikōura Canyon. A deeply incised channel that reaches depths of 1200 metres and slices 60 kilometres across the continental shelf to within a few hundred metres of the shore. A complex mix of currents create particularly rich feeding grounds.

Kaitiakitanga. Shared responsibility and awareness of actions in the present and their effect on the future. This message is celebrated by SeaWeek, an event promoted annually by the New Zealand Association for Environmental Education.

Kina barren. An undersea desert where the natural balance has gone awry and the kina (sea urchin) population has outstripped the capacity of the environment to support it.

Krill. A form of zooplankton that includes small crustaceans. Krill are an important food for many animals including baleen whales and many seabirds.

Kupe. The first Polynesian explorer to reach the shores of Aotearoa/New Zealand.

Marine protection areas (MPAs). Inshore and offshore marine parks, marine reserves, marine mammal sanctuaries and areas covered by regulation directed towards Māori customary fisheries management.

Marine reserve. A permanent 'no-take' zone, with no fishing, removal of any material, no dredging, dumping, construction or any other activity that might disturb natural processes.

Mātaitai. Marine protected area administered under Māori protocols by a nominated kaitiaki or guardian.

Nekton (cf plankton). Creatures that move through the water under their own steam. Many ocean animals have life stages that are first planktonic and later nektonic.

Offshore plateaus. A number of large plateaus are part of Zealandia. They lie at depths of 500 to 1500 metres and include the Campbell Plateau, the Chatham Rise, the Hikurangi Plateau, the Northland Plateau and the Challenger Plateau.

Otariidae. The family of New Zealand fur seals and New Zealand sea lions.

Pelagic. Open ocean as opposed to coastal or inshore waters. It is further broken down to: epipelagic (from the surface to 200 metres); mesopelagic (from 200 to 1000 metres); bathypelagic (from 1000 to 4000 metres); hadal or hadopelagic (more than 6000 metres deep).

Photic zone. Surface or epipelagic layer: the distance light will penetrate, approximately 200 metres.

Phytoplankton. Single-celled floating plants (millions per litre) that harness the light in the sunlit upper waters and are the basis of the food web powering the whole ocean. Phytoplankton include diatoms (microscopic algae with ornate silica shells), dinoflagellates (weak swimmers with small, whip-like tails), phaeophytes (brown algae) and cyanobacteria (blue-green algae).

Picoplankton. The smallest of the plankton, less than one micron (one thousandth of a millimetre) across.

Plankton. The myriad of microscopic plants (phytoplankton) and animals (zooplankton) that drift at mercy of the movements of the sea.

Plate tectonics. The description of the solid outer crust of the earth as a mosaic of giant plates. New Zealand straddles the Australian Plate to the west and the Pacific Plate to the east. A deep trench marks the marine boundary between the two, with the 10,000-metre-deep Kermadec Trench in the north and the Puysegur Trench in the south. The Southern Alps are the result of the converging plates on land.

Rāhui. Tapu or sacred and forbidden area, prohibiting or limiting the quantity, size and season of gathering, depending on the circumstance.

Rhodoliths. Coral-like structures formed when coralline red algae deposit calcium carbonate inside their cell walls.

Salt water. One kilogram of water contains approximately 35 grams of mainly common salt (sodium chloride). The salinity of water determines its density.

Seamount. An underwater mountain or volcano. Like their terrestrial counterparts they may be solitary, in clusters or in chains.

Sponges. Colonies of individual cells that survive through cooperative specialisation.

Subantarctic Islands. The Snares, Auckland Islands, Antipodes Islands, Bounty Islands and Campbell Island lie on the vast Campbell Plateau, but are widely separated, each with a different geology and distinctive combination of plant, terrestrial and marine life.

Taiāpure. Marine areas of customary importance to an iwi or hapū that are administered by a committee under provisions of the Fisheries Act 1996. They are a broader option than mātaitai involving wider community consultation.

Tangaroa. In Māori lore, the turbulent ocean god and father of fish.

Tannin. An astringent, yellow-brown compound derived from plants.

Taonga. A treasured object in Māori culture.

Territorial sea. A nation's maritime domain, extending 12 nautical miles from land.

Test. The hard shell of sea urchins (kina).

Thermocline. The temperature and hence density boundary between two bodies of water.

Tikanga. Customary protocols

Titanomagnetite. The iron-bearing mineral found in the black sands of the North Island's west coast.

Trophic cascade. The domino effect triggered when an animal at or near the top of the food web is removed or replaced and there is a ripple of consequences. The trophic level is the position an organism occupies in the sequence of food production. In a simple marine food chain, the first trophic level is that of primary producers, phytoplankton; immediately above are herbivores, tiny zooplankton that eat the phytoplankton; on the third level are carnivores, the creatures that eat the zooplankton. There might be several of these layers, each successive one having larger creatures but fewer numbers.

UNCLOS. The United Nations Convention on the Law of the Sea (1982), the constitution by which the seas are governed.

Water column. The water from sea surface to ocean floor.

Wellings. Vertical movements of large bodies of water, either from depths of hundreds of metres to the surface or the reverse. Wellings mix water layers and move nutrients from one area to another. When there are higher nutrient levels phytoplankton increase, which triggers a cascade of fruitfulness right across the food web.

Zealandia. The underwater continent of which New Zealand is the emergent portion.

Zooplankton (see plankton). Microscopic oceanic animals. Some, such as fish larvae, will ultimately transit to another phase of existence. Zooplankton include foraminifera (single-celled organisms with calcite-rich shells), radiolarians (shells made of silica) and various ciliates (with tiny hairs around their bodies) and zooflagellates (with long thread-like structures that give them a limited amount of propulsion). Zooplankton also include larger creatures such as jellyfish, siphonophores (colonial animals such as Portuguese man-o'-war) and copepods — 10,000 or so species that in total form the greatest protein source in the ocean.

BIBLIOGRAPHY

Many sources were referenced for *Our Big Blue Backyard*. People with a lifetime's passion and expertise in matters marine were, of course, a first port of call, as was the ocean itself. They were closely followed by a wide, somewhat eclectic range of books, papers and articles that were also invaluable, both for general and specific information. Selected publications that were on hand for the duration of the project are listed below. And, of course, the internet, an awesome repository of collective knowledge; it opens windows into the past even as it is up-to-the-minute. Those in the list of online resources are among those most consulted.

BOOKS & PAPERS

Andrew, N. & Francis, M. (eds.) *The Living Reef: The Ecology of New Zealand's Rocky Reefs*, Craig Potton Publishing, 2003

Baker, A. N. *Whales and Dolphins of Australia and New Zealand: An Identification Guide*, Victoria University Press, 1999

Ballantine, W. J. *Marine Reserves for New Zealand*, University of Auckland, Leigh Laboratory Bulletin No. 25, 1991

Ballesta, L. *Planet Ocean: Voyage to the Heart of the Marine Realm*, National Geographic, 2007

Batson, P. B. *Deep New Zealand: Blue Water, Black Abyss*, Canterbury University Press, 2003

Biggar, K. & Fitzgerald, J. *First Crossings: Historic NZ Adventures Brought to Life*, Random House, 2013

Bishop, N. *Natural History of New Zealand*, Hodder & Stoughton, 1992

Bradstock, M. C. *Between the Tides: New Zealand's Shore and Estuary Life*, Bateman, 1989

Campell, H. & Hutching, G. *In Search of Ancient New Zealand*, Penguin and GNS Science, 2007

Campbell, H. et al. 'New Zealand Geology', online issue of *Episodes*, International Union of Geological Sciences, 2012

Carter, L. 'Currents of Change: The Ocean Flow in a Changing World', online pdf, NIWA, 2001

Cox, G. J. *Whale Watch: A Guide to New Zealand's Whales and Dolphins*, Collins, 1990

Doak, W. *Deep Blue: A South Pacific Odyssey*, HarperCollins, 1996

Doak, W. *City Under the Sea: Portrait of a Reef Fish Community at the Poor Knights Islands*, 1990

Doak, W. *The Cliff Dwellers: Poor Knights Marine Invertebrates*, online pdf, 1979

Enderby, J. & Enderby, T. *A Guide to New Zealand's Marine Reserves*, New Holland, 2006

Enderby, J. & Enderby, T. *Know Your New Zealand Fishes*, New Holland, 2012

Francis, M. *Coastal Fishes of New Zealand: Identification, Biology, Behaviour*, Craig Potton, 2012

Goff, J. R., Nichol, S. L. & Rouse, H. L. *The New Zealand Coast. Te Tai o Aotearoa*, Dunmore Press and Whitirea Publishing, 2003

Hauraki Gulf Maritime Park Board. *The Story of Hauraki Gulf Maritime Park*, 1983

Hayward, B. 'Geology and Geomorphology of the Poor Knights Islands, Northern New Zealand', *Tane*, Auckland Institute and Museum, 1991

Hirt-Chabbert, J. *Fish Species of New Zealand: A Photographic Guide*, Penguin, 2006

Hutching, G. *The Penguin Natural World of New Zealand*, Penguin, 1998

Jacob, W. *Coastlines of New Zealand*, New Holland, 2000

Jones, M. B. & Marsden, I. D. *Life in the Estuary: Illustrated Guide and Ecology*, Canterbury University Press, 2005

Kerr, V. & Kamo High School Y13 Geography Class. *Whangarei Harbour Marine Reserve Proposal*, Kamo High School, 2002

Kingsford, M. J. *Studying Temperate Marine Environments: A Handbook for Ecologists*, Canterbury University Press, 1998

Kirkwood, R. *Fur Seals and Sea Lions*, CSIRO Publishing, 2013

Koslow, J. A. *The Silent Deep: The Discovery, Ecology and Conservation of the Deep Sea*, University of Chicago Press, 2007

Le Guern Lytle, C. 'When Mermaids Cry: The Great Plastic Tide', online paper, undated

Matsen, B. *Descent: The Heroic Discovery of the Abyss*, Pantheon Books, 2005

Miller, M. & Batt, G. *Reef and Beach Life of New Zealand*, Collins, 1973

Morton, J. & Miller, M. *The New Zealand Sea Shore*, Collins, 1968

Mulcahy, K., Peart, R. & Bull, A. *Safeguarding Our Oceans: Strengthening Marine Protection in New Zealand*, Environmental Defence Society, 2012

Natusch, S., Doak, W. & Gibb, J. *The Edge of the Land: The Coastline of New Zealand*, Penguin, 1983

Orbell, M. *The Illustrated Encyclopaedia of Maori Myth and Legend*, Canterbury University Press, 1995

Peat, N. *The Tasman: Biography of an Ocean*, Penguin, 2010

Peart, R. *Castles in the Sand: What's Happening to the New Zealand Coast?* Craig Potton and Environmental Defence Society, 2009

Probert, K., Jillet, J. & Carson, S. *Southern Seas: Discovering Marine Life at 46o South*, Otago University Press, 2005

Rose, P., & Laking, A. *Oceans: Exploring the Hidden Depths of the Underwater World*, BBC Books, 2008

Scofield, P. & Stephenson, B. *Birds of New Zealand: A Photographic Guide*, Auckland University Press, 2013

Sefton, A. *Sir Peter Blake: An Amazing Life*, Penguin, 2004

Sobel, J. A. & Dahlgren, C. P. *Marine Reserves: A Guide to Science, Design, and Use*, The Ocean Conservancy, 2004

Sim-Smith, C. & Kelly, M. *A Literature Review on the Poor Knights Islands Marine Reserve*, Department of Conservation, 2009

Te Ara/Ministry of Culture and Heritage. *New Zealanders and the Sea*, Bateman, 2009

Thomas, D. N. & Bowers, D. G. *Introducing Oceanography*, Dunedin Academic Press Ltd, 2012

Turbott, E. G. (convenor). *Checklist of the Birds of New Zealand and the Ross Dependency, Antarctica*, Random Century and The Ornithological Society of New Zealand Inc., 1990

Wing, S. *Subtidal Invertebrates of New Zealand: A Divers' Guide*, Canterbury University Press, 2008

Wood, R. et al. *New Zealand's Continental Shelf and UNCLOS: Article 76*, Institute of Geological and Nuclear Sciences Information Series 56/NIWA Technical Report 123, 2003

Wood, Rev. J. G. *The Common Objects of the Sea Shore: Including Hints for an Aquarium*, Routledge, 1859

ONLINE RESOURCES

The oceanic quantity of online resources includes sites that are often beautifully and informatively illustrated and which increasingly include video clips. The following are among the most frequently consulted but even so are only a small selection.

Government departments and related agencies (both national and international) have vast resources and are founts of reliable information. They include the Department of Conservation (DOC), Maritime New Zealand, the Ministry for the Environment (MFE), the Ministry of Foreign Affairs and Trade (MFAT), the National Aquatic Biodiversity Information System (NABIS), the National Institute of Water & Atmospheric Research (NIWA), New Zealand Biodiversity, Parliamentary Commissioner for the Environment (PCE), GNS Science (GNS), Landcare Research, the Parliamentary Counsel Office (PCO), US Geological Survey (USGS), and National Oceanic and Atmospheric Administration (NOAA). A number of regional councils and local authorities have published first rate documents on marine and coastal management, such as *Sea Change: The Hauraki Gulf Marine Spatial Plan*.

Centres of learning are equally excellent, among them the University of Auckland Institute of Marine Science, Auckland Museum, Victoria's New Zealand Electronic Text Collection and New Zealand Marine Studies Centre, Otago University.

Publications, online encyclopedia, newspapers and specialist technical services include Te Ara/The Encyclopedia of New Zealand and its 1966 predecessor, NZ Topo Maps, Papers Past, *New Zealand Geographic*, the Museum of New Zealand/Te Papa Tongarewa, the State Library of Victoria, Encyclopaedia Britannica, *New Zealand Listener*, *Scientific American* and *New Scientist*. And Wikipedia has its uses.

Conservation organisations and societies provide on-the-spot insight to immediate conditions, concerns and activities, especially through online newsletters. There are many, such as Algalita, the Center for Ocean Solutions, Ocean Conservancy and World Wildlife Fund. Numbered among local equivalents are Experiencing Marine Reserves, Forest & Bird, the Ornithological Society of New Zealand, the New Zealand Association for Environmental Education, Marine NZ, the NZ Plant Conservation Network, the Sir Peter Blake Trust and envirohistory NZ.

Then, with an even closer focus, many marine reserves have an associated care group such as Whangateau HarbourCare, Friends of the Taputeranga Marine Reserve, Sustain Our Sounds, Friends of Mangarākau Swamp, Island Bay Marine Education Centre and Ngā Motu Marine Reserve Society.

Special interest groups such as Option4 or Kiwis Against Seabed Mining (KASM) provide useful alternative perspectives, while businesses including dive sites and tourism operators such as Dive! Tutukaka, Wrybill Birding Tours, Aerius Helicopters and Whale Watch Kaikōura offer yet another angle on the ocean.

Finally, specialist sites are invaluable for their precision and erudition. Among them, for instance, are a site devoted to New Zealand molluscs, Riley Elliott's site on Shark Research and Conservation and, from overseas, A Cabinet of Curiosities, dedicated to diatom art.

ILLUSTRATION CREDITS

KEY: t = top; m = middle (l–r); c = centre (t–b); b = bottom; l = left; r = right; JH = Janet Hunt; NHNZ = Natural History New Zealand; MNZ = Maritime New Zealand; DOC = Crown Copyright: Department of Conservation Te Papa Atawhai; Turnbull = Alexander Turnbull Library, National Library of New Zealand/Te Puna Mātauranga o Aotearoa.

pp.2–3, 4, 7, 12, 3: JH; pp.14–15: Darryl Torckler; p.16: JH, based on GNS Science data, base layer from Koordinates Limited; p.18: Jacques Callot, 'Firing the Cannon', ca.1634/1635, National Gallery of Art, Washington; p.20: John Arthur/State Library of Victoria; p.21t: Albert Günther, *Report on the Scientific Results of the Voyage of HMS Challenger During the Years 1873–76, Zoology*–Vol. XXII (1887); p.21b: NIWA; p.22: NIWA; p.23tl: Corbis; p.23tr: Arthur Mee's *Children's Encyclopaedia*; p.23b: Vince Kerr/Fish Forever; p.25: Brent Stephenson/eco-vista; p.26: JH; p.27: GNS Science; p.28: JH; p.29 Vivian Ward, Igor Ruza and Adrian Turner/University of Auckland; p.31: *Kaikoura Star*/Fairfax Media; p.32: Howard Lynk, info@victorianmicroscopes.com; p.33: Ernst Haeckel, Wikimedia Commons; pp.35, 36, 38–39 all images: JH; p.43: Darryl Torckler; p.44: Cynthia Vanderlip/Algalita Marine Research & Education; p.46: JH; pp.48–49, 51: Roger Grace; pp.52–53, 54 (x2): JH; p.57: Roger Grace; pp.58–59: JH; p.60: NHNZ; p.63: Samara Nicholas; p.65 (x2): JH; p.66tl, bl & br: Roger Grace; p.66tr & m: Vince Kerr/Fish Forever; p.67: Roger Grace; pp.68, 69, 71: Experiencing Marine Reserves/Samara Nicholas; p.72: Vince Kerr/Fish Forever; pp.74, 75, 77: NHNZ: p.78tl, tr, bl, br: NHNZ; p.78m: Roger Grace; p.79: NHNZ; p.80: JH; p.82: NHNZ; p.83: JH; p.84: NHNZ; p.85: photonewzealand/Darryl Torckler; pp.86, 87: JH; pp.88, 90, 91: NHNZ; p.92: JH; p.93: Ian Skipworth; p.94: JH; p.95: Dave Aboott/NHNZ; p.97: Ian Skipworth; p.99: JH; pp.100–101 (x 4): JH; p.101 (octopus): Roger Grace; p.102: JH; p.105 (x2): JH; p.107 (x2): Brent Stephenson/eco-vista; p.109 (x2): Winston Cowie/NHNZ; p.110: Charles Heaphy watercolour, Turnbull; p.111: Northwood Collection, Turnbull; p.113: JH: p.114: artist unknown, Cowan collection, Turnbull; p.117: Rob Suisted/naturespic.com; pp.118–119: JH; pp.120, 121: JH; p.122: Roger Grace; p.123: JH; p.124: courtesy of Mike Lee; p.125t: Eugenie Sage/greens.org.nz; p.125b: Wade Doak; p.128: Roger Grace; p.129: Ian Skipworth; p.131t & bl: NIWA/John Booth: pp.131br, 133, 134: JH; p.135 (x2): Long Bay Marine Education Centre; pp.136–137: Haru Sameshima/Motu Manawa Restoration Group; pp.137, 138 (x3), 139m, 139b: Kent Xie/Motu Manawa Restoration Group; p.139t: Jeremy Painting/Motu Manawa Restoration Group; pp.140, 141, 142, 143 (x2): JH; pp.144–145: Brent Stephenson/eco-vista; p.148: Ian Skipworth; p.151: Dave Rayner/Aerius: pp.152: Maritime NZ; p.153t: NZ Defence Force; pp.154 (x2), 155: Maritime NZ; p.157: Auckland Art Gallery Toi o Tāmaki; pp.158, 159 (x2): Maritime NZ; p.161: photonewzealand/Darryl Torckler; p.162: Riley Elliott; p.163: Ian Skipworth; pp.164–165, 166, 168–169: JH; p.170: Elise Smith/Ngā Motu

Marine Reserve Society; pp.171, 172: JH; p.174: Brent Stephenson/eco-vista; p.175: Aeronavics/Whāingaroa Environment Centre; p.177: JH; p.179: Brent Stephenson/eco-vista; p.181: JH; p.182: Ian Skipworth; p.183: Roger Grace; pp.184 (x3), 184–185: Jamie Quirk/DOC; p.184b: Debbie Freeman/DOC; pp.186, 187: Jamie Quirk/DOC; pp.189, 190: Debbe Freeman/DOC; p.191: NHNZ; pp.192–193, 194–195: JH; p.197: photonewzealand/Darryl Torckler; p.198: Ed Skelton; p.199: NIWA/Tracy Farr/Kate Neill; pp.201, 202: JH; p.203: Ian Skipworth; pp.204–205: photonewzealand/Rob Brown; p.207: photonewzealand/Craig Potton; p.208: Danny Boulton/Sustain Our Sounds; p.209: Ian Skipworth; p.211: photonewzealand/Hedgehog House; p.213: photonewzealand/Derek Morrison; pp.215, 217: Jo-Anne Vaughan, John Gilardi/Friends of Mangarākau Swamp; pp.218–219: photonewzealand/Colin Monteath/Hedgehog House; p.222: NHNZ; p.225: Max Quinn/NHNZ; pp.226, 227: Lindsay Davidson/NHNZ; p.229: Max Quinn/NHNZ; pp.230–231: Stefan Mutch/NHNZ; p.235: Whale Watch Kaikōura; p.236: NHNZ; p.237: Stefan Mutch/NHNZ; p.238: Ian Skipworth; p.242: NHNZ; p.243: Michaël Catanzariti/National Oceanic and Atmospheric Administration; p.244: photonewzealand/David Wall; p.245: Greg Bowker/Fairfax Media; pp.246–247, 248, 250: Brent Stephenson/eco-vista; pp.251, 252, 253 (x3), 254: Ian Skipworth; p.255 (x2): Fiordland Marine Guardians; pp.257, 259, 260 (x2): NHNZ; p.261: Brent Stephenson/eco-vista; p.262: Ian Skipworth; p.263: Max Quinn/NHNZ; pp.264–265: Brent Stephenson/eco-vista; pp.266, 269, 270, 271: Ian Skipworth; p.272: Samara Nicholas; pp.273, 274: Brent Stephenson/eco-vista; p.277: Ian Skipworth; pp.278, 279, 281: Brent Stephenson/eco-vista; pp.282, 283: Ian Skipworth; pp.284, 285: Scott Hein/Hein Natural History Photography; p.286: Brent Stephenson/eco-vista; p.287: Joe Dodgshun/*Otago Daily Times*; p.288: NHNZ; p.291: NHNZ; p.304: Ian Skipworth.

TEXT CREDITS

p.6: 'The Sea, Our Saviour', Hone Tuwhare, courtesy of the estate of Hone Tuwhare, honetuwharepoetry@gmail.com. Tuwhare's poetry is available in *Small Holes in the Silence: Collected Works*, Godwit, 2011; p.40: Bill Bryson, *A Short History of Nearly Everything*, Black Swan, 2003; p.42: 'Viewpoint for New Zealand Geographic: A Marine Reserve Manifesto', Bill Ballantine, Leigh Marine Laboratory, 2004; p.54: Bill Ballantine, pers. comm., December 2013; pp.72, 77, 78: Dave Abbott, NHNZ; p.84: Wade Doak, pers. comm., January 2014; pp.96, 97: Winston Cowie and Dave Abbott, NHNZ; pp.125, 128: Roger Grace, pers. comm., January 2014; p.139: Bill Ballantine, *Marine Reserves for New Zealand*, University of Auckland, Leigh Laboratory Bulletin No.25, 1991; p.146: C.S. Lewis, *The Lion, the Witch and the Wardrobe*, Penguin, 1950; p.202: Murray Hosking, taputeranga.org; p.232: *Kaikōura Marine Strategy, Sustaining Our Sea*, 2012; p.262: Dave Abbott, NHNZ; p.268: Steve Hathaway, NHNZ; p.273: 'Special Report Two: Footnote From Peter', sirpeterblaketrust.org.

INDEX

Bold numbers indicate photographs

Abel Tasman National Park 206, 212
Abbott, Dave 72, 77, 79, 84, 96–97, 253, 262–63
adelie penguins **21**
Akaroa Harbour Taiāpure 245
Akaroa Marine Reserve 12, 13 (map), 244–45
albatrosses 30, 45, 115, **264**, 267, 273, 278, **278**, **282**, 283, **284**, **285**, 286, **286**
 Antipodean 264, 267, 286
 Campbell 278
 Laysan 45
 light-mantled sooty (toroa pango) **286–87**
 Salvin's **284**, **285**
 southern royal 278, **278**, **282**, 283
 wandering 278
algae — see seaweeds
Anderton, Jim 126
anemones 62, 64, **66**, **93**, 132, 147, 180, **183**, 187, 188, 191, **191**, 197, 202, 208, **208**, 209, 210, 213, 228, 251, 252, **252**, 286, 291
angelfish, black 98, 147
annelid worms 183
Antarctic blue whale 178
Antarctic cod 286
Antarctic tern 285
Antipodean albatross **264**, 267, 286
Antipodes Islands 19, 275–76, 286, 293
Antipodes Island (Moutere Mahue) Marine Reserve 12, 13 (map), 267, 275–76, 286
Aorangi — see also Poor Knights Islands 81, 87, **88**, 89, 90
arrow worms 23
Arthur, John 20
Astrolabe Reef — see also *Rena* disaster 152, 157
Auckland Islands 19, 126, 129, 262, 267, 275, 276, 278–81, 293
Auckland Islands (Motu Maha) Marine Reserve 12, 13 (map), 267, 278–80
Australasian bittern (matuku) 140, 216
Australasian gannet 90, 154, 195

Bactra moth 139
baleen whales 30, 278, 292
Ballantine, Dr Bill 28, 41, 42, 47–48, 53–55, **54**, 62, 64, 70, 124, 139
banded dotterel 189, 216
banded kōkopu 64, 216
banded rail 64, 67, 90, 138, 216
banded wrasse 187, 188, 197, 202, 208, 210, 213, 259
Banks Peninsula 36, 42, 173, 176, 220, 240, 241, 243, 244
Banks Peninsula Marine Mammal Sanctuary 243
barnacles 64, 72, 84, 95, 132, 141, 213, 242, 251, 285
barracouta 115
barracuda 226
Barton, Otis 23, **23**
basking shark 41
Bates, Abbie **172**
Battershill, Chris 180
beaked whale 174, 234
Beebe, William 23, **23**, 30
bellbirds 90

Berntsen, Jessica **171**
black angelfish 98, 147
black-bellied storm petrel 106, 107
black-billed gull 195
black shag 115, 195
black-winged petrel 271
Blake, Sir Peter 134, 272, 273
 Blakexpeditions 273
 Sir Peter Blake Emerging Leader award 63
 Sir Peter Blake Marine Education & Recreation Centre 132, 134, **135**
 Sir Peter Blake Trust 63
 Young Blake Expeditions 63, 272
blue cod (rāwaru; pākirikiri) 169, 189, 197, 198, 202, 203, **203**, 208, 210, 211, 213, 236, 242, 259
blue knifefish 161
blue maomao 50, 63, 151, 161, 269
blue moki 161, 169, 188, 202, 208, 211, 259
blue shark 161, 162–63, **162**, 175, 197
blue whale 9, 173, 178, **179**, 234, 278
Bornholdt, Felix 272
bottlenose dolphin 123, 124, 208, 251
Bounty Island shag 285
Bounty Islands (Moutere Hauriri) Marine Reserve 12, 13 (map), 267, 275–76, 284–85
Bouwman, Carlijn **159**
brachiopods (lamp shells) 251, 253, **253**, 259, 291
British Natural History Museum, Tring 106
brittle stars 56, 183, 208, 210, **251**, 252, **252**, 291
brown creeper 258
Buller's shearwater 89, 94, **94**
butterfish 50, 64, 147, 187, 188, 198, 202, 242, 259

Campbell albatross 278
Campbell Island 19, 24, 275–76, 279, 280, 282–83, 286, 293
Campbell Island daisy **283**
Campbell Island (Moutere Ihupuku) Marine Reserve 12, 13 (map), 267, 275–76, 282–83, 284
Cameron, James 23
Cape Rodney–Ōkakari Point Marine Reserve — see also Goat Island Marine Reserve 12, 13 (map), 47–55, 121 (map), 122, 123
caramel drummer 269
Carlton, Dave 189
carpet shark 96, 209, **209**, 259
Carter, Chris 62, **63**
Caspian tern 138, 141, **184**, 189, 195
Cathedral Cove — see Te Whanganui-a-Hei (Cathedral Cove) Marine Reserve
Chapman, Professor Val 47–48
'China Shops' 251–52, 254
cockles 115, 117, **125**, 138, 141, 210, 216
cod 115, 169, 189, 197, 198, 202, 203, **203**, 208, 210, 211, 213, 236, 242, 259, 286
 Antarctic 286
 blue (rāwaru; pākirikiri) 169, 189, 197, 198, 202, 203, **203**, 208, 210, 211, 213, 236, 242, 259
 rock 115
common dolphin 174, 208
conger eel 64
Contiguous Zone 19
Convention on Wetlands of International Importance (Ramsar Convention) 217
Cook, Captain James 17, 86–87, 157, 168, 206–207
corals 41, 147, 180, 187, 191, 199, 251, 252–53, **252**, **253**, 269, 291, 293
Cousteau, Jacques 81

Cowie, Winston 73, 77, 79, 96, 97, 109, **109**, 122
Crabb, Peter **170**
crabs 64, 74, 84, 95, 115, 131, 141, 183, 202, 210, 216, 232, 242, 282, 285
 'false' 236, **236**
 giant masking 285
 giant spider 282, 285
 paddle 74
crakes, spotless 90, 138, 216
crayfish **38**, 40, **42**, 47, 50, 56, 61, 68, 70, 84, 96, 109, 115, 125, 128, 129, **129**, 130–31, **131**, 132, 147, 180, **184**, 186, 187, 188–89, **190**, 197, 198, 202, 208, 209, 211, 213, 251, 259, 289
 packhorse (green) 96, 129, 131
 red rock lobster 129, **131**
crested blennies 64
crested penguins **227**
Cruz, Catarina **159**
Cruz, Marco **159**

deepwater nurse shark 41
demoiselles 64, 98, **99**, 161, **271**
 two-spot 98, **99**, 271
Department of Conservation (DOC) 40, 57, 67, 68, 69, 109, 116, 126, 176, 178, 186, 189, 198, 216, 232, 242, 268, 286, 290
diatoms — see plankton
Dive! Tutukaka 92, 94
diving petrel 195
Doak, Brady 84, 96
Doak, Jan 83, **83**
Doak, Wade 62, 70, 74, 82, 83, **83**, 124, 125, 126, 163, 182, 186, 270
dogfish 259
dolphins 75, 115, 123, 124, 151, 173–76, 200, 208, 212, 223, 233, 238–39, **238**, 242, 243, 245, 251, 272, 278, 289, 291
 bottlenose 123, 124, 208, 251
 common 174, 208
 dusky 208, 238–39, **238**, 278
 Hector's (upokohue) 173–76, **174**, 208, 223, 238, 243
 Māui's 173–76, 243
 Yangtze River 176
dotterels 67, 72, 138, **138**, 141, 142–43, **142**, **143**, **159**, 189, 212, 216
 banded 189, 216
 New Zealand (tūturiwhatu) 67, 138, **138**, 141, 142–43, **142**, **143**, **159**, 189
Dowding, John **159**
Drains to Harbour 69
drummers 50, 197, 269
 caramel 269
 silver 50, 197
d'Urville, Dumont 106, 157
dusky dolphin 208, 238–39, **238**, 278

East Coast Bays Coastal Protection Society 134
eastern bar-tailed godwit 72, 138, **139**, 141, 216
eastern rockhopper penguins 283, 286
Edith Winstone Blackwell Interpretive Centre 53
eels 30, 64, 97, **97**, 161, 183, 216, 226
 conger 64, 226
 long-fin 216
 moray 97, **97**, 161, 183
Environment Canterbury 233
Environment Southland 57
Environmental Protection Agency 177
erect-crested penguins 285, 286, **286–87**
Exclusive Economic Zone (EEZ) 9, 16 (map), 17, 19, 20, 24, 27, 129, 291

Experiencing Marine Reserves programme 62–63, 68–69, 70, 200
Extended Continental Shelf 16 (map), 19, 24, 291

fairy prions 90, 242
'false crabs' 236, **236**
fantails 90
fanworms 72, **72**, 253
Farrelly, Warren 62, 74
feather-duster worms **253**
fernbird 138, **139**, 216
fin whale 273, 278
Fiordland 246–254
Fiordland Marine Conservation Strategy 254
Fiordland Marine Guardians 57, 254, 255
Fiordland National Park 248
first people 108–114
flax snail 90
flax weevil 90
flesh-footed shearwater 45
Flood, Bob 106–107
flounder 141, 216
fluttering shearwater 94, 115, 207
Forest & Bird 129, **138**, 158, 233
  Motu Manawa Restoration Group **138**
Francis, Dr Malcolm 191
Friends of Mangarākau Swamp 217
Friends of Matakohe 67
Friends of Taputeranga Marine Reserve 200, 202
fulmar prions 285

Galapagos shark 269
gannets, Australasian 90, 154, 195
Garrett, Ross 134
Gartrell, Dr Brett 154
geckos 67, 90, 104
  forest 67
  Duvaucel's 90
giant centipede 90
giant grouper 41
giant kōkopu 223
giant limpet 269
giant masking crab 285
giant salp **23**, 83
giant spider crab 282, 285
giant squid 31, **31**, 234, 235
giant wētā 90, 104
GNS Science 17, 20, 149
Goat Island 9, 40, 42, 47–55
  Goat Island (Cape Rodney–Ōkakari Point) Marine Reserve 12, 13 (map), 42, 47–55, 62, 121 (map), 122
  Goat Island Marine Discovery Centre 40, 54
goatfish 64, 72
godwit guardian sculpture 143
godwits 72, 138, **139**, 141, 212, 216
  eastern bar-tailed 72, 138, **139**, 141, 216
golden limpet 188
Goldsmith, Eric 150
Gondwana 25, 291
Grace, Dr Roger 41, 124–127, **125**, 128, 129
Great Barrier Environment Strategy Planning Committee 127
Great Barrier Island (Aotea) 50, 81, 83, 89, 103, 104, 126, 156, 289
Great Pacific Garbage Patch 44
grey ternlet 271
groper — see hāpuku
grouper 41, 161, 270, **270**, 272
  giant 41
  spotted black 41, 270, **270**, 272
  toadstool 161
gulls 41, 72, 115, 132, 138, 143, 195, 216, 226,
237, **237**, 241, 242, 245, 285, **290**
  black-billed 195
  red-billed 195, 237, **237**
  southern black-backed 41, 132, 138, 216, 285
Günther, Albert 21

Haeckel, Ernst 32
Haika, Puke 128
Hammonds, Barbara **170**
Hancock, Eli **172**
hāpuku (groper) 125–26, **125**, 127
harrier hawks 90
Hathaway, Steve 84, 96, 269
Hauraki Gulf 49, 60, 107, 112, 115, 121, 146, 199, 217
  Hauraki Gulf Forum 121
  Hauraki Gulf Marine Park/Tīkapa Moana 100–143, 147
    marine reserves 121–43, 121 (map), 146–48
  Hauraki Gulf Maritime Park 89
Hauturu/Little Barrier Island 90, 103–104, 106, 107, 150
Hautai Marine Reserve (proposed) 12, 13 (map), 221, 223
Hāwea (Clio Rocks) Marine Reserve 12, 13 (map), 248
Heaphy, Charles 110
Heather, Melanie **287**
Heatley, Phil 221
Hector's dolphin (upokohue) 173–76, **174**, 208, 223, 238, 243
herons 64, 72, 90, 141, 189, 195, 212, 216
  reef 141, 195
  white-faced 90, 216
hihi (stitchbird) 104
Hikurangi Marine Reserve (proposed) 12, 13 (map), 234
hiwihiwi 187
Hohneck, Mook 109, **109**
hoiho (yellow-eyed penguin) 242
Hooker, Sir Joseph 280, 283
Hooker's (New Zealand) sea lion 226–27, **262**, 263, 276, 278, 279–81, **279**, **281**, 283, 292
Horoirangi Marine Reserve 12, 13 (map), 206, 210–11, 212, 214
Hosking, Murray 202
Hudson, Steve 96
hūmenga (wandering anemone) 191, **191**
humpback whale 83, 173, 196, 234, 270, 272, 278

inanga 216, 223, 291
Irwin, Steve 76
iwi and hapū
  Kāi Tahu 241
    Te Rūnaka o Koukourarata 241
  Kāti Māmoe 255
  Ngā Puhi 112
  Ngāi Tahu 220, 233, 254, 255, 258
    Kati Kurī Māori 235
    Ngāti Kurī 233, 236
  Ngāi Tara 215
  Ngāi Tumatakōkiri 215
  Ngāi Te Hapū 156
  Ngāi Te Rangi 150
    Te Whānau-a-Tauwhao 150
  Ngāti Awa 160, 161
  Ngāti Hei 146
  Ngāti Kere 188
  Ngāti Konohi 186, 187
  Ngāti Manuhiri 109
  Ngāti Paoa 112

Ngāti Rārua 215
Ngāti Tai 113, 114
Ngāti Tama 180
Ngāti Tama Manawhenua Ki Te Tau Ihu 211, 214
Ngāti Te Whiti 171
Ngāti Toa 196
Ngāti Wai 89, 90, 129,
Ngāti Whātua 112
Ngāti Whatuiāpiti 188
  Tamatea Taiwhenua 188
Te Ātiawa 215
Waikato 112
Waitaha 241, 255

jellyfish 21, 23, 30, 75, 94, 130, 183, 191, 293
John Dory 63, 115

kahawai 64, 115, 169, 216
Kahukura (Gold Arm) Marine Reserve 12, 13 (map), 248
Kahurangi Marine Reserve (proposed) 12, 13 (map), 221, 222
Kaikōura 9, 30, 42, 201, 232–39, 241, 254, 290
  Kaikōura Boating Club 233
  Kaikōura District Council 233
  Kaikōura Marine and Coastal Protection Society 233
  Kaikōura Marine Strategy 233, 236
  Kaikōura Whale Sanctuary 234
kākā 196
kākāriki (parakeets) 90, 104, 207
  red-crowned 90
  yellow-crowned 207
Kamo High School 61, 63
Kapiti Island Nature Reserve 194, 196
Kapiti Marine Reserve 12, 13 (map), 194–99, 216
kekeno (New Zealand fur seals) 169, 200, 212, **213**, **222**, 224–26, 227–28, **227**, **228**, 236, 242, 257, 276, 283, 284, 285, 286, 292
kelps and kelp forests 47, 50, **51**, 56, **57**, 64, 70, 76, **93**, 123, **128**, 132, 147, 151, 161, **182**, 187, 188, 190, 191, 197, 202, 213, 228, 236, 240, 241, 242, 259, 260, 263, 269, 277, **277**, 286, 291
Kermadec Islands 19, 63, 265–72, 275
  Kermadec Islands Marine Reserve 12, 13 (map), 126, 267–71
  Kermadec Ocean Sanctuary 268
  Kermadec little shearwater 271
  Kermadec scalyfin 269
  Kermadec storm petrel 271, 272
  Kermadec triplefin 269
Kerr, Vince 68
Key, John 233
kina (sea urchins) 47, 50–52, **51**, 56, 57, **57**, 84, 123, 128, 131, 186, 188, 197, 208, 209, 213, 228, 252, 259, 269, 289, 291, 292, 293
kina barrens 50–52, **51**, 56, **57**, 128, **128**, 292
King, Virginia 103
kingfish 64, 115, 150, 151, 161, 169, 269, 272
kingfishers 64, 72, **78**, 90, 189, 216
kiwi 67, 104, 196, 207, 258, 260, **260**
  little spotted 207
  Stewart Island brown (tokoeka) 258, 260, **260**
kōaro 195, 291
kōheru 161
kokako 104
kōkopu 64, 195, 216, 223, 291
  banded 64, 216
  giant 223
  shortjaw 195, 291

kororā (little blue penguins) 104, 115, **152**, 152–54, **153**, 171, 195, 208, 212, 241–42, **242**
krill 21, 30, 94, 178, 234, 237, 238, 292
Kupe 17, 292
Kutu Parera (Gaer Arm) 12, 13 (map), 248

lamp shells (brachiopods) 251, 253, **253**, 259, 291
Land Information New Zealand (LINZ) 20
Lardelli, Professor Derek 186
Lawrieston, David 225, 226
Laysan albatross 45
leatherjackets **148**, 187, 208, 210, 213, 242, 259
Lee, Mike 123–24, **124**
Leigh Marine Laboratory 47, 52, 53, **52–53**
lichens 64, **67**, 109, 251
light-mantled sooty albatross (toroa pango) **286**
Lilley, Callum 178
Little Barrier Island — *see* Hauturu
little blue penguins (kororā) 104, 115, 152–54, **152**, **153**, 171, 195, 208, 212, 241–42, **242**
little shag 90, 195, 216
little spotted kiwi 207
limpets 54, 188, 213, 242, 269
    giant 269
    golden 188
ling 259, 286
leopard seals 276
Long Bay–Ōkura Marine Reserve 12, 13 (map), 121 (map), 122, 132–35
Long Island–Kokomohua Marine Reserve 12, 13 (map), 206–208, 212
long-fin eels 216

mackerels 64, 226
mako shark 150
manaia — *see* seahorses
Mangarākau Swamp 215, 216–217
mangroves 60, 61, 63, 64, 70, **78**, 79, 136, **136–37**, 138, 140, 141
maomao 50, 63, 151, 161, **184**, 269
    blue 50, 63, 151, 161, 269
    pink 151
maps
    bathymetric map of Zealandia 22
    marine reserves 2014 13
    marine reserves in and around Hauraki Gulf Marine Park 121
    New Zealand Territorial Waters, Exclusive Economic Zone, Extended Continental Shelf, NZ–Australia 2004 Delimitation Treaty 16
    New Zealand's ocean currents 35
marblefish 147, 187, 188, 202, 208
marine reserves 2014 — *see also* individual names
    list of reserves, areas and years of establishment 12
    map of New Zealand showing reserves 13
    map showing reserves in and around Hauraki Gulf 121
MarineNZ 69
Marlborough Sounds 37, 206, 208, 210
marlin 150
masked booby 271
mātaitai 40, 116, 117, 221, 233, 236, 258, 292, 293
    Ōkārito Mātaitai Reserve 223
    Tauparikākā Mātaitai Reserve 223
    Te Whaka-a-Te Wera (Paterson Inlet) Mātaitai Reserve 258

Matheson, Roddy 53
Māui's dolphin 173–76, 243
Maxted, John 134
megaherbs 283, **283**
Mickleson, Rose 272
Mimiwhangata Marine Park 127–29
Ministry for the Environment 233
Ministry of Fisheries 116, 188, 220
Ministry of Foreign Affairs and Trade 20
Ministry of Primary Industries (MPI) 40, 116, 176, 233
minke whale 234, 278
Moana Uta (Wet Jacket Arm) Marine Reserve 12, 13 (map), 248
moki 50, **66**, 70, 147, 161, 169, 187, 188, 197, **197**, 202, 208, 210, 211, 213, 236, 242, 259, 262, **266**
    blue 161, 169, 188, 202, 208, 211, 259
    painted **266**
    red 50, **66**, 70, 147, 187, 188, 197, **197**, 208, 210, 213, 236, 259
mollymawks 278, 283, 285
    Salvin's 278, 285
    shy 278
    white-capped 278
Moore, Charles 44–45
Moorish idol **266**
moray eels 97, 161, 183
Morton, Professor John 47
mosaic moray eel **97**
Motu Manawa (Pollen Island) Marine Reserve 12, 13 (map), 121 (map), 122, 136–139, 200
Motu Matakohe (Limestone Island) 63, 64
Motukaroro — *see also* Whāngārei Harbour Marine Reserve 62, 63–64, **65**, **66**, **67**, 74
Moturoa School 171
Motutapu 104, **110**, 112–14, **113**, **114**
    Motutapu Restoration Trust 114
Mountains to Sea Conservation Trust 69
mullet **14–15**, 64, **78**, 132, 141
    yellow-eyed **14–15**, **78**
Murman, Geordie 107
Museum of New Zealand Te Papa Tongarewa 106
Musgrave, Captain Thomas 279–80
mussels 55, 64, 109, 115, 121, 122, **122**, 123, 132, 197, 199, 209, 210, 213, 228, 242, 251, 285
muttonbird — *see* sooty shearwater

National Institute of Water and Atmospheric Research (NIWA) 20, 21, 198, 256, 291
National Oiled Wildlife Response Centre 154
Natural History Museum, Paris 106
Natural History New Zealand (NHNZ) 9, 74, 82, 84, 95, 96, 227
nekton 130–31, 292
New Zealand Association for Environmental Education (NZAEE) 172, 292
New Zealand bigeye 72–73
New Zealand Continental Shelf Project 20
New Zealand dotterel 67, 138, **138**, 141, 142–43, **142**, **143**, **159**, 189
New Zealand Federation of Commercial Fishermen 254
New Zealand fur seals (kekeno) 169, 200, 212, **213**, **222**, 224–26, 227–28, **227**, **228**, 236, 242, 257, 276, 283, 284, 285, 286, 289, 292
New Zealand (Hooker's) sea lion 226–27, **262**, 263, 276, 278, 279–81, **279**, **281**, 283, 292
New Zealand Native Forest Restoration Trust 217

New Zealand Oceanographic Institute 198
New Zealand storm petrel 106–107, **107**
Ngā Motu/Sugar Loaf Islands Marine Protected Area 127, 167, 168–71
Ngā Motu Marine Reserve Society 170, 171, 172
Nicholas, Samara 61–63, **63**, 64, 68–69, **69**, 70, **272**, 289
noddy 271
North Island robin 104
northern scorpionfish 96, 161
nudibranchs 64, 83, **93**, 160, 169, 188, 202, 208, 210, 213, 228, 251, **254**
NZ–Australia 2004 Delimitation Treaty 16 (map)

oceanic white-tip shark 41
octopus 30, 64, **78**, 79, 83, 84, 188, 197, 202, 226, 242
    paper nautilus 83
Ōhau Point New Zealand Fur Seal Sanctuary 236
Ōkārito 222, 223
    Ōkārito Mātaitai Reserve 223
Open Bay Islands 9, 224–28
orca 73, **74**, 75, **76**, 76, 124, 173, 174, 175, 200, 208, 239, 278
Ornithological Society of New Zealand 158
oysters 64, 115, 123, 127
oystercatchers 72, 108, 115, **120**, 132, 132, 138, 141, 189, 195, 212, 216

packhorse (green) crayfish 96, 129, 131
paddle crab 74
Paikea 235
painted moki **266**
pākirikiri (blue cod; rāwaru) 169, 189, 197, 198, 202, 203, **203**, 208, 210, 211, 213, 236, 242, 259
Palmer, Bill 163
paper nautilus octopus 83
parakeets (kākāriki) 90, 207
    red-crowned 90
    yellow-crowned 207
Parininihi Marine Reserve 12, 13 (map), 180–81, 182
parore 50, 63, **122**, 132, 187
Patagonian toothfish 286
pāteke (brown teal) 104
pāua 47, 127, 188, 197, 198, 208, 211, 242, 259
penguins 21, 30, 75, 104, 115, 152–54, **152**, **153**, **158**, **159**, 171, 195, 197, 208, 212, **227**, 241–42, **242**, 245, **274**, 277, **277**, 278, 283, 285, 286, **287**
    adelie 21
    crested **227**
    eastern rockhopper 283, 286
    erect-crested 285, 286, **287**
    little blue (kororā) 104, 115, **152**, 152–54, **153**, 171, 195, 208, 212, 241–42, **242**
    Snares crested **274**, 277, **277**
    white-flippered 241–42, 245
    yellow-eyed (hoiho) 242
perch 115, 161, 189, 203, 208, 259
    butterfly 189, 208, 259
    sand 203
    sea 189, 208, 259
    yellow-banded 161
Peters, Pamela **69**
petrels 90, 106–107, **107**, 115, 154, 195, 271, 272, 278
    black-bellied storm 106, 107
    black-winged 271
    diving 195
    Kermadec storm 271, 272

New Zealand storm 106–107, **107**
white-faced 106, **107**
white-naped 271
phytoplankton — *see* plankton
Piccard, Jacques 23
picoplankton — *see* plankton
pied shag 7, 90, 195
pied stilt 64, 189
pilot whale 173, 234
pink maomao 151
Piopiotahi (Milford Sound) Marine Reserve 12, 13 (map), 248
pipi 8, 79, 141, 216
pipits 90
plankton 23, 44, 82, 98, 130–31, 191, 232, 252, 272, 291, 292
diatoms 29, **29**, 32, **32**, 291, 292
phytoplankton 28, 29, 30, 32, 34, 37, 50, 177, 178, 292, 293
picoplankton 29, 292
zooplankton **29**, 30, 50, 224, 238, 292, 293
Pōhatu (Flea Bay) Marine Reserve 12, 13 (map), 220, 241–42, 244
pōhutukawa 7, 47, **87**, 90, 104, 147, 149
Pollen Island — *see* Motu Manawa (Pollen Island) Marine Reserve
Poor Knights Islands 9, 60, 77, 80–99, 115, 147, 163, 169, 182, 183
Poor Knights Islands Marine Reserve 12, 13 (map), 60, 68, 92, 121 (map), 125–26
Poor Knights rengarenga 89
pōrae 115
porcupine fish 115
porpoises 75, 174, 243, 291
prions 90, 94, 242, 285
fairy 90, 242
fulmar 285
Punakaiki Marine Reserve (proposed) 12, 13 (map), 221, 222

Queen Charlotte Sound 206
Quinn, Max 90, 228
Quota Management System 40, 163

rāhui 40, 115–16, 129, 233, 293
rāhui pou **186**, 187
rails 64, 67, 90, 115, 138, 216
banded 64, 67, 90, 138, 216
Rākaihautū 241
Rakiura — *see* Stewart Island/Rakiura
Ramsar List/Convention 217
Rangaunu Harbour 79
rāwaru (blue cod; pākirikiri) 169, 189, 197, 198, 202, 203, **203**, 208, 210, 211, 213, 236, 242, 259
Raynal, François 279–81
rays 41, 68, 73, 75, **75**, 76–77, **77**, 83, 85, **85**, 115, 124, 162, 259
eagle 73, 76, 77, **77**
electric 259
manta 41, 83
spinetail devil 41
stingray 68, 73, **75**, 76, 77, 124, 162
red-billed gull 195, 237, **237**
red moki 50, **66**, 70, 147, 187, 188, 197, **197**, 208, 210, 213, 236, 259
red rock lobster 129, **131**
red-tailed tropicbird 271
reef heron 141, 195
Rena disaster 152–59
Rewa, Huriwaka **159**
rhodoliths 197, 199, **199**, 293
right whale 173
southern right whale 173, 200, 234, 243, **243**, 278
robins (toutouwai) 104, 207, 258
North Island 104
South Island 207
Stewart Island 258
rock cod 115
roughy, common 189
Royal Forest & Bird Protection Society — *see* Forest & Bird
royal spoonbill 64, 72, **78**, 138, 195

saddleback — *see* tieke
salmon farms 208
salps 23, **23**, 83, 94, 291
Salvin's albatross **284**, **285**
Salvin's mollymawks 278, 285
Sandager, Andreas 96
Sandager's wrasse **84**, 95–97, **95**, 98, **161**, 289
Saville, Sav 106
scallops 115, 210, 259
scarlet wrasse **148**, 187, 189, 202, 208, 259
Schuler, Zeta **159**
Scollay, Kina **228**, **228**
scorpionfish 96, 161, 187
northern 96, 161
Scott, Andrew 262
Scott, Anne **170**
sea anemones — *see* anemones
sea cucumbers 20, 56, 210, 262, 291
sea lions 115, 224, 226–27, 242, **262**, 263, 276, 278, 279–81, **279**, **281**, 283, 292
New Zealand (Hooker's) 226–27, **262**, 263, 276, 278, 279–81, **279**, **281**, 283, 292
sea pens 251, 253, **253**
sea slugs — *see also* nudibranchs **66**, 254
sea urchins — *see also* kina 163, **163**
seahorses (manaia) 62, 64, 202, 262, **260**, 270
seals 30, 83, 115, 151, 152, 169, 197, 200, 208, 212, **213**, **222**, 224–28, **227**, **228**, 233, 236, 242, 243, 257, 276, 283, 284, 285, 286, 289, 292
leopard 276
New Zealand fur (kekeno) 169, 200, 212, **213**, **222**, 224–28, **227**, 228, 236, 242, 257, 276, 283, 284, 285, 286, 289, 292
Ōhau Point New Zealand Fur Seal Sanctuary 236
southern elephant 276, 283, 286
seal hunting 224–26, 258, 275, 276, 284
seaweeds (algae) — *see also* kelps and kelp forests 50, 56, 57, 64, **67**, **93**, 132, 151, 187, 188, 190–91, **190**, **191**, 199, **199**, 200, 202, **208**, 209, 213, 220, 226, 236, 238–39, 251, 259, 260, **260**, 269, 282, 286, 291
SeaWeek 172, 292
sei whale 278
seven-gill shark 226, 262
shags 2, 7, **38**, 40, 47, 64, 90, 115, 195, 212, 216, 242, 245, 285
black 115, 195
Bounty Island 285
little 90, 195, 216
pied 2, 7, 90, 195
spotted 115, 195, 242, 245
sharks 41, 75, 76, 85, 96, 115, 150, 161, 162–63, **162**, 209, **209**, 226, 239, 256–57, **257**, 259, 262, 268, 269, 272
basking 41
blue 161, 162–63, **162**, 175, 197
carpet 96, 209, **209**, 259
deepwater nurse 41
Galapagos 269
mako 150
oceanic white-tip 41
seven-gill 226, 262
whale 41
white pointer (great white) 41, 226, 256–57, **257**, 262
Shaw, Edith 216
shearwaters 89, 45, 90, 94, **94**, 115, 154, 195, 207, 261, **261**, 271, 277
Buller's 89, 94, **94**
flesh-footed 45
fluttering 94, 115, 207
Kermadec little 271
sooty (tītī; muttonbird) 115, 195, 261, **261**, 277
shellfish — *see also* cockles, kina, mussels, oysters, paua, pipi, scallops, tuatua 30, 64, 72, 84, 96, 108, 116, 121, **122**, 123, 126, 131, 134, 198, 210, 216, 226, 233, 236, 254, 258
shortjaw kōkopu 195, 291
shrimps 23, 30, 64, 84, 95, 130, 161, 183, 210, 216, 251
shy mollymawks 278
silver drummer 50, 197
Skelton, Ed **198**
skinks 67, 104
Smith, Dr Nick 233, 244, **245**
snails 64, 90, 115, 132, 141, 210, 216, 226, 228, 251
snapper 47, 50, 52, 56, 62, 63, 64, 68, **68**, 84, 86, 115, 129, 132, 147, 161, 169, 197, **198**, 213, 216
golden 161
Snares — *see* The Snares
Snares cape pigeons 285
Snares crested penguins **274**, 277, **277**
sooty shearwater (tītī; muttonbird) 115, 195, 261, **261**, 277
South Island robin 258
South Pacific Centre for Marine Science 53
southern black-backed gulls 41, 132, 138, 216, 285
southern elephant seals 276, 283, 286
southern pigfish 259
southern right whale 200, 234, 243, **243**, 278
southern royal albatross 278, **278**, **282**, 283
Spanish lobster 161
sperm whale 31, 174, 234, **235**, 270, 278
sponges 32, **43**, 47, 62, 64, **66**, 70, **93**, 132, 147, 160, 169, 180, 182–83, **182**, **183**, 187, 188, 197, 202, 210, 242, 251, 282, 285, 286, 293
finger **66**, **183**
golf ball **66**
organ pipe **66**
spoonbill, royal 64, 72, **78**, 138, 195
spotted black grouper 41, 270, **270**, 272
spotted shag 115, 195, 242, 245
spotties 63, **122**, 132, 187, 202, 208, 210, 213
squat lobsters (kōura rangi) 236, 237, 238
squid 21, 30, 31, **31**, 45, 75, 84, 162, 226, 234, 257, 280
starfish 31, 54–55, 56, 84, 131, 147, 197, 202, 209, 210, 213, 216, 228, 251, 252, 269, 291
stargazers 72, 79
Stephenson, Brent 106, 107
Stewart Island/Rakiura 9, 42, 143, 203, 256–63, 277, 284, 286, 289
Stewart Island brown kiwi (tokoeka) 258, 260, **260**
Stewart Island weka 258
stilts 64, 72, 189
pied 64, 189
stitchbird — *see* hihi
Subantarctic Islands 262, 275–86, 293
Sugar Loaf Islands — *see* Ngā Motu/Sugar Loaf Islands Marine Protected Area
Sutherland, Samara — *see* Nicholas, Samara
sweep **122**, 169, 187, 188

Taiapa, Nikita **171**
taiāpure 40, 116, 117, 233, 236, 245, 293
  Akaroa Harbour Taiāpure 245
  Whakapuaka Taiāpure 211
Taipari Roa (Elizabeth Island) Marine Reserve 12, 13 (map), 248
takahē 104, 105, **105**, 196
Tāmaki makaurau 111–12
tangata kaitiaki 116
Tapuae Marine Reserve 12, 13 (map), 170–72, 180
Taputeranga Marine Reserve 12, 13 (map), 194, 200–202, 206
tarakihi 115, 169, 189, 208, 210, 211, 213
Taumoana (Five Fingers Peninsula) Marine Reserve 12, 13 (map), 248
Tauparikākā Marine Reserve (proposed) 12, 13 (map), 221, 222, 223
Tauparikākā Mātaitai Reserve 223
Tāwharanui 49, 109, 121
  Tāwharanui Marine Reserve 12, 13 (map), 121 (map), 122, 123–24, **124**, 127, 128–31
  Tāwharanui Open Sanctuary 123
Tawhiti Rahi — *see also* Poor Knights Islands 81, 87, 89, **99**
Te Angiangi Marine Reserve 12, 13 (map), 188–89, 191
Te Awaatu Channel (the Gut) Marine Reserve 12, 13 (map), 248
Te Hāpua (Sutherland Arm) Marine Reserve 12, 13 (map), 248
Te Huruhi Primary School **38**, 40
Te Korowai ō te Tai Marokura/the Kaikōura Coastal Marine Guardians (Te Korowai) 233
Te Matuku Marine Reserve 12, 13 (map), 121 (map), 122, 140–43, 147
Te Paepae-o-Aotea (Volkner Rocks) Marine Reserve 12, 13 (map), 146, 160–61, 162, 186
Te Pātaka-o-Rākaihautū (Banks Peninsula) 240
Te Rauparaha 196
Te Rohe o te Whānau Puha/ Kaikōura Whale Sanctuary 234
Te Rūnanga o Kaikōura 233
Te Rūnanga o Ngāi Tahu 233
Te Tai-o-Marokura 236
Te Tapuwae-o-Hua (Long Sound) Marine Reserve 12, 13 (map), 248
Te Tapuwae-o-Rongokako Marine Reserve 12, 13 (map), 186–87, 188, 190
Te Wāhipounamu–South West New Zealand Heritage Area 223
Te Wera 258
Te Whaka-a-Te Wera (Paterson Inlet) Mātaitai Reserve 258
Te Whanganui-a-Hei (Cathedral Cove) Marine Reserve 12, 13 (map), 121 (map), 122, 146–48, 200
Tennyson, Alan 106
terns 115, 138, 141, 154, **184**, 189, 195, 242, 245, 271, 285
  Antarctic 285
  Caspian 138, 141, **184**, 189, 195
  white-fronted 195
Territorial Sea (Territorial Waters) 16 (map), 19, 24, 293
The Snares/Tini Heke 275–76, 277, 278, 280, 293
Thomas, Bryan 106–107
Thompson, Bubba 255
Thompson, Brayden **171**
thornfish 259
tī kouka (cabbage tree) 134, 138
tīeke (saddleback) 104, 196, 207, 258
  North Island 104, 196
  South Island 207, 258
Tindall Foundation 69
Tiritiri Matangi 104–105, 132, 289
tītī (sooty shearwater; muttonbird) 115, 195, 261, **261**, 277
toadstool grouper 161
tokoeka (Stewart Island brown kiwi) 258, 260, **260**
Tonga Island Marine Reserve 12, 13 (map), 206, 212–13, 214
toothed whales 174, 234, **235**, 278
toroa pango (light-mantled sooty albatross) **286**
Torres, Leigh 178
toutouwai (robin) 104, 207, 258
  North Island 104
  South Island 207
  Stewart Island 258
Tregidga, John 121
trevally 64, 115, 169
triplefins 64, **66**, 69, 188, 208, 210, 213, 242, 269
Trnski, Dr Tom 268
tuatara 90, 94, 104, 207
tuatua 115, 132
tubeworms 31, 72, 141, **141**, 242, 251, 253
Tūhua (Mayor Island) Marine Park 12, 13 (map), 121 (map), 146, 149–51
tuna 150, 161, 163
  yellowfin 161
turtles 45, 75, 83, 270, 272
Turver, Chris 198
Tūtakahikura 241
tūturiwhatu (New Zealand dotterel) 67, 138, **138**, 141, **142**, 142–43, **143**, **159**, 189
Tuwhare, Hone 6, 10, 261
two-spot demoiselles 98, **99**, **271**

Ulva Island/Te Wharawhara Marine Reserve 12, 13 (map), 256–59
UNESCO World Heritage sites 221, 223, 236, 276
United Nations Convention on the Law of the Sea (UNCLOS) 18, 20, 293
United Nations Environment Programme 273
upokohue (Hector's dolphin) 173–76, **174**, 208, 223, 238, 243

Victoria University Coastal Ecology Lab 200
Visser, Dr Ingrid 73, 75
Volkner Rocks — *see* Te Paepae-o-Aotea (Volkner Rocks) Marine Reserve

Waetford, Kawiti **90**
Waiau Glacier Coast Marine Reserve (proposed) 12, 13 (map), 221, 222–23
Waiheke Island 103, 104, 121, 122, 140, 142, 289
Waikanae Estuary Scientific Reserve 194
Waikaraka — *see also* Whāngārei Harbour Marine Reserve 63, **65**, 69
Walsh, Don 23
wandering albatross 278
wandering anemone (hūmenga) 188, 191, **191**
Waterhouse, Captain 286
weka 226, 258
  Stewart Island 258
West Coast Marine Protection Forum 220–21, 233
West Coast North Island Marine Mammal Sanctuary 176
Westhaven (Te Tai Tapu) Marine Reserve 12, 13 (map), 206, 214–17
Westhaven (Whanganui Inlet) Wildlife Management Reserve 216
Westland Tai Poutini National Park 223
wētā 90, 104, 285
  cave 90
  giant 90, 104
Whakanewha Regional Park 142, 143
Whakapuaka Taiāpure 211
whales — *see also* dolphins 75, 115, 121, 123, 151, 233, 234, 235, 243, 270, 273, 278, 291
  Antarctic blue 178
  baleen 30, 278, 292
  beaked 174, 234
  blue 9, 173, 178, **179**, 234
  fin 273, 278
  humpback 83, 173, 196, 234, 270, 272, 278
  Kaikōura Whale Sanctuary 234
  minke 234, 278
  orca 73, 74, **74**, 75, **75**, 76, 124, 173, 174, 175, 200, 208, 239, 278
  pilot 173, 234
  right 173
  sei 278
  southern right 173, 200, 234, 243, **243**, 278
  sperm 31, 174, 234, **235**, 270, 278
  toothed 174, 234, **235**, 278
whale hunting 83, 173, 178, 196, 258, 275
whale shark 41
Whale Watch 235
Whananaki Primary School 62
Whanganui Inlet 206, 214–15, 217
Whāngārei Harbour 60, 61–67, 69, 72, **72**, 73, 75, 76
  Whāngārei Harbour Marine Reserve 12, 13 (map), 60, 61–64, **65**, 68, 121 (map), **183**
White Island (Te Puia-o-Whakaari) 160–61, 267
white pointer (great white) shark 41, 226, 256–57, **257**, 262
white-capped mollymawks 278
white-faced heron 90, 126
white-faced petrel 106, **107**
white-flippered penguins 241–42, 245
white-fronted tern 195
white-naped petrel 271
whitebait 195, 216, 220, 291
Whitebait Connection 69
Whiting, Cliff 255
Wilkinson, Kate **124**, 221
World Oceans Day 244
worms 23, 30, 31, 64, 72, **72**, 84, 95, 132, 141, **141**, 183, 203, 210, 216, 242, 251, 253, **253**
  annelid 183
  arrow 23
  fan 72, **72**, 253
  feather-duster **253**
  tube 31, 72, 141, **141**, 242, 251, 253
wrasses — *see also* spotties 64, **84**, 95–97, **95**, 98, 115, **148**, 161, 187, 188, 189, 197, 202, 208, 210, 213, 242, 259, 272, 289
  banded 187, 188, 197, 202, 208, 210, 213, 259
  Sandager's **84**, 95–97, **95**, 98, **161**, 289
  scarlet **148**, 187, 189, 202, 208, 259
Wrybill Birding Tours NZ 106

Yangtze River dolphin 176
yellow-eyed mullet **14–15**
yellow-eyed penguin (hoiho) 242
yellowfin tuna 161

Zealandia (continent) 17, **22**, 24, 25, 27, 291, 292, 293
zooplankton — *see* plankton

ABOUT THE AUTHOR

Janet Hunt grew up with two big blue backyards — Mount Taranaki immediately outside the door and the ocean gleaming in the distance on the North Island west coast. She was in her teens before she woke up to the fact that not all sand is black and that a swim in the ocean does not always entail a joyous romp in wild surf.

Although she is again resident in Taranaki, she has lived for long periods on Waiheke Island, where she had an ongoing love affair with the estuaries, wetlands, islands and waters of the Hauraki Gulf and all the creatures and plants that live in them.

So, without really knowing it, she was poised and ready when asked to write this book. She describes the process as a fascinating journey, involving many new friends and acquaintances and full of fresh experiences and apprehensions. At times she felt like the little fur seal in the book, looking for its first time into the sea, an astonishing, different, other world.

Janet is the award-winning author and graphic designer of *Hone Tuwhare: A Biography* (Godwit, 1998), *A Bird in the Hand: Keeping New Zealand Wildlife Safe* (Random House, 2003), *From Weta to Kauri: A Guide to the New Zealand Forest* (Random House, 2004), *A Kindness to the Land: Don Chapple's Conservation Scrapbook* (2006), *Wetlands of New Zealand: A Bitter-sweet Story* (Random House, 2007), *Three Cheers Fifty Years: Inglewood High School 1957–2007,* and *E3 Call Home: A True Story of Godwit Migration and Misadventure* (Random House, 2009). *A Bird in the Hand* was the 2004 New Zealand Post Book of the Year, and *Wetlands of New Zealand* won the 2008 Montana Medal for Non-fiction.